362.2   Irvine, Leslie.
IRV   Codependent
1999   forevermore : the
           invention of self in
           a twelve step group

CODEPENDENT
FOREVERMORE

CODEPENDENT FOREVERMORE

The Invention of Self in a
Twelve Step Group

LESLIE IRVINE

The University of Chicago Press
Chicago & London

LESLIE IRVINE is assistant professor of sociology at the University of Colorado.

The University of Chicago Press, Chicago 60637
The University of Chicago Press, Ltd., London
© 1999 by The University of Chicago
All rights reserved. Published 1999
08 07 06 05 04 03 02 01 00 99   1 2 3 4 5
ISBN (cloth): 0-226-38471-3

Library of Congress Cataloging-in-Publication Data

Irvine, Leslie.
   Codependent forevermore : the invention of self in a twelve step
group / Leslie Irvine.
     p.   cm.
   Includes bibliographical references and index.
   ISBN 0-226-38471-3 (alk. paper).
   1. Codependency—Social aspects—United States. 2. Co-Dependents
Anonymous. 3. Self—Social aspects. 4. Identity (Psychology). I. Title.
RC569.5.C63I78 1999
362.2′04256—dc21   99-10350
                                        CIP

I owe a very special debt of gratitude to Lynn Appleton and Robert Zussman. *Codependent Forevermore* began its life as a paper in one of Lynn's graduate seminars, and it was she who suggested that I might enjoy this topic. When the paper grew into a master's thesis under Lynn's direction, I also benefited from the insights of Helen Bannan and the late Martin Levine. Marty's last set of comments to me close with him saying how much he looked forward to seeing the work become a book. It saddens me that he did not live long enough to do so.

I was fortunate to arrive at Stony Brook the very semester that Robert Zussman offered a seminar on The Self, and it was he who introduced me to the study of narrative. Throughout the research and writing, he had an uncanny sense for offering just the right amount of guidance. Sincere thanks are also due to Michael Kimmel, Ian Roxborough, and Diane Barthel for their critical and timely comments.

I would also like to thank Doug Mitchell, Matt Howard, Russell Harper, Liz Demeter, and Erin Hogan of the University of Chicago Press, as well as the Press's incredibly thorough anonymous reviewers. In addition, I thank the members of Codependents Anonymous who gave of their time and so candidly told me their stories. Although the Twelve Step tradition of anonymity prevents me from thanking them by name, I could not have completed this research without them.

This is a study of how disrupted lives can be made livable again. It draws on ethnographic research in Codependents Anonymous, a Twelve Step group known simply as CoDA. CoDA is a psychospiritual, self-help program that attracts people who have experienced a divorce or the breakup of a committed relationship—or a series of such events. CoDA offers people a way to account for their experience, and, consequently, a way of making sense of their lives. What dedicated members claim to gain from the group is a sense of self. I took their claims seriously, and tried to understand what makes that sense possible. This, then, is primarily a study of the experience of selfhood.

There are many competing notions of the self, in popular culture as well as academic scholarship. The self has been equated with the soul (versions of which include the "inner child"), with the collection of roles that we play, and with an "audience's" response to a competent social "performance." This book portrays the self as a story, or, more accurately, as *stories*, and people as narrators of *selves*. I think of selfhood as a narrative accomplishment, created in the stories people tell about themselves—and this includes the stories that they tell *to* themselves. The self is both the premise and the result of the stories people tell. As Arthur Frank writes in his study of making sense of serious illness, "Stories do not simply describe the self; they are the self's medium of being" (1995, 53). Likewise, psychiatrist Roy Schafer adds that "the self is a telling" (1981, 31). A "person can only *tell* a self or encounter it as something *told*" (Schafer 1992, 27, emphasis original; see also MacIntyre 1984). Our experience of "having" a self is contained in an "internal conversation" (Gagnon 1992) about who we are. The self cannot be experienced except as mediated by words and narrative. Conventional means of talking about the self suggest otherwise, however. We describe the self as something "within" us. We try to "know" the self. We "tell ourselves" something. So heavily are these images used that they are not recognized as the narrative conventions that they are. Nevertheless, when I speak of "having" a self, I am telling myself a story that there is a self to tell a story to (see Schafer 1981, 31).[1]

A narrative concept of the self does not mean that people simply make up stories of themselves. To be sure, some people do precisely this; depending on the circumstances, we call them liars or phonies or something less polite, or else we institutionalize and medicate them. The narrative concept of self that I use here is not so much a matter of people making up stories as it is of stories making people. As Frank (1995) explains, "The stories we tell about our lives are not necessarily those lives as they were lived, but these stories become our experience of those lives" (22). The events of people's lives are reshaped according to the storytelling norms of given situations, and, through telling and retelling, those stories become the events of those lives. The "truth" of an experience is what emerges from the telling. Moreover, the stories you tell depend on the institutions within which you are embedded, as well as the resources that you bring to the telling. Institutions impart guidelines or formulas for what constitute acceptable stories. People reshape their experiences to fit. Rough edges are planed down, or even exaggerated, depending on the setting. The job interview, for example, distills your sense of who you are into your strengths and your shortcomings. The medical history answers the question of how you feel with a list of symptoms and their onset. Each person brings a variety of experiences and circumstances to the telling, and thus tells a unique story—but one that nevertheless follows the formula.

CoDA is a storytelling population. The group exists so that people may talk about themselves, through what is referred to as "sharing." But the opportunity to talk is not an opportunity to say anything that comes to mind. CoDA offers a characteristic formula into which its members import their own experiences. They must use codependency's language and its chronology of "abusive childhoods" and "dysfunctional relationships." Those who find the discourse convincing *become* codependent—not because they have a particular "condition," although that is how they understand it. Rather, they become codependent because they believe in and use the discourse to make sense of their lives. As Frank (1995) explains, "The truth of stories is not only what *was* experienced, but equally what *becomes* experience in the telling and its reception" (22, emphasis original). For people who identify with the codependency discourse, it offers a means of explaining why their lives have turned out the way they have. Consequently, it offers them a meaningful sense of self. This is not to say that it offers everyone the same kind of self. Rather, it offers them a way of piecing together stories of themselves, and these stories can vary according to the circumstances of those who tell them. This book examines the internal logic of these stories and explores what they can do for those who use them.

In addition to examining what makes the sense of self possible, this book engages in two other, related projects. One of these has to do with explaining what codependency is, as a cultural phenomenon, with tracing its origins and popularity, and with understanding how CoDA works. As a psychospiritual "condition," codependency has an intellectual history. More importantly, however, the meaning of codependency has been shaped by what people have used it to explain. People who identify with codependency share a language but differ profoundly in how they use it. Because they use the language of codependency to account for a variety of experiences and circumstances, they have a hand in reconstructing its meaning. Its content mirrors what people use it to explain. Likewise, as a group, CoDA has an organizational history. What I find more interesting is the way it serves as what I call an Institution "lite," which offers all the benefits of traditional institutions, but makes fewer demands on those within its purview. The chapters that immediately follow this one focus on codependency as a discourse, and on CoDA as an Institution "lite."

Another project focuses less on codependency and more on a set of ideas that were illuminated by the research. Specifically, these ideas have to do with the role of institutions, social structure, and culture in shaping the self. It seems likely that the discourse of codependency would offer hyperindividualistic answers to the ontological questions that CoDA members pose. Indeed, this has been the thrust of much of the criticism of this self-help phenomenon. In contrast, however, I found that the discourse of codependency helps members of CoDA create narratives of the self that are simultaneously individual and social. "Becoming codependent" involves an interaction between structure and agency, or between the circumstances of your life and the resources that you can draw upon to make sense of them. A single discourse with a prescribed set of concepts can be used to create lives with very different meanings. This theme runs throughout the book, but constitutes the central focus of part 2.

John Steadman Rice (1996) has written that codependency "is not something that one 'has,' but rather, something one believes" (10). Recognizing this, I have not, as a sociologist, set out to test the "truth" of codependency, just as I could not test the "truth" of religion. If I were to study religion, however, I could learn about what it means to believe without delving into questions of religious "truth." I have sought to do exactly this with codependency. Although I do not use it as a means of understanding my own life, I have attempted to learn from those who do. Much of what has been written about codependents has dismissed them as weak, gullible, or silly. Throughout the research, I kept in mind what W. I. Thomas said when he encountered questions about whether Wladek Wisniewski had told him a true story. Thomas explained that the truth or accuracy of the story made no difference; what mattered was that it was true *then,* for Wisniewski (see Plummer 1983, 105). Although I do not presume to equate myself with Thomas and Znaniecki, or my work with the classic *Polish Peasant,* I have borrowed the wisdom of Thomas's position. The people I encountered during my research called themselves codependents. For my purposes, it matters only that the idea *was true for them at the time.* I have tried to understand the consequences of holding that idea as truth.

A FEW WORDS ABOUT VOCABULARY

I use the terms "discourse," "ethos," and "narrative" so often that it would serve me well to clarify what I mean by them at the outset. For the definition of "discourse," I turn to *The Penguin Dictionary of Sociology,* which defines it as "a domain of language-use that is unified by common assumptions." *The Penguin Dictionary* also refers readers to the definition of "ideology," in that both ideologies and discourses offer "ready-made way[s] of thinking." Swidler's means of conceptualizing ideology may help here. She maintains that ideology "offer[s] a unified answer to the problems of social action" (1986, 279). When I refer to the "discourse of codependency," I invoke Rice's claim that codependency is not something "one 'has' but rather, something one believes." I prefer "discourse" to "ideology" because it emphasizes the characteristic use of language. In CoDA, one's vocabulary becomes rife with terms and phrases such as the "dysfunctional family," "abuse," "unhealthy relationships," and so on. *The Penguin Dictionary* also points out that the "ready-made" quality of a discourse "closes off" alternatives. Just so, when I refer to the "discourse of codependency," I connote a closed system, in which everyone is codependent—even those who are "in denial"—and all families are dysfunctional. Because of its persuasive, all-or-nothing quality, I sometimes use "rhetoric" in place of "discourse," mostly for variety of language.

I use "therapeutic ethos" to refer to a collection of discourses about self-fulfillment that has developed over the past thirty years or so. "Therapeutic ethos" does not refer to any particular therapeutic technique or orientation. Rather, it refers to a characteristically American "spirit" in which everyone is allegedly entitled to happiness, high self-esteem, and personal satisfaction. Others have dubbed this "liberation psychotherapy" (Rice 1996), the "triumph of the therapeutic" (Rieff 1966), the "awareness movement" (Schur 1976), the "culture of narcissism" (Lasch 1979), and "expressive individualism" (Bellah et al. 1985). Although I hesitate to add yet another term to the mix, I think that "therapeutic ethos" concisely sums up the collection of activities, beliefs, and general interest in the fulfillment of an inner self.

Finally, "narrative." I refer to the "narratives" that codependency generates through its "narrative formula." A narrative "describes what happened, defines outcomes, or presents the stages of a social process . . . [narratives] usually relate events or describe processes step by step. First this happened, then that happened" (Rubin and Rubin 1995, 24). When I interviewed members of CoDA, I asked them to tell me about codependency and recovery. They explained, step by step, how their lives had changed. They told me what they believed had happened. They put events and situations together to give their experience meaning— for themselves as well as for me. Indeed, narrative is "the primary form by which human experience is made meaningful" (Polkinghorne 1991, 1; see also Chase 1995). I refer to codependency as a "narrative formula" because it provides a characteristic sequence through which codependents order the events of their lives. The content may differ, but the order—the "dysfunctional" family that set you up for codependency, the "unhealthy" relationships, the crisis, and recovery—is formulaic and provided by the discourse. Much of what it means to "be" codependent centers on adoption of this narrative formula. In addition, I sometimes refer to codependency as a "narrative strategy." By this, I mean that the discourse offers a means of making sense of entire lives in a big picture; it is not simply a means of justifying discrete experiences or events. For those who identify with its discourse, codependency becomes a way to integrate an entire life into one more or less coherent assemblage, or "narrative strategy." As Swidler (1986) explains, "Strategies are the larger ways of trying to organize a life . . . within which particular choices make sense" (276; see also Bourdieu 1977). "Narrative strategy," then, connotes a means of organizing a life, and within the one offered by codependency, particular choices (avoiding certain people because they foster "unhealthy" behavior, for example) make sense.

THE SETTING

CoDA meets at approximately fifty locations in the greater New York area, where this research took place. Most of these are rooms in churches, community centers, and the occasional library or hospital. The House of Life, where I did the bulk of the fieldwork, hosts three meetings each week. This community outreach center affiliated with the Catholic Church serves a largely white, local population that has, according to Census data, a median household income of just under $55,000. Within a cluster of colonial-style buildings that occupy two suburban blocks, The House provides residential drug and alcohol rehabilitation, shelter for battered women and their children, and free counseling for a host of other troubles. The building that houses its administrative offices has a multipurpose room that becomes home to Codependents Anonymous groups three times each week.

For twenty-five dollars a month—fifty for the group that meets on Friday evenings—each group rents a room that, at other times, accommodates other sorts of meetings. The room has three large windows, but curtains always cover them, and the only natural light comes through the glass doors at the entrance. Recessed lighting creates pools of harsh light that contrast with pockets of relative darkness. At one end of the room, a connecting corridor leads to the community center offices, and, during the morning meetings, the sounds of typing and copying leak into the meeting room. Most of the area of the room is taken up with rows of metal chairs with vinyl seats. Extras are stacked against a rear wall. Imitation wood paneling covers the walls. Light-brown commercial carpeting covers the floor. Wooden sliding doors conceal three closets filled with coffee pots, styrofoam cups, and craft supplies. Because of The House's Catholic affiliation, a crucifix hangs on one wall and a large statue of the Virgin Mary stands on a table in one corner. Photographs of the center's founders and a picture of Martin Luther King hang on other walls, along with felt banners bearing quotations from Scripture and inspirational sayings. An upright piano sits to one side of the room, its top decorated with secondhand knickknacks and dusty artificial flowers. A few mismatched tables, two sofas, and a podium stand in various corners of the room.

As CoDA members arrive for a meeting, they move the chairs out of the rows and into a circle. Once the circle is formed, they sit and talk, or sit quietly by themselves. In good weather, some stand outside, keeping the smokers company. One of the "home group members"—those who attend a particular group regularly—gets the notebook containing the printed meeting text and the container for donations out of the storage closet. Someone else arrives with the box of literature, tapes, meeting and telephone lists, and other materials that CoDA makes available at meetings. Although meeting locations often provide storage areas for those that rent their space, groups often do not want to risk having their materials disappear, as happened to one New York City group. Someone broke into a locked closet and stole several years' accumulation of CoDA literature. The group had to reestablish its stock—a costly process in terms of both money and time. To avoid this, a volunteer usually takes responsibility for this cache of literature. Upon arriving, he or she unpacks the box and arranges the material on a table. Others look through the literature, page through a book, or help set things out. Unlike AA, CoDA meetings do not provide coffee or snacks for members. As I explain in more detail later, codependency constitutes a "master addiction" that can express itself in a number of ways. In order not to encourage anyone's addiction to food, caffeine, sugar—or to providing such items for others—CoDA eschews AA's custom of serving food and beverages.

Meetings usually start within a few minutes of the scheduled time. A volunteer leader opens the meeting with introductions—first names only—and the Serenity Prayer, which reads, "God, grant me the serenity to accept the things I cannot change, the courage to change the things I can, and the wisdom to know the difference."[2] Next comes a statement about the purpose of CoDA. The group is "a fellowship of men and women whose common problem is an inability to maintain functional relationships" (CoDA 1988). The leader then asks if anyone is attending for the first, second, or third time. If so, the newcomers are asked to give their names and the group welcomes them in unison: *"Hi, Leslie. Welcome."* After this, the leader asks if there are any announcements, and those who want to publicize Twelve Step events chime in. Someone might announce a new group forming, or a CoDA dance or picnic in the works. After announcements, the leader asks if anyone is celebrating a CoDA anniversary. These are commemorated with bronze coins that mark milestones in years. They are used in all Twelve Step groups; Alcoholics Anonymous offers them for smaller increments of sobriety. This part of the meeting concludes with a collection, with each person usually putting a dollar in a coffee can or wicker basket.[3]

Next, a volunteer, usually scheduled beforehand, "shares" his or her experience of codependency and recovery in front of the entire group for about ten minutes. In closing, he or she proposes a recovery topic for group discussion. Topics I heard during my research include "Getting in touch with feelings," "My relationship with my Higher Power," and "How I'm taking care of myself," just to name a few. Then, the group either splits up into small groups for individual sharing or remains intact for sharing by turns. CoDA groups have the freedom to decide on the style of their particular meeting, whether remaining in a large group and volunteering to share by show of hands, or breaking up into small groups to give every person an opportunity to share. Most of the meetings I attended used the small-group format. Beginner's groups, very small groups, and all the groups in Manhattan used the show-of-hands method. During the sharing, no one offers advice or responds to what another is saying. CoDA prohibits "crosstalk," which is feedback or criticism explicitly or implicitly directed at what another has said. Before the sharing begins, the leader reminds members to speak only about themselves, and to limit their sharing to five minutes.

After about thirty minutes of sharing, the meeting closes with members individually voicing positive affirmations ("I am right where I need to be," or "I am enough," for example) or with the Lord's Prayer said in unison. Finally, members join hands for an enthusiastic chant of "Keep coming back. It works if you work it, so work it. You're worth it." They then break into applause, and some of the more demonstrative members give hugs around the room. After this, the members return the room to its original order, chatting as they move chairs. Some conversations continue outside the building; others move to diners and coffee shops.

THE MEMBERS

Although I refer to the "members" of CoDA—and that is how they refer to themselves—the criteria for membership are ephemeral and subjective. The CoDA Preamble, recited at every meeting, explains that the "only requirement for membership is a desire for healthy and fulfill-ing relationships with others and ourselves" (CoDA 1988). Thus, you may consider yourself a member of CoDA simply by attending a single meeting.

The anonymous character of Twelve Step groups makes demographic data difficult to obtain. Members introduce themselves using first names only, and although they may talk about work or family in their sharing, they conscientiously omit identifying references. Nevertheless, some descriptive information was available through observation. For each meeting, I recorded the number of people attending, noted the sex dis-tribution, and made a guess at ages. Meetings draw about twenty people on average, but this number can dip down to six in beginners' meetings and climb to forty or higher on Friday nights. Women constituted 58 percent of a total of 626 members I observed. This figure approximates the 61 percent observed by Rice, who studied groups in other parts of the country. Judging by the sharing, most members were heterosexual, although some could simply have been careful about their choice of pronouns. More likely, gay men and lesbians attended the "closed" meetings dedicated to their concerns, but I did not visit any of these.

Judging by appearance, members came mostly from the Baby Boom generation and were predominantly white, also consistent with Rice's findings. At The House of Life, only one member came from a minority group, but this is in an area that, by Census data, is about 95 percent white. Racial composition varied somewhat more in New York City, but even there, membership remained mostly white. In an effort to locate meeting sites that offered more demographic heterogeneity, I used Cen-sus data to determine the racial and income characteristics of the areas in which each of the groups met. I found that, even in neighborhoods with relatively high percentages of Asians, Blacks, and Hispanics in resi-dence, the groups themselves drew only a small proportion of minori-ties. For example, at one Manhattan meeting site that had relatively high proportions of Blacks and Hispanics in the surrounding neighborhood (about 20 percent), minorities composed only about 15 percent of those attending the meetings. I saw no one who appeared to be Asian, al-though Asians composed nearly 12 percent of the local population. Moreover, I saw no Asians at any of the CoDA sites I visited.

The Twelve Step norm of anonymity made determining the occupa-tions and incomes of members a bit more complicated. With the excep-tion of The House of Life, I did not attend any particular group's meet-ings long enough to learn what members did for a living. Using dress, appearance, and demeanor as very rough gauges, I would place most members in the ambiguous category of the middle class, although more towards lower than higher. Checking again with Census data, I found that no groups met in areas with median household incomes below $25,000 a year. Most took place in areas with incomes between $45,000 and $55,000 a year. I found only one exception to this: a meeting on Manhattan's Upper East Side, where the median household income is over $100,000. Even there, however, I did not find that the composition of the membership differed significantly from that of other meeting sites.

At The House of Life, I became well enough integrated into the group to know what some of the members did for a living. I also asked that question of the thirty-six people I interviewed. Glass ceilings and downward mobility struck me as predominant experiences. A few people at the bottom of the ladder collected disability income. Some women lived on support from ex-husbands, supplementing it with "under the table" work, such as babysitting and housecleaning. I would describe several of the men as "underemployed," having taken any work available after losing careers with the defense industry when a large area employer closed down. The number of people who worked two and three jobs to make ends meet amazed me, and talk of hunting for a house, apartment, or job arose quite often at meetings. Some members seemed to live quite comfortably, however, having avoided the job losses and divorces that can ravage one's economic status. A number of men that I place in this category worked in the building trades, and the women worked in professions such as dental assisting and nursing.

THE MECHANICS OF THE RESEARCH

Collecting the data

During the seventeen months that I studied CoDA, I attended over two hundred meetings on Long Island and in New York City. This represents over four hundred hours of observation. Much of the time, I participated in the meetings, which is to say that I talked about myself. I did not have to make up a story about codependency, as I would have if I had tried to "pass" in AA. As I explain in more detail later, the meaning of codependency is sufficiently open that it can accommodate the events of any life. Each individual has the freedom, indeed the right, to decide what his or her codependency means. Thus, I was able to share without lying. Moreover, I am convinced that, in this setting, participation was the sociologically ethical thing to do (see the Appendix). CoDA's norms make continuous detached observation impossible, and I wanted to spend sufficient time in at least one group to learn about its culture. Therefore, in most meetings, I participated as well as observed. In groups that I visited only once or a few times, I was able to observe without participating.

I attended only what Twelve Step groups refer to as "open" meetings, meaning those that interested members of the public may attend. CoDA has "closed" meetings for gay men and lesbians and for in-depth study of the Twelve Steps in sequence. I did not attempt to attend any of these. I went to at least two open meetings a week, sometimes as many as four. I attended the particular meeting at the location that I refer to as The House of Life consistently over the course of the research, tapering off my attendance towards the end. I attended a second weekly meeting at The House for about six months. The rest of the time, I drove to other locations to visit a total of eighteen different groups. I also attended a CoDA picnic and an all-day event called a CoDA-thon, a combination of meetings, meals, and entertainment orchestrated once a year by the regional CoDA committee known as "Intergroup." I took notes as soon as possible after each meeting or event, usually within an hour. I wrote down what I had seen and heard, as best I could recall. I made up pseudonyms and removed all identifying references.

After I had attended meetings at The House long enough to recognize the regular members, I began to approach some of them for interviews. The norms of Twelve Step groups prevented me from recruiting people for interviews by making an announcement at meetings (see the Appendix for an account of what happened when I attempted to do so). The norms of anonymity also ruled out recruiting people through ads and flyers, although I initially tried that, too. Presuming that I could ask people who attend an anonymous group to identify themselves to a stranger only indicates the depth of my naïveté about Twelve Step culture. The only workable strategy was to approach people as I became familiar with the group. I chose people for interviews along "theoretical sampling" guidelines (Glaser 1978; Glaser and Strauss 1967). I first approached people who had several years of involvement with CoDA, believing that I could learn more—and more quickly—from them. I then approached people who had raised topics about which I wanted to learn more. I re-interviewed several people a year after the first interview. Moreover, my rapport with the members made it possible to speak to them informally after meetings to explore some of their comments directly. I interviewed until my coverage of topics had reached "saturation," meaning that I interviewed until I began to hear the same things repeatedly and stopped learning anything new.[4]

The interviews lasted from an hour and a half to three hours. Most took place in people's homes, but I also conducted some in local diners or coffee shops. All who agreed to an interview signed a standard consent form. I transcribed all the interviews myself and gave each person a copy of the transcript. Because of the norms of anonymity in Twelve Step groups, I felt a responsibility to make sure that I had disguised identities well. I also wanted to thank those I interviewed for their time in some way, and the transcript was a means of doing so. I asked interviewees to read their transcripts and contact me within thirty days if they saw any problems. No one did. After a month's time, I erased each tape.

Analyzing the data

One of the criticisms of ethnography centers on its susceptibility to selective observation. The researcher has a limited capacity to observe, and his or her attention is inevitably drawn to what seems most interesting, according to idiosyncratic criteria. This criticism is not without grounds. Nevertheless, no method is ideal, and the suitability of any one technique must not be judged in the abstract, but in the particular setting in which it was used. Participant observation attempts to understand aspects of social life from the perspective of those who engage in them. It is, therefore, better suited to deciphering the social organization of groups than are more formal data collection procedures. Although the techniques for analyzing ethnographic data cannot be codified to the extent available for data derived more formally, there are widely used and highly respected analytic techniques available in the grounded theory methods (see Glaser and Strauss 1967; Glaser 1978; Charmaz 1983; Strauss and Corbin 1997). In attempting to create order in my data, I used several aspects of grounded theory, especially constant comparative analysis, theoretical sampling, theoretical coding and memoing, and the development of theoretical concepts. The grounded theory method "stresses discovery and theory development rather than logical deductive reasoning which relies on prior theoretical frameworks" (Charmaz 1983, 110). It works deductively, prompting the researcher to ask "What do I see going on here?" and "What do these people seem to be doing?"

When answers suggest themselves, the researcher looks for more data that might shed more light on the question. New answers produce new data, which generate new questions, and so on. Analysis and data collection proceed simultaneously, and the researcher must develop a sensitivity for when to stop. Some specific examples might help illustrate my procedures.

In the initial stages of my fieldwork, I developed simple codes for my notes from meetings. At first, I coded what appeared to be parts of the meeting, such as "Setting up," "Leading," "Speaking," and "Sharing." Before long, I began to develop more sophisticated codes within each of these coded categories. For example, within "Speaking" and "Sharing," I developed codes for "Dysfunctional Childhood," "Abuse," "Hitting Bottom," and "First Steps in Recovery," among others. Through these more detailed codes, I found the similarities that constitute an acceptable account, by CoDA's standards, of codependency and recovery. Once aware of these similarities, I was then able to verify their importance by watching for what happened when they were missing. Gradually, I refined this set of codes into the theoretical concept I call the "narrative formula" of codependency. I simultaneously compared my developing theoretical concept with interview material and with the books on codependency, especially *Codependent No More, Beyond Codependency and Getting Better All the Time,* and *Codependents' Guide to the Twelve Steps* (Beattie 1987, 1989, 1990); *Understanding Co-Dependency* (Wegscheider-Cruse and Cruse 1990); *Co-Dependence: Misunderstood-Mistreated* (Schaef 1986); and *Co-Dependence: Healing the Human Condition* (Whitfield 1991). Having heard the same elements in the same order in three sources of data—and having heard no new ones—I decided that I had found the formula for telling a story of "becoming" codependent, and not simply a few coincidental similarities.

I was also interested in finding out how recovery served as a narrative strategy in individual lives. I wanted to know what people did with the codependent label once they had chosen it. I probed this in the interviews. I began by asking how long each person had attended CoDA and what was happening in their lives when they first arrived in the group. I developed simple codes from the initial interview transcripts, such as "Getting in touch with emotions" and "Taking care of myself." From these, I developed more refined codes that became questions in later interviews. "Getting in touch with emotions" became "Moderating intensity" and "Seeking serenity." "Taking care of myself" branched off into "Self-indulgence" and "Ending relationships." Over time, a set of four topics emerged that constitute the narrative themes I address in part 2. These themes are the product of analyzing individual stories for the social processes they reveal, rather than preserving each story in its uniqueness. In other words, I sought to learn how the "narratives embodied general cultural phenomena" (Chase 1996, 53).

For the more quantitatively minded, narrative themes are similar to the factors that emerge in a factor analysis.[5] This is a statistical technique that identifies similarities, or factors, that underlie a set of items. Attitude scales that address a variety of topics, such as politics, inequality, gender, and the family, may contain a single underlying factor, such as conservatism, that contributes to all the items. Other factors may appear, but only those that meet given statistical criteria are considered. Likewise, although other topics appeared in my notes, these four were most heavily "weighted." For example, one of these narrative themes is emotion management. After I had created codes for "Moderating intensity" and "Seeking serenity," I began to notice two things: I saw that these codes appeared frequently in my notes, and that some of my interview transcripts read as if they were stories of managing emotions. In other words, when I summed up given interviews, they were summaries of emotion management. I then began to seek out people who raised emotion-related topics at meetings. I found that some people seemed to "use" their codependency primarily as a strategy of emotion management. Of course, they mentioned other issues, but emotion management emerged as a dominant topic.

Three other topics made a particularly strong showing. One is the use of codependency to adopt more egalitarian gender standards. Another has to do with using codependency to present oneself as a victim, justifying considerable self-indulgence in the process. A third is the use of codependency to make a transition from one set of commitments to another, in other words, to "detach" from a relationship that now seems problematic.

Certain social-structural circumstances predispose one's choice of particular narrative themes. In part 2, I examine the linkages between structure and narrative strategy through case studies of each of the four predominant narrative themes. Each theme applies not only to the story, but to the self experience by the teller, since "stories give direction to lives" (Rosenwald and Ochberg 1992, 6). In each of the case studies, social structure influences the use of a particular narrative. The narrative then shapes the interpretation a person gives of the events of his or her life, and this becomes the point of that life.

I should point out that the single instances in the four case studies by no means constitute my sole source of evidence of a given narrative. I should also say that there is no "pure" narrative of codependency, and that no one person uses codependency *only* for the purpose suggested by a single theme. Most members express a bit of one theme and a bit of another. This is where the metaphor of factors is particularly helpful. Several codependency narratives may intersect in one person. Those that I treat at length account for most of the patterned variation among the narratives that I observed. What remains is, more or less, noise.

Although I have just drawn on a statistical metaphor, I make no statistically generalizable claims about this research. I did not—and could not—sample a representative population of codependents. I describe a phenomenon that seems to appeal largely to white, middle-class Baby Boomers. Since most Americans either aspire to or are judged by middle-class standards, the issues raised and illuminated by codependency have resonance among many other groups, as well. Moreover, since selfhood can be considered an American entitlement, the efforts undertaken by men and women conspicuously in search of the self can reveal what makes this taken-for-granted experience possible.

PART ONE

NOT JUST ANOTHER ADDICTION: THE ROLE OF INSTITUTIONS

CoDA is a very recent 12-Step offspring of AA.
(Mitchell-Norberg, Warren, and Zale 1995)

THIS IS THE MOST COMMON ASSUMPTION about the appearance of the support group for codependents: In the beginning, there was Alcoholics Anonymous. Americans supposedly appreciate following programs and steps, and this predilection has been exploited through the spawning of innumerable offshoots. Though not entirely inaccurate, this origin story is an oversimplification. It obscures important differences between the claims made by the codependency discourse and those contained in AA's more traditional stance toward addiction. In several significant ways, codependency and CoDA represent far more of a *departure* from AA's claims than an *extension* of them.[1] The failure to recognize this has meant that the broader set of social circumstances that codependency addresses has been ignored or underestimated. This is one reason why it is important to clarify its origins. It is important to know that most people who identify with codependency do so in circumstances that range far afield from alcoholism or addiction. Codependency, as a discourse, and Codependents Anonymous, as a group, respond to very real concerns that are unique to these times. The rising divorce rate and the fragility of relationships, to name just two such circumstances, help to account for the mostly generational character of codependency's appeal. Those who identify themselves as codependent use the designation and the discourse to restore meaning to disrupted lives. It makes sense to understand what they are doing and how.

Another reason why it is important to understand CoDA's origins is that it has percolated into the American cultural landscape. When I began this research, it had already generated cartoons, jokes (*What does a codependent say after sex? "That was good for you. How was it for me?"*), and satirical books, such as *Cat-Dependent No More. Saturday Night Live* has created skits around codependency, complete with caricatures of the members of a "dysfunctional" family. The comic performer Reno had spoofed it in her one-woman off-Broadway show, *In Rage and Rehab*, which ran for three months and then became an HBO special. "Thank you for sharing" has become a successful snide remark.

If getting the jokes and understanding its strategic uses provide insufficient motive for taking codependency seriously as a cultural phenomenon, a third reason might be more compelling. Regardless of one's opinion of the vision of personhood and social relationships it offers, it nevertheless informs much of everyday life. The humor is only possible because many of the assumptions underlying the discourse of codependency are taken for granted. They have been incorporated into other discourses that address new and related problems, and will continue to reproduce in this manner. In many ways, I am already looking at codependency in the rear-view mirror. For these three reasons, along with others that will unfold throughout this book, it is important to get its origins right. The first two chapters that constitute part 1 will help clarify how and why the discourse and its support group appeared when they did. The following two chapters examine what the group and the discourse offer those who use them.

CHAPTER ONE

CODEPENDENCY, ADDICTION TREATMENT, AND THE THERAPEUTIC ETHOS

The discourse of codependency and the support group Codependents Anonymous exist today because of the trail blazed by Adult Children of Alcoholics, or ACoA. It makes more sense to understand CoDA as the offspring of ACoA rather than AA. Nevertheless, the three groups make significantly different claims about the "conditions" to which they respond. Members of each group make sense of their lives in very different ways. The failure to examine these differences has meant that groups with subtle yet significant schisms are erroneously combined into a monolithic recovery "movement."

Until the founding of ACoA, Al-Anon constituted the sole source of group support for relatives and close friends of alcoholics. Al-Anon was formed in 1951 by the wives of two AA members. The group adopted AA's Twelve Steps and offered support for women married to alcoholics. Although Al-Anon had long recognized the impact of alcoholism on family members, it did not do so in the way that the Adult Child discourse eventually would. The audience for a support group for people who claimed to experience the intergenerational effects of alcoholism would not emerge until the advent of a particular understanding of the dynamics of the family. This would come with the incorporation of concepts from the field of family therapy, as developed by Virginia Satir and others. Until roughly the 1970s, addiction treatment and family therapy existed as separate discourses. Then, theories used in the latter arena were integrated into the former.

Although I cannot possibly do justice to the field of family therapy here, I can sketch out a few of its core premises. The term "family therapy" does not connote a particular therapeutic technique or approach, but its many variants do share a belief in the family as a system. In this view, each family member plays a role that makes the whole more than the sum of its parts. Day-to-day interactions manifest a cumulative shared history that follows a circular causality: Each generation grows up to "become" its parents, for better or for worse. Families develop rules to hide their secrets, their embarrassments, and their black sheep from outsiders. Children internalize these rules to please their parents. Eventually, the collusion inhibits intimacy, trust, and self-confidence. Adult life consists of re-enacting your childhood, and unresolved conflicts rear their ugly heads throughout.

During the 1960s and '70s, a few trendsetting therapists and addiction treatment professionals had begun to advocate the view that treatment of an alcoholic should involve his or her spouse and children, as well. Purportedly, "family members get caught up in the consequences of the illness [of alcoholism] and become emotionally ill themselves" (Woititz [1983] 1990, xv). This view gained legitimacy when the well-funded National Institute for Alcoholism and Alcohol Abuse (NIAAA) took an interest in the impact of alcoholism on children. The NIAAA sponsored the first study of the services provided to children of alcoholics—services provided largely by family therapists. Gradually, the discourse of family therapy percolated into addiction treatment. Where Al-Anon had maintained that the family could remain healthy despite the presence of alcoholism, the introduction of family systems thinking called that possibility into question. Then, Janet Woititz, the acknowledged "mother" of the Adult Child movement, began to popularize the idea that "the child of an alcoholic has no age. The same things hold true if you are five or 55" ([1983] 1990, ix). Within a few years, the treatment of the "children" of alcoholics began to include grown men and women. The term "adult child" entered mainstream vocabulary with the publication of *Adult Children of Alcoholics* (Woititz [1983] 1990). The book reached the *New York Times* bestseller list and remained there for a year, without formal promotion. It put Health Communications, Inc., now the leading recovery publisher, on the map.

The concerns of those who identified themselves as Adult Children did not articulate well with the tenets of AA and Al-Anon, the existing avenues of support for alcohol-related troubles. The Adult Child does not belong in AA for at least three reasons. First, AA exists solely for the alcoholic who wishes to become or remain sober. Some Adult Children have drinking problems themselves, but many do not. Discussion in AA focuses on firsthand experience with alcohol, not on problems once removed, which are the primary concerns of Adult Children. Second, in AA, blaming the constitution of your family for your drinking indicates a type of self-justification called "stinkin' thinkin'." AA maintains that the alcoholic simply needs to put down the drink; no one else needs to change. The Adult Child discourse, in contrast, locates alcohol-related problems in intergenerational family dynamics, some of which must change in order for the Adult Child to recover. The Adult Child must sometimes "detach" from family members whom he or she recognizes as troublesome. The hardship and distress of detachment can be so painful, Woititz claims, that AA's admonition to stop drinking and go to meetings "is a piece of cake" by comparison ([1983] 1990, 130). Third, the Adult Child discourse reverses AA's "conformist" logic of recovery. In AA, the "disease" of alcoholism allegedly causes the alcoholic's failure to conform to existing normative standards, which are considered essentially sound. AA's discourse directs attention to the harm done by the alcoholic as a result of this failure, and recovery, in AA, comes through conforming to existing norms. The Adult Child discourse reverses this causal sequence. It focuses on the harm inflicted through conforming to repressive family rules that hid the presence of alcoholism.[1] Consequently, it takes an especially critical perspective on the institution of the family and its norms. AA, in contrast, says nothing about the institution and respects its norms. For the alcoholic, conformity *is* recovery. For the Adult Child, conformity cannot be recovery; it can only be dysfunction.

In short, the Adult Child discourse did what AA advised against doing: It took the focus off the alcoholic and placed it on outside factors, such as the dynamics of the family. It also imported a critical, anti-institutional perspective into an essentially conservative discourse. AA, with its emphasis on active drinking, could not accommodate the issues for which Adult Children sought help.

Al-Anon, the more likely source of support for children of alcoholics, did not welcome them, either. Al-Anon is for family members living with active alcoholism, which does not describe most Adult Children. The alcoholism that affected the family system that, in turn, affected the Adult Child may have existed generations ago. Or, an Adult Child may have an alcoholic parent. In either case, however, he or she does not typically live with active drinking. Al-Anon, meanwhile, has had some difficulty figuring out what to do with Adult Children, and the organization has issued several statements saying that, like AA, it sees the importation of a nontraditional Twelve Step perspective as problematic (see Rice 1996, 60–61; see also Asher and Brissett 1988, 345).

Since the concerns of Adult Children did not fit into either of the existing support groups, they created their own. Woititz explains that

> [because Al-Anon] is designed primarily to serve the newest member living with an active problem, and rightly so, others who are in different life circumstances have to do some translating in order to relate what is being said to their own lives and to gain the benefit. So adult children, although equally needy, don't quite connect. The development of a much-needed support group for ACoA's fills that gap ([1983] 1990, ix).

The ACoA groups that filled the gap Woititz speaks of did not simply expand on what already existed. Their new claims about the intergenerational impact of alcoholism moved beyond what standard addiction rhetoric could address. But the importation of therapeutic principles does not automatically make ACoA a creation of a therapeutic culture, either. For while its causal logic came from therapy, its discourse departed from therapeutic mainstays.

The Adult Child concept owes a great deal to widespread diffusion of the therapeutic ethos over roughly the past three decades. This way of understanding personhood uprooted older, more traditional beliefs about the relationship between the individual and society. The older beliefs had portrayed norms and institutions as essentially good, and psychological health involved fitting in and conforming. Within this context, a program such as AA, founded in 1935, made sense. AA's discourse maintained that, when a problem occurs, society does not need to change; the individual alone must bring his or her behavior back in line with normative standards. The therapeutic ethos reversed this perspective. It portrayed the self as innately good, with "needs" that deserve priority over conforming to society's norms. From this perspective, trying to "fit in" warps the development of the self. Problems occur *because of* conformity to normative standards. Psychological health, in the form of self-actualization, comes through freedom from social conventions. Mainstream society, with all its repressive forces, makes people sick. Compelling evidence suggests that large numbers of Americans have accepted the therapeutic ethos as a means through which to think about their lives (see, for example, Bellah et al. 1985; Veroff, Douvan, and Kulka 1981a, 1981b; Yankelovich 1981; Zilbergeld 1983).[2] The timing of the diffusion of the therapeutic ethos makes the members of the Baby Boom—those born between 1946 and 1964—most likely to have adopted its tenets, intentionally or otherwise.

The idea of a self repressed by conformity represents the first point

at which Adult Child discourse departs from its therapeutic roots. While self-actualized, or -actualiz*ing*, individuals require the freedom to explore the needs of the self, Adult Children claim to lack a sense of self altogether. When Woititz first came up with this idea during the 1970s, she had trouble getting anyone to take her seriously. "It was a time of I–I–I," she writes. "So the idea that there were millions of people being profoundly impacted by the behaviors and attitudes of others and who had no self to indulge ran contrary to the flow of the time" (Woititz [1983] 1990, vii–viii). She and the other founders of ACoA did not claim that Adult Children need to fulfill a self that had simply suffered repression; they argued that the experience of growing up with alcoholic family dynamics destroys the sense of self altogether. This claim represents a significant departure from, not the further development of, the dominant therapeutic ethos. The discourse of codependency would continue along this path. One of its advocates calls it "the disease of lost selfhood" (Whitfield 1991), and Rice refers to codependents as "the symbolic opposites of self-actualized individuals" (1996, 84).

ACoA's second departure from its therapeutic heritage would make group membership possible. The therapeutic ethos manifests an explicitly anti-institutional orientation. It assumes a pre- or extrasocial self, and blames institutions and norms for repressing its innate goodness. Because family, friendship, and community constitute the primary means through which norms, values, and beliefs pass from one generation to the next, it has subjected these informal institutions to especially harsh attack. Consequently, the therapeutic ethos cannot recommend group membership, with its roles, norms, and obligations, as an aid to fulfillment. Yet, ACoA discourse does exactly this. Because Woititz and others have a background in alcoholism treatment, and because groups constitute the treatment of choice for alcoholism, the founders of ACoA legitimated group membership at a time when it had largely fallen into disrepute. The first step an Adult Child is advised to take—after reading *Adult Children of Alcoholics*—is to find a support group suited to his or her individual situation. The therapeutic ethos, in its pure, anti-institutional form, could not possibly have made this recommendation.

The establishment of ACoA groups in the 1980s represented a divergence from the major tenets of the therapeutic ethos by recommending a distinctly institutional form of recovery. Moreover, ACoA deviated from the discourse of its Twelve Step progenitors by bringing concerns other than alcohol or substances into play. This double departure paved the way for Codependents Anonymous.

THE BIRTH OF CoDA

Until roughly 1980, the term "codependent" had meant "co-alcoholic" or "co-chemically dependent." It remained largely an "insider" term used by addiction treatment professionals. Initially, it referred to "anyone who has been affected by the person who has been afflicted by the disease of chemical dependency" (Larsen 1983). Being "affected by" usually meant trying to find the one elusive thing that could ostensibly put an end to the drinking or drug use. This involved a nearly obsessive attempt to make everything just right—including oneself. Spouses of addicts or alcoholics often complained that they had become so engrossed in trying to meet the ephemeral "needs" of their significant others that they had "lost touch with" themselves and their feelings. Eventually, they felt that the lives of others had taken precedence over their own—a state that could only be considered problematic in the era of the therapeutic ethos.

In the 1980s, treatment professionals began to notice that the characteristics that had been described as codependency often appeared in people who had no addictions or close associations with addicts or alcoholics at all. In counseling, they saw people who claimed they:

—have difficulty identifying feelings

—minimize, alter, or deny their feelings

—have difficulty making decisions

—are embarrassed to receive recognition, praise, or gifts

—are very sensitive to others' feelings and assume the same feelings

—are extremely loyal, remaining in harmful situations too long

—put aside personal interests and hobbies to do what others want

—accept sex as a substitute for love

—think [sic] and feel responsible for other people—for other people's feelings, thoughts, actions, choices, wants, needs, well-being, lack of well-being, and ultimate destiny

—anticipate other people's needs

—think they're not quite good enough. (selected from CoDA 1995, 4–5; Beattie 1987, 37)

What led people who were "extremely loyal" or who "anticipate other people's needs" to seek help? In many cases, the therapeutic ethos seems to have produced some of the very problems it aimed at correct-

ing. It placed the needs of the self over and above institutional demands and expectations. As a consequence, it directed considerable criticism at institutions such as marriage, the family, and friendship. Its prescriptive literature often advised people to break free of these obligations, if necessary, in order to discover their full potential. Yet, it offered nothing to replace them, no indication of how to be a social being and simultaneously remain unencumbered by mainstream social patterns. For many people, this combination of condemnation and a lack of alternatives

> translated into a seemingly endless string of disillusionments and disappointments: failed relationships, friendships, marriages; an overarching and pervasive ambiguity about how to decide among all but limitless courses of action; the demise of the established social and cultural foundations from which most people, historically, have arrived at some stable sense of themselves, of their world, and of their place in that world. (Rice 1996, 35)

The "endless string of disillusionments and disappointments" left demographic landmarks among the Baby Boomers, in particular, as they came of age under the therapeutic ethos. Demographer Cheryl Russell, who has studied Baby Boomers extensively, describes them as the first generation of "free agents" (1993). In 1969, baseball player Curt Flood, the world's first free agent and himself a Baby Boomer, sued the St. Louis Cardinals for trading him to the Philadelphia Phillies. Flood lost the battle but won the war. Six years later, an arbitrator ruled that players should have freedom of choice, and free agency gradually became a part of not only baseball, but basketball and football, as well. This victory, Russell argues, symbolizes the moral stance of a generation. For free agents,

> the interests of the individual take precedence over the needs of the family, the rights of an organization, or the power of the state. This perspective is more emotional than intellectual, more psychological than political. It is not a conscious belief, but an unconscious force, shaping the relationships between free agents and their families, friends, neighbors, employers, and the community at large. . . . As individualistic Baby Boomers came of age over the past thirty years, they withdrew from the institutions of American society. (Russell 1993, 27–28)

Of course, "free agency" and the therapeutic ethos did not exist in a vacuum. Therapeutic language alone was not responsible for divorce. Indeed, it is a mistake to believe that the therapeutic ethos was fundamentally at odds with larger societal trends that were somehow stable.

The first generation of "free agents" faced a confluence of social and economic changes, as well. The therapeutic ethos was helping them adapt to this concurrent change. Simultaneously, however, it was also changing the understanding of personhood and one's relationship to society. It is in this particular change that the origins of the codependency discourse can be found.

The therapeutic ethos promised fulfillment, but could not make good on its promises. It offered its believers two choices: submit to the collective constraints of the established social order, or try for fulfillment on a voyage through uncharted waters. You could either be a conformist or an individual. While the former choice exacted its toll in the form of "sickness," the latter resulted in unprecedented divorce rates, increased rates of cohabitation, and decreased interest in parenthood, at least within this particular generation. Herein lies the paradox of "free agency": Putting self-fulfillment first justifies ending bad marriages and intolerable commitments. This freedom comes at a cost, however; it jeopardizes the institutional anchors that create a secure sense of self. As the first Baby Boomers were reaching their thirties and forties, they paid the price for "free agency." The generation before them had begun to seek professional help for personal problems in unprecedented numbers, and the Baby Boomers continued that trend. The number of Americans seeking professional counsel nearly doubled between 1957 and 1976, when the first Boomers reached age thirty (see Veroff, Douvan, and Kulka 1981a, 1981b). Simultaneously, therapists and others developed various ideological tools to respond to their clients' concerns. They diagnosed the feeling of having no sense of self—but having no alcoholic parents to blame—as codependency.

The creators of the codependency discourse believed that addiction, in the classic sense of alcoholism or substance abuse, need not exist for people to identify with the sorts of problems that codependency addresses. Codependency, they claimed, constitutes *a disease in its own right,* purportedly brought on by living in a "dysfunctional" society. The logic behind this view is important for understanding how those who identify with codependency see the world and their relationship to it. In an ideal world, or at least one that is ideal in a psychotherapeutic sense, everyone would have a sense of self-fulfillment. However, vast numbers of people claim to lack a sense of self altogether, not to mention the attendant fulfillment. Since the family system serves as the main conduit of values and norms, and since, in this view, learning these values and norms requires overwhelming conformity, it follows that the family *must* deprive children of healthy selves. Since people are "meant"

to have healthy selves, depriving them in this way amounts to the deprivation of a basic right, which is tantamount to "abuse." The "abuse" suffered in the family allegedly produces people who spend the rest of their lives trying to heal their wounded "inner children." They seek compensatory fulfillment in sex, drinking, drugs, work, people-pleasing, and other diversions. It is the act of looking for other sources of fulfillment that is of concern here, because you should, ideally, be satisfied with who you are. In this view, turning to potentially addictive substances and behaviors can itself be addictive, apart from the substances and behaviors themselves. Recovery author Charles Whitfield describes codependency as an "addiction to looking elsewhere" (1991, 4). This addiction—which underlies and produces all others—is called codependency. It is a "master" addiction, or, as *The CoDA Book* puts it, "the root of all addictions" (1995, 117). As Rice explains, codependency "conceptualizes the psychological condition that is caused by cultural repression of the self as an addiction" (1996, 103).

Since codependency purportedly lies at the root of all other addictions, and since any behavior can be an addiction if it is a substitute for "true" fulfillment, all behaviors can be attributed to codependency—including those that indicate its presence. Its causes depend on which of its popularizers one consults. As a former addict, Melody Beattie gives causal priority to alcoholism and drug addiction, but claims that "many other circumstances seemed to produce [codependency] also" (1987, 31). These "other circumstances" include "having a relationship, personally or professionally, with troubled, needy, or dependent people" (31). Sharon Wegscheider-Cruse's depiction (1985) reflects her therapeutic background. For her, codependency can afflict "anyone who grew up in an emotionally repressive family." Likewise, family therapist Robert Subby attributes it to oppressive family rules. Anne Wilson Schaef imputes society's "addictive process," especially as it plays out in churches, families, and schools. Whitfield, a physician and psychotherapist, claims that codependency can cause "many physical, psychological, and spiritual conditions" (1991, 8).

Not only do its *causes* depend on whom one asks, its *symptoms* do, as well. Consider how these members of CoDA described their codependency:

> I have a tendency toward dysfunctional relationships. I usually pick people who are not working, or who don't have transportation. So this puts me up on the pedestal, and I can control it. I can come and go and see them when I want to and when I need them. And I can withdraw at any time. *(woman, forty-two)*

For me, it's a people addiction and it's a food addiction. *(man, forty)*

Sometimes my feelings are very large, and I know that they're inappropriate, and I don't know where to hang them, and that's what it is, what
codependency is, for me. *(woman, forty-five)*

One man told me that his codependency "was under everything." He
said, "It made me need these outside things [food, alcohol, and relation-
ships] to go to." Later in our conversation, he reversed the causal relationship he had just implied. Codependency, he said, "is doing something outside of myself to make me feel good on the inside." In short,
it can act as both cause and symptom of *a disease in its own right.*

Cause *and* symptom? How can this be? What kind of "disease" is
this? Codependency is not a "disease" in any usual sense of the term.
It is a discourse, with "disease," "addiction," "dysfunction," and other
terms serving as ways of talking about yourself and the formative events
of your life. Although it is typically described in medical terms of causes
and symptoms, it cannot be adequately understood as a singular entity
of any kind. It is better understood as an "open text" (Eco 1979; Fish
1980). It allows various audiences to generate meanings that serve their
equally varying interests and identities. It contains unresolved contradictions that each person can explore in order to locate similarities to his
or her own interests or experiences. Thus, people in different social
locations activate the many potential meanings of codependency differently. Its popularity depends on this definitional ambiguity.[3] It must appeal to a wide and potentially unlimited audience. Whitfield (1991)
seems to have recognized the necessity of openness, although surely for
very different reasons, when he wrote that "people who identify as being
co-dependent . . . are equally entitled to any use that they can make of
the concept and experience of being co-dependent" (52).

This does not imply that the meaning of codependency, or of any
"open text," is "anarchically" open (Fiske 1986). Any and all meanings
cannot be drawn from it. But what constitutes any one person's codependency depends on what that person sees as troublesome in his or
her own history. In one case, it may refer to a pattern of alcoholic or
substance-abusing partners. In another, it may mean "neglected spirituality" or a "wounded inner child." Moreover, codependency can stand
for different things within a single life. It can articulate with the range
of circumstances and situations that people bring to it. Even in a setting
most likely to engender a monolithic concept of what it means to "be"
codependent—one designed specifically for wives of alcoholics—researchers found that

the very definitional ambiguity of the concept allowed the women to pick and choose among the varied characteristics of codependency. They could, so to speak, choose the kind of codependent they wanted to be. For some, the assumption of the identity "codependent" involved a lifelong commitment to a fundamental change of self. To others, it resulted in a relatively mild alteration of behavior, attitude, and identity. (Asher and Brissett 1988, 347)

Codependency's "definitional ambiguity" does not suggest that it has become "so vague as to be meaningless" (Krestan and Bepko 1990). Almost everyone who has written about it has taken a shot at its "freely shifting definitions" (Babcock 1995, 3). A proliferation of definitions does not make a concept meaningless, however; if in doubt, ask any social scientist about "culture." The people who nonetheless understood that they had this ambiguous "disease" could not bring their complaints to AA, Al-Anon, or even ACoA, which were all more or less dedicated to alcoholism. They experienced the same difficulty that the Adult Children had encountered: No existing group welcomed discussion of their concerns. Ken, one of the founders of CoDA (his last name omitted in keeping with Twelve Step anonymity), describes the situation:

Mary and I had been in counseling for co-dependency for about two years and were finding it increasingly difficult to gain support from and talk about our co-dependency in A.A. meetings. And rightfully so, for A.A. is a program of recovery from alcoholism, not codependency. In my work during those two years, I had completed hundreds of evaluations for co-dependency on patients and family members and found a great many of these people *were not adult children or friends, family members, or relatives of alcoholics.* Many were extremely uncomfortable in attending [ACoA] or Al-Anon as they felt they didn't quite fit in, and eventually left these programs and were left without support for their recovery from co-dependency. (CoDA 1987, emphasis added)

People who identified with codependency did not fit in at AA or Al-Anon because the discourse is twice removed from traditional Twelve Step thinking. Not only does it focus on family systems issues that AA members consider "stinkin' thinkin'," it does not address alcohol or specific substances. Ken and his wife Mary recognized that this "disease" did not fit neatly into the paradigms of the existing support groups. To fill the gap, they got together with some others and founded Codependents Anonymous as a "fellowship of men and women whose common problem is an inability to maintain functional relationships." They adopted and adapted AA's Twelve Steps as guides for assessing and changing one's life. They borrowed AA's Twelve Traditions, which outline the group's voluntaristic, democratic, anonymous principles. The Traditions ensure that CoDA, like all other Twelve Step groups, would endorse no outside causes and draw support entirely from member contributions. CoDA also adopted AA's organizational structure, consisting of a nested series of voluntary committees and a National Service Organization.

About thirty people attended the first CoDA meeting on October 22, 1986. Within a month, the number had increased to over a hundred (CoDA 1987, 1995). One hundred and twenty new groups were established the first year. At the time of this writing, the number of groups approaches four thousand in the United States alone, with meetings in all fifty states. The National Service Office has these data because new groups are formed by registering with them. There is no cost to starting up a group beyond the rental of a meeting facility. CoDA charges no fee to register a group; the registration simply assures that a new group will be included in the national and local directories of meetings. While there may be "underground" CoDA groups, it is not likely that their numbers are significant. Anyone sufficiently motivated to run a meeting would also want to gather enough people, and registering a group allows newcomers to locate the meetings. Beyond numbers of groups, however, demographic data about codependents do not abound, not least because CoDA has not conducted a survey of its membership. The guarantee of anonymity precludes any valid demography of Twelve Step groups.

In its wholehearted adoption of anonymity and other aspects of the Steps, CoDA clearly emulates AA. Beyond this, however, the two groups have little in common. Several members of CoDA echoed Ken in describing discomfort they have experienced in other Twelve Step groups. To be sure, many people felt quite comfortable attending an assortment of meetings. More often, however, people said that "codependent issues" were particularly unwelcome in AA. For example, one man said that "feelings and stuff like that wasn't [sic] very accepted at most [AA] meetings." Another told me that he found AA "stuffy" when it came to talking about relationships. A woman who sometimes attended AA with her boyfriend agreed. AA, she said, "sticks to drinking . . . people go to AA to talk about drinking. You don't mention relationships or feelings. It's very specific. They'll steer you back if you talk about anything else. They'll shame you, so you learn what they're about." [4]

The problems that people bring to CoDA have necessitated several changes in the way that Twelve Step meetings are conducted. You will find no coffee served at CoDA meetings, for example, while the coffee

31

pot is a fixture in AA, along with the occasional cake or donuts. Because CoDA members may have various "addictions"—including feeling responsible for the coffee pot—no food or drink is offered. A few meetings in New York City even request that members bring no food or beverages other than water to meetings. Whether this reflects "weaknesses" within those particular groups or simply a means of keeping rented facilities clean, the absence of coffee nevertheless distinguishes CoDA from AA.

Another difference is the absence of sponsors. In AA, a new member will typically have regular contact with someone far enough along in recovery to offer support and encouragement for sobriety. Although CoDA does not prohibit sponsorship, I never encountered any evidence of it during my research. Several members I spoke with believe that sponsoring another could place you at risk for lapsing into the over-concern for others that indicates codependency. CoDA members become captains of their own recoveries. Your "inner child" or "true self" is the only guide to what you "need" to do. The idea that one person could, and should, advise another on recovery is heresy in CoDA. In contrast, AA explicitly distrusts the self as a guide to behavior. AA's "text," the *Big Book,* claims that the root of the alcoholic's problem is "a philosophy of self-sufficiency," sometimes called "selfishness," "self-centeredness," and "self-will run riot." CoDA members, in contrast, see these qualities as praiseworthy. As one woman told me, in terms that, although perhaps exaggerated, still highlight her preoccupation, "I like CoDA because it helps me to stay focused on myself. Worrying about everybody else nearly killed me." To be sure, people are free to call one another between meetings using the voluntary phone lists that circulate within groups. But the motivation for reaching out is "What do I need?" not "How can I help someone else?" To ask the latter question would be to encourage your "disease."

The vision that established CoDA is decidedly *not* the same one that established AA. Understanding the two groups as one runs roughshod over several decades of discursive change that generated different support groups. CoDA is not the result of churning out ever more specialized versions of a group originally designed for alcoholics. For, as Kuhn and Foucault have made clear, new ideas do not come from the continuous development of established models. Rather, they come from the combination of models previously considered incommensurable. There are ideological miles between AA and CoDA that allow CoDA to open its meetings with the statement that "many of us were raised in families where addictions existed—some of us were not" (CoDA 1988).

CHAPTER TWO

IN SEARCH OF THE RECOVERY "INDUSTRY"

Ever new branches of the recovery system are being spawned every day it seems.
(Rapping 1996, 90)

Codependency and its treatment lie at the heart of how the recovery industry seeks to manipulate and control women.
(Tallen 1990, 20)

How do people get into CoDA? There is, according to some, a movement afoot. Somewhere, a "recovery system" or "industry" endlessly spins out newer, more profitable addictions. This juggernaut allegedly targets people who are looking for easy answers to the questions of adult life and draws them into the growing ranks of a "recovery movement."

This is the assumption made by what I call "middlebrow" analysts of popular culture, who complain that America has become a nation of whiners and victims (see, for example, Sykes 1992). "Middlebrow" criticism exists largely outside the universities. Most appears in popular periodicals. Some makes it further up the scale, into *Harper's* or the *New York Times Book Review*. Instances include Faludi's *Backlash*, Kaminer's *I'm Dysfunctional, You're Dysfunctional*, or Babcock and McKay's collection of feminist critiques by journalists, therapists, and substance abuse treatment professionals.

"Middlebrow" critics have used the "recovery movement" to air their own pet social peeves without considering the circumstances to which such a "movement" might respond. They claim that if Americans would just get back to—and here the substance varies—they would not accept Band-Aid solutions like codependency for deeper problems. Codependency is a cop-out, they argue. It tells the wrong story to gullible people who are manipulated by a greedy "recovery industry." The feminist slant to this line of thinking argues that women are especially susceptible to this manipulation, and that codependency represents a retreat from the advances of feminism.[1]

It is easy to dismiss Americans as gullible, in general, and women as particularly susceptible to certain kinds of manipulation. It is also easy to mistake the proliferation of Twelve Step groups for a "movement." But this does not mean that people—women in particular—are being herded into CoDA by a "recovery industry," or that their concerns are somehow not "real." At the risk of empirical solipsism ("If I haven't heard of it, it must not exist"), consider, for a moment, what I had to do to locate CoDA groups in which to do this research. Given my background, if there were a recovery "movement" at work, surely it would have targeted me. But I had no idea how to find CoDA. Although I had seen posters for local AA and Al-Anon meetings, I had never seen one for CoDA. They had no listing in my local phone book at the time, although they did soon after, and a web site now makes contact even easier. Lacking a local phone number, I had to use ingenuity. Fortunately, I was not motivated by personal crisis, because it took several weeks of persistent effort to find a group.

Codependents' Guide to the Twelve Steps lists addresses and phone numbers of various Twelve Step resources. I called the number listed for CoDA's National Service Office and left a message asking about meetings in my area. After a few days, a volunteer called back and gave me the number for the local Intergroup. I called it and received instructions for getting a meeting list by mail. Once I received it, I had to locate the meeting site, and—as a shy person, something that cannot be overemphasized—I had to gather the courage to walk into a room full of strangers without knowing what to expect. Each time I went to a new meeting I had to do much the same thing. Granted, I began to know what to expect at the meetings, but finding the churches and other buildings in which they were held took consistent dedication. Sometimes the printed schedule I had was outdated and a group had moved to another location. Finding it required another phone call to Intergroup and further puzzling over a map.

Such is research, some might say. Dedication comes with the territory. To be sure, but this strengthens my point: I was highly motivated to exert this level of effort. Yet, the people who are not doing research get there through much the same route. No one takes them by the hand. They, too, must send self-addressed, stamped envelopes and locate parish halls in unfamiliar towns. Even when a therapist refers them to a group, they still must find it on their own and risk feeling foolish as they mistakenly walk into a meeting of AA or the missions committee taking place in another room.

The point bears repeating: because this was research, I was highly motivated to persist. Someone without my particular motivation must therefore have some equally pressing concerns. Going to the first meeting takes dedication and courage; it also implies a level of hurt that overpowers potential apathy. Given what it takes to get people to a meeting of any sort, I consider it nearly miraculous that CoDA has flourished. It would be far easier to stay home and read books or listen to tapes. Indeed, if people were taking this easier route, or taking it more often, instead of going to meetings, this would be evidence of the "recovery industry" at work. If people were being manipulated by a profit-oriented "recovery industry," it would hardly be in that "industry's" interest to lead them into a voluntaristic group that does not stand to gain economically from their participation.

Yet, the middlebrow critics suggest that the people who go to CoDA do not have "real" problems. These are people who simply refuse to face the realities of adult life, and a multimillion-dollar business caters to their weaknesses. This view is wrong on several counts. As my efforts to find meetings made clear, without sufficient motivation, no one would bother. This does not mean that people have not been influenced by, say, the marketing efforts of recovery publishers. Nor does it mean that money has not been made from codependency. Rather, it means that the middlebrow critics have created a poor basis from which to dismiss—much less understand—what CoDA offers. Let me address their claims systematically.

First, the term "recovery industry" evokes a vast network that comprises helping professionals, publishers, authors, treatment facilities, insurance companies, and manufacturers of Twelve Step paraphernalia, all working to sell the message of codependency. The idea of an "industry" conflates several different economic and professional sectors, some that indeed overlap, and others that do not. Publishing, for example, sometimes overlaps with the therapeutic community. During the 1980s, many mainstream publishers entered into co-marketing agreements with the educational divisions of substance abuse treatment centers. Harper and Row affiliated with Hazelden Treatment Center in Minneapolis to publish and distribute the Harper/Hazelden line that includes Beattie's *Codependent No More.* Prentice-Hall established a similar venture with Parkside Medical Services Corporation, a national chain of rehabilitation centers for alcoholism, drug addiction, eating disorders, and psychiatric illness. Prentice-Hall/Parkside Recovery Books publishes *Codependents' Guide to the Twelve Steps* (Beattie 1990). Obviously, publishers profited from these affiliations; usually, the treatment center did direct-mail advertising, contacted local book stores, and made an expert available for the media (see Bethune 1990). In these instances, publishers simply engaged in sensible marketing strategies: they detected a trend and followed it, taking advantage of available resources along the way. However satisfying politically, interpreting this as manipulation seems to me a naive understanding of publishing's raison d'être.[2]

Publishing also overlaps with the therapeutic community in that most recovery authors write from experience. Yet dismissive blanket labeling, such as Elizabeth Kristol's "therapy-cum-publishing phenomenon" (1990), leaves little room for serious consideration of the connections—and lack thereof—between these two domains. Within the culture of substance abuse treatment, people who have "been there"—who have themselves been alcoholics or addicts—purportedly make the best counselors. Many people in that arena believe that only recovering addicts and alcoholics have the qualifications to counsel others about the experience. These "professional ex-s," as one observer calls them, capitalize on a deviant biography by transforming it into a career in counseling (Brown 1991).[3] The majority of the professional counselors in substance abuse centers—72 percent, according to one national survey—entered the counseling profession after themselves undergoing treatment for substance abuse (NAADAC 1986). Several of the leading advocates of codependency—Melody Beattie, John Bradshaw, and the founders of CoDA, for example—came from backgrounds of addiction and underwent treatment. Research among "professional ex-s" suggests that substance abuse counselors typically enter the profession through their exposure to formal treatment, not through involvement in a Twelve Step program (Brown 1991), which is the primary vehicle through which most people come to identify with codependency. Moreover, thousands of counselors have not become authors with the celebrity of Beattie and Bradshaw. Assailing the success of a few "professional ex-s" as a marketing device reveals a certain condescension: Because they only want to make money, we should not take them seriously. This accusation is seldom leveled at other "professional ex-s." Former prisoners and gang members counsel delinquent youth, and some have written books about their criminal pasts. Yet one hears no accusations of how these "experts" only want to peddle the straight life to a vulnerable target market.

Second, and related to the issue of "professional ex-s," is the middle-brow critique that most of the advocates of codependency do what they do because there is money in it. Without question, many along the line have grown rich on codependency. But economic success hardly constitutes evidence of intention. At the risk of sounding naive, I believe them when they say, as Melody Beattie has, that their primary objective is not profit but helping others see their way clear to a better life. I also believe what Gary Seidler, cofounder and president of Health Communications, Inc. (HCI), the leading publisher in the recovery niche, had to say:

> And that's something else—where Kaminer tears us apart in one chapter where she talks about conferences and the conference boutique, and implies how much money was made in conferences and doesn't name us, but meant us because we were doing all the conferences. All I can tell you is the conferences were very expensive to produce. And, yes, we made a lot of money on them, but only because we had such tremendous numbers of people who came. There were many other conferences that we did before and after where we didn't have those kinds of numbers but we had the same overheads, and we lost a lot of money on those conferences. The only reason these conferences made a lot of money is because there were a lot of people. But the bottom line for me is were people helped? Were people helped through all of this stuff? Support groups and reading books and listening to tapes and going to conferences—were people helped? And if anybody wants to suggest that no, people really weren't helped, I can't respond, because that is so ridiculous.

If someone were to look for evidence of a "recovery industry," it is easy to see why they might point to HCI. It has, in addition to its book publishing branch, other branches that publish magazines for therapists and substance abuse professionals and organize the conferences Seidler mentioned. These conferences provide continuing education credits that attendees can use to meet criteria for professional certification in the "helping professions," which include counseling, addiction treatment, therapy, and related occupations. With its separate companies, not to mention its rapid growth, HCI is an obvious target for the "recovery industry" label. Seidler admits that recovery is profitable; HCI is, after all, a business. Yet despite his company's success, he claims to be concerned about helping people.

Even those conspicuously engaged in "helping" have been accused of being part of a "recovery industry." Therapists, for example, have had a role in popularizing codependency. But this does not mean that, "for therapists, the marketing of codependency has become big business" (Lodl 1995, 210). To the contrary, at least one scholar who has charted the course of therapy as a profession refers to its recent history as "the triumph of the therapeutic *and its decline*" (Philipson 1993, emphasis added).

There is no question that the number of Americans who seek psycho-therapeutic care has increased. An increase in the number of therapists has paralleled this trend. The number of doctorates conferred in psychology nearly doubled between 1971 and 1987, making for more Ph.D.'s in psychology than all the other social sciences combined (Anderson, Carter, and Malizio 1990). In sheer numbers, therapy has an impressive presence. However, recent trends in the actual practice of counseling make it less so. As one observer puts it, "After three decades of growth, the 1980s stands as a decade of reversal, compromise, and significantly lowered expectations for psychotherapists and their clients" (Philipson 1993, 39). Professional publications refer to a "mental health care revolution" in which cutbacks at every level have changed the delivery of psychotherapeutic care (see, for example, Zimet 1989). Mental health problems increasingly receive treatment with medication, rather than one-on-one therapy. Because it involves less time and money to medicate patients, third-party payers, the state, and managed forms of health care increasingly endorse drug therapy as the treatment of choice. Patients who seek psychotherapy, either in addition to or instead of medication, may find sustained treatment hard to come by. This is especially so for the growing numbers of Americans enrolled in HMOs. Because HMOs operate on a prepaid, fixed payment basis, they limit the treatments defined as not "medically necessary." While they must provide short-term psychotherapy in order to meet federal requirements, many HMOs actually provide their enrollees with far fewer than the twenty visits mandated by federal statute. In a study of California HMOs, for example, Ilene Philipson found that, in practice, "a person must be suffering a major situational crisis to be seen for any more than 6 sessions" (1993, 42). Six visits hardly constitute evidence of exploitive profit-making. Moreover, the *Diagnostic and Statistical Manual of Mental Disorders* that mental health professionals use to certify diagnoses for insurance purposes does not include codependency among its conditions. A therapist can diagnose a patient with any number of personality disorders that may then "point to" an informal diagnosis of codependency. For example, one therapist told me that her codependent clients typically "lined up under" a particular set of traits. But a "certifiable" diagnosis of codependency does not exist. Even a leading addiction treatment facility such as Hazelden does not recognize codependency as a diagnostic entity. Their family program, which is not covered by insurance, provides treatment and counseling for the wide range of problems that may accompany close association with an addict or alcoholic, but makes no diagnosis of codependency.

Of the thirty-six members I interviewed, just under half had come to CoDA at a therapist's suggestion. Those who came to CoDA in this way said that the therapist had suggested CoDA, but not as a condition of successful treatment. Granted, it could be that, for various reasons, the people I spoke to wanted to believe that coming to CoDA was their own choice. Nevertheless, they said that their therapy focused on particular problems, and CoDA provided a supplement—if they wanted one. Moreover, some who saw therapists found their way to CoDA on their own, and one man attended despite his therapist's advice. (She told him that his "addictive personality" might cause him to become addicted to the group.) A few stopped going to therapy while they continued with CoDA, some for financial reasons, some because they saw no reason to continue. One man said that therapy "wasn't helping" him. One woman told me that she did not think therapy "works." Another, who had grown tired of group therapy, preferred CoDA because, in her own words, "I can go to a meeting and drop a dollar in a basket and talk about what I've got to talk about instead of paying forty dollars out of my pocket to sit here and listen to someone else talk about the same shit they've been talking about forever." Claims about codependency as therapeutic entrepreneurialism weaken in this light. Therapists do not stand to profit economically when their clients attend CoDA, and clients typically continue with the group long after the therapy ends.

Third, the image of a "recovery industry" has often meant that commonplace business practices have been assailed as manipulation through their association with recovery. This is the case with substance abuse treatment. To an observer writing around 1990, the rapid growth of treatment facilities probably seemed like cause for alarm. That initial phase of growth, however, did not reach the prophesied proportions. Recent transformations in American health care in general have influenced the course of addiction treatment in particular.

During the ten or fifteen years following the 1965 passage of Medicare and Medicaid, the number of for-profit hospitals increased as investor-owned hospital companies began to purchase and build propri-etary hospitals.[4] The Health Maintenance Organization Act of 1970 sought to subject health care providers to "the discipline of the market" (Starr 1982) by defining providers as corporate entities. Enterprising hospital corporations seized upon this new opportunity. By the early 1980s, the prospective payment system, designed to reduce hospital costs under Medicare, spread to private insurance programs and made hospital ownership much less profitable than it had been. Consequently, investment companies looked for opportunities elsewhere. A combina-tion of fortuitous circumstances made specialty facilities, especially those offering psychiatric and substance abuse treatment, a lucrative option. The passage of the 1970 Comprehensive Alcohol Abuse Act es-tablished a federal bureaucracy—the NIAAA—with a vast budget to combat alcoholism. The Act effectively institutionalized the disease model of alcoholism, which then became the accepted explanation for other substance dependencies, as well. The disease model justified hos-pitalization for addiction treatment. The Act also required insurance companies to offer coverage for alcohol treatment in health care pack-ages. A federal survey of drug and alcohol treatment facilities reports that their numbers more than doubled between 1979 and 1989 (NIDA and NIAAA 1990). The growth of specialty facilities simply mirrored the earlier growth of acute-care hospitals. Health care corporations, in-terested in maximizing profit, concentrated their investments where conditions favored them.

The atmosphere began to change as cutbacks in state funding and third-party payments, combined with the rise of managed health care, made substance abuse facilities less profitable. Until the mid-1980s, most of the insurance reimbursements for substance abuse treatment had gone to hospitals. Then, employers began to seek more cost-effective alternatives to hospitalization, especially Employee Assistance Programs that provide counseling directly (see Duggar 1991). Even when hospitalization becomes necessary, most insurance plans typically provide only a seven-day stay for detoxification; providers, after all, de-mand quick results that minimize reimbursements, and hospital compa-nies want to maximize profits with high turnover rates. This makes it unlikely that many codependents have spent languorous weeks in treat-ment centers. During the time I spent attending CoDA meetings, I knew of no one who had undergone residential treatment for codepen-dency. I did meet people who had histories of such treatment for drug addictions or mental illness, but these occurred years prior to association with CoDA. Most people in the group had never seen the inside of a treatment facility.

Fourth, the middlebrow feminist claim that the "recovery industry" targets women has several problems. There is no way of assessing how many people—male or female—identify with codependency. CoDA would be the most reliable source of data on the total number of co-dependents, and it has not, and will not, survey its membership. Yet, one often reads that women constitute 85 percent of CoDA's sixty thousand members (see Mitchell-Norberg, Warren, and Zale 1995).[5] Presumably, the total is an estimate based on three thousand CoDA groups having twenty members each. The 85 percent is a stock feminist statistic that first appeared in a 1990 *New York Times Book Review* essay written by Wendy Kaminer, a version of which appears in her book *I'm Dysfunctional, You're Dysfunctional* (1991). When Kaminer interviewed HCI's cofounder and president, Peter Vegso, he estimated that women composed 85 percent of their market. Kaminer positioned the figure in her article such that a reader gets the impression that 85 percent of codependents are women. When the statistic appeared in print, observers of codependency—myself included—went on to use and abuse it. For example, Walters (1995) writes that "publishers report that 85 percent of the readership of codependent materials are women," yet cites no source for the figure (184). Babcock (1995) writes that "the membership of 'codependency self-help groups' is predominantly female," citing Kaminer, but also Haaken's research (1993, 1995) on ACoA, even though the two groups make significantly different claims. Others, like Simonds (1992), have extrapolated the figure to sales of other types of books. Simonds, for example, reckons that women buy more books on New Age religion than men, based on Kaminer's figure (117).

I asked Vegso's partner, Gary Seidler, about the figure. He repeated that 85 percent of their market does indeed consist of women; that much Kaminer gets right. But this does not represent either their book market or self-identified codependents. The company has no data on the demographic characteristics of their book market. Nor, for that matter, do most publishers. None of the publishing firms Simonds researched in her study of women's self-help reading conducted any after-purchase market studies. While doing this research, I could not find a publisher that had any demographic data on their markets, or knew whether men or women bought more books. Publishers simply seem to believe that the bulk of the book-buying public consists of women, period. An editor at HCI told me that "women tend to read more, or at least buy more reading materials than men. . . . It's always been that way." Perhaps codependency books do "speak primarily to women," to use Kaminer's words, but then so, it seems, do novels of various categories, cookbooks, home health guides, and magazines. And, for that matter, so do groceries and clothing. In this sense, the market for codependency books simply mirrors many other markets, and the 85 percent reveals nothing exceptional about the relationship between codependency and gender.

Seidler explained that, at least for HCI's market, occupation explains away part of the relationship between gender and codependency. The surveys that yielded the 85 percent represent conference attendees and magazine subscribers, both of which, in this case, consist largely of helping professionals, an occupational niche composed largely of women. Perhaps this 85 percent also happens to identify personally with codependency, but the figure does not represent a proportion of self-identified codependents.

Given that I initially accepted the feminist truism of 85 percent at face value, the actual proportion of women I observed at CoDA meetings surprised me. Among the eighteen groups that I studied, women accounted for 58 percent of those in attendance (a total of 626). At no point did I begin to think of them as "girl groups," as Rapping had during her research (1996). Moreover, among the twenty groups that Rice observed, women constituted 61 percent (a total of 547). Neither of these figures even approximates the percentage of women reported by Kaminer, and cited by others. In addition, studies of small groups, in general, suggest that women constitute a slightly greater proportion of their membership than do men, making CoDA's appeal to women less exceptional (see Wuthnow 1994, 47).

Most feminist critics are not interested solely in pointing out, albeit inaccurately, that women constitute the majority of codependents; they maintain that the codependency discourse harms women. They have most often read codependency's key treatises and used a version of content analysis to argue for the overdetermination of female address. For example, characteristics such as being "overinvolved," "depending upon others for approval," "having poor boundaries," and being "too willing to assume blame" could only describe women, claims one critic (Walters 1995, 184). Another writes that many of codependency's "themes—the lack of self-esteem and self-identity, the people-pleasing behavior, and the problems with control and dependency—are typically referred to in other literature as 'female' issues" (Martin 1988, 391). Yet, stereotypically "masculine" characteristics such as control, anger, and shutting off feelings appear on lists of "symptoms" as often as do "feminine" ones. Irresponsibility, workaholism, and emotional withdrawal—traits not considered stereotypically female—are also said to indicate the presence of codependency. The feminist critics overlook these more "masculine" characteristics and present the discourse as the latest instance in a history of labeling women's traits as defective.

One of the lessons I learned early in this research is that one cannot speculate about the characteristics and motivations of an audience from a selective reading of texts. I began this project by analyzing texts, and in so doing, I, too, concluded that codependency was another example of the oppression of women by professionals allegedly working in their best interests (Irvine 1992). Once I began the fieldwork and talked to women—and men—who claimed to be codependent, I learned otherwise. The meaning of codependency "is not explicable through a literal reading of [the] treatises themselves" (Rice 1996, 199). Since most of the feminist critics believe that only one true meaning of codependency exists, however, they assume they can recover that meaning through the texts without going to the trouble of locating real codependents in order to hear their views. They simply announce that "codependency is harmful to women" (Babcock and McKay 1995, xvii) without defining "harm" and without finding women who can substantiate the claim.

Regardless of where it is directed, the claim that people are herded into groups by a profiteering "recovery industry" implies that the problems to which codependency responds are not real. On the contrary, therapists and treatment professionals may have created the vocabulary with which people come to describe their problems, but they did not create the problems themselves (see de Swaan 1981). "Professional ex-s" may have popularized that vocabulary and publishers reproduced it, but they did not create the problems, either. The problems that lead people to CoDA, and to the codependency discourse as a way of making sense of their lives, are not only real, they are compelling. They inspire intricate quests to locate meetings. They draw people out of their homes and into the halls of churches that have long since lost their ability to generate equivalent commitment. Given what it takes to get into CoDA, I consider it remarkable that the meetings are consistently filled. If a "recovery industry" were indeed at work, surely it would have left much less to individual initiative.

CHAPTER THREE

Uncoupling and Narratives
of the Self

People are not pulled into CoDA by a corrupt recovery juggernaut. They are pushed there by the disruption that comes with "uncoupling," or ending a relationship. If codependency is "about" anything, it is about resolving the disruption that uncoupling does to the self. With very few exceptions, people seek out CoDA after the breakup of a serious, committed relationship or in a relationship's terminal stages. Every one of the thirty-six people I interviewed had done so. Breaking up was a constant theme in the meetings I attended. In some cases, the breakups had to do with children. A divorce separates a father from his children and he must adjust to seeing them only on weekends. Or, a sporadically employed, alcoholic, thirty-something son wants to move back home for the third time, and his mother, tired of having money stolen from her purse, wants to bring herself to say "no." This kind of uncoupling certainly differs from separation and divorce. Nevertheless, it can bring similar social and emotional disruption. Consequently, some people in this situation also seek support in CoDA. More often, however, the breakups involved divorce. Since people who divorce typically remarry within a few years, and since one divorce increases the likelihood of a second, some of the people I encountered had experienced the end of two or more marriages. The same logic applies to cohabiting relationships. People who cohabit usually split up or marry within about a year and a half (see Cherlin 1992; see also Blumstein and Schwartz 1983). If cohabiting couples marry, the somewhat "liberated" attitude that allowed them to cohabit also increases the likelihood that they will eventually divorce. This first divorce, in turn, increases the likelihood that they will remarry and divorce again. By the time a person reaches forty or forty-five—roughly the most common age range of the CoDA members I observed—he or she may have a history of several failed relationships.[1] Melody Beattie noted this characteristic—although she attributed it differently—when she observed that "multiple marriages are common in people recovering from codependency" (1990, 209). (I argue that multiple relationship failures may lead certain people to consider the codependency discourse as a means of making sense of what went wrong; I do not believe that there is an underlying codependency that leads them into unhappy relationships, which is how Beattie would put it.) Actual marital status is largely irrelevant, however. As Weiss explains, "It is separation, not divorce, that disrupts the structure of the individual's social and emotional life" (1975, 4). That disruption, and the hope of resolving it, draws people to CoDA.

Of all the disruption that uncoupling causes, the disruption of the experience of selfhood is no doubt the greatest. Peter Marris (1974), who has done one of the few extant studies on responses to loss, concurs that "the fundamental crisis of bereavement [and here he includes divorce] arises, not from the loss of others, but the loss of self" (33). When two people begin a commitment, their identities gradually merge so that the two form the single social unit known as a "couple." They make common friends, usually other couples. They lead a joint social life; a host or hostess does not consider extending an invitation to one partner, but not the other. They establish a common household. They open a joint bank account. The phone listing appears under both names. They may pay joint income taxes. They plan a common future. They coordinate schedules; individual departures from the routine require explanation, if not a form of permission. In short, two separate individuals become *a couple*.

Doing so involves far more than settling these practical and "administrative" details, however. Love songs often contain the phrase "I've built my whole world around you," and for good reason. The other person increasingly becomes part of the stories you tell about yourself and, consequently, that person becomes a part of you. Initially, the other person is an audience for the storytelling that begins during courtship, with the revealing of histories, likes, and dislikes. The audience role continues with the daily recounting of events that occurred at home or work, but the other person gradually joins those events, and a shared history emerges. Storytelling of this sort has a purpose beyond merely conveying information. Stories enclose narratives of the self within them. In the telling, people reassure themselves that they exist. As their stories unfold, they reaffirm the existence of the self as audience to themselves (see Schafer 1981, 1992). The stories people tell about themselves include significant other people—as audiences, co-authors, participants, and critics. The level of disclosure that characterizes intimacy means that this is all the more so for couples.

Studies of uncoupling describe breaking up as reversing the merger that took place during the relationship's formation. The process involves "confirm[ing] an identity independent of the coupled identity created with the other person" (Vaughan 1986, 28; see also Weiss 1975; Riessman 1990). Two people who had publicly and privately merged their identities have to establish themselves once more as separate individuals. Again, this manifests itself in tangible or practical acts, such as finding separate places to live, separate bank accounts, and new telephone listings. For women, it can mean a change of name, which in turn involves innumerable bureaucratic inconveniences. It can entail serious economic loss, especially for women with children.[2] Moreover, it can require rethinking the structure of your day. Simple acts of eating and sleeping lose their taken-for-granted quality. When do you eat, without the "cues" from a partner who has prepared or shared your meals? When do you sleep, without signals from the other that the day has ended? Uncoupling also requires filling a "skill gap" by doing things, such as cooking or keeping track of bills, that the other had done while the relationship was intact.

But just as becoming a couple involves more than sharing a phone number and checking account, uncoupling, too, involves more than establishing physical separation.[3] Some of the members of CoDA described the experience to me in these words:

It was completely draining. I lost my whole life. *(woman, thirty-six)*

Absolutely a nightmare. *(woman, thirty-nine)*

What does it feel like? It feels empty. That you can't figure a freaking thing out. That you feel so . . . so helpless. *(man, forty-two)*

I was devastated. My life stopped for about four months. *(woman, forty-five)*

Everything all of a sudden just . . . everything fell apart. *(man, fifty)*

The language is telling: "I lost my whole life." "It feels empty." "My life stopped . . ." What they are describing, although no one put it in these particular words, is the loss of selfhood. They had lost the ability to tell stories of themselves that made sense. Marriage and committed relationships provide formulas and contexts for your stories. They are not free-floating, as others have argued (see Baudrillard 1983). People do not simply make up stories about themselves on a whim. Rather, they draw plots, scripts, casts, and audiences from institutions. Although I will refine my use of the term somewhat in the following chapter, I mean "institution" to refer to patterns of activities organized around a similar goal. Marriage and relationships, as institutions, provide opportunities for people to "be" or "become" themselves because they anchor the stories told by those within them. When a relationship ends, that institutional anchor is dislodged. This is at the heart of the "narrative wreckage" that the members of CoDA described.[4] Uncoupling disrupted the continuity in their existing stock of stories. It derailed the plots. It removed key characters. It made future chapters or episodes unimaginable. It meant that two people whose language had evolved from "I" to "we" must now think of themselves as "I" again. Doing so does not come easily:

> During the time that we were splitting up, when Gina hadn't left yet, I ran into an acquaintance of hers. She said, "Aren't you Gina's boyfriend?" I didn't know what to say. I think I said, "Well, I'm her future ex-boyfriend," or something. But I hadn't thought about what to call myself, and it felt really strange. (*man, age forty-two*)

> You know, society seems to have this rule about talking about ex-s. You're not supposed to bash them, but you're not supposed to go around saying good things about them either. I mean, if your ex- was so great, why aren't you still together, right? So you can't really say anything about them. So here's this person, who's been an important part of your life for years, maybe, and you can't even talk about them. What do you do with those memories? It's like you have to deny them, and it's so screwed up. (*woman, age thirty-nine*)

Implicit in becoming an "I" again is the question of *"Who will I be now, without this other person?"* In this sense, uncoupling does have a positive side to it, in that it offers opportunities to pursue avenues not possible within the relationship. But there are often obstacles to taking hold of those opportunities and answering the question of "Who will I be?" For with the loss comes the specter of self-doubt: *Can I trust my judgment, in light of having failed?*

The implication of failure may seem implausible in times when divorce and separation have become commonplace. Yet, even today, "relationships are almost universally viewed in success/failure terms," writes

McCall (1982). The ability to maintain a relationship is "a major test of adulthood" (Vaughan 1986, 160). Therefore, "any party to a terminated or even a spoiled relationship is tarred by failure" (219). Even if you do not take your *own* divorce as a sign of failure, others often see it in that light.[5] Research suggests that, while divorce *itself* has become more accepted, divorced *people* have not (Gerstel 1987). The process is still widely held as indicative of some personal flaw. For example, socializing with couples becomes difficult after uncoupling, and not only because of the inevitable "splitting of friends" (see Gerstel 1987; see also Spanier and Thompson 1984; Weiss 1975). Divorced people report feeling that married friends exclude them from social interaction because they seem to find them threatening in some way (see Gerstel 1987). Married couples may fear that the experience will "rub off" on them, or that a now-single friend will move in on a husband or wife. As a woman in CoDA explained, even the act of telling others elicits their judgment:

> There's no booklet that comes with your divorce papers, you know, telling you how to be a divorced person. Marriage comes with a set of rules, more or less. Even if there are no rules, everything is pretty optimistic. It's cute and giggly when you have to decide things like what name to take. People smile at you. Divorce doesn't work like that. You have to figure it out on your own. You tell people you're using a different name now and they don't smile. They look down and go, "Ohhh." *(age thirty-eight)*

The stories that people tell after uncoupling must redeem this experience of failure. On the way to answering the question of "Who will I be now," they must also answer the question of *What happened?* Lurking beneath this are questions such as *Why me? What's wrong with me? And what am I really like?* (McCall 1982; La Gaipa 1982).[6] To provide satisfying answers, uncoupling stories must take the form of "accounts" (Scott and Lyman 1968). Accounts are "linguistic devices [that] explain unanticipated or untoward behavior" (46). They either mitigate responsibility for your conduct or accept responsibility but neutralize the consequences of doing so. Accounts that accomplish the former are known as "excuses"; those that accomplish the latter are called "justifications." By either relieving or neutralizing personal responsibility, accounts help to diminish blame and, therefore, reduce the effects of stigma. Moreover, accounts not only convey information to *others;* they also explain your own conduct *to yourself.* In so doing, they restore your own sense of self-approval.[7]

For accounts to be honored, they have to use vocabulary that is "anchored in the background expectations of the situation" (Scott and Lyman 1968, 53). Self-consciously or not, audiences have standards for what they will find credible. Anyone who has been late for an important engagement or stopped for speeding knows this well. Accounts must be consistent with what "everybody knows" about what they purport to explain, or at least with what "everybody" in a particular setting "knows." In the case of uncoupling, accounts have to convey legitimate reasons for breaking up. In middle-class, American culture, it is generally legitimate to emphasize the importance of the individual over the relationship. Although few people would give fulfillment as the sole reason for breaking up, the sense of obligation to oneself constitutes an appropriate explanation for doing so. Studies suggest that even those who do not have this view initially come to acquire it eventually as a means of making positive sense of the loss (Weiss 1975; Vaughan 1986; Riessman 1990). People repair the "narrative wreckage" of uncoupling, and, consequently, redeem damaged selves, using accounts that follow standards set by their audiences—including themselves. These standards—and new audiences—then become important in the revision of the story of who they are.

There are, then, crucial ways that selfhood, as a narrative accomplishment, depends on institutions. Marriages and relationships, as institutions, provide anchors for the stories of the self. When these anchors are lost, others must replace them. Until then, life "feels empty," and "everything falls apart."

This is not how the contemporary self is supposed to work. For some time, and from a variety of perspectives, scholars have charted the declining importance of institutions for the experience of selfhood.[8] In a classic essay on the experience of "The Real Self," Turner (1976) documented "a long-term shift" away from locating the self socially, in institutions, roles, and values.[9] Alongside this pre-therapeutic ethos, "institutional" self, an "impulsive" orientation had gained strength. The "impulsive" locates the experience of "real" selfhood in "deep, unsocialized, inner impulses" (992).[10] The image evokes the romanticism of the nineteenth-century concept of the self, and some would characterize the "impulsive" type as neo-Romantic (see Anderson 1997).[11] I would add that it is a pillar of the therapeutic ethos.

In both the "institutional" and "impulsive" types, belief in a "real" self still exists. The distinction lies in where people locate it. Recently, however, some have claimed that even the belief in a "real" self, as a permanent, continuous entity, has "cease[d] to be intelligible" (Gergen 1991, 170). The idea of a "real" self has allegedly evolved into an awareness that we are all "populated with *fragments of the other*" (172, emphasis original). This fragmentation is ostensibly well-suited to life in these "postmodern" times. "The cumulative result," writes Kenneth Gergen, "is that we are readied for participation in a world of incoherence, a world of anything-goes" (173).

Perhaps. But judging from the evidence in CoDA, the idea of a "real" self remains inviolable. While the idea of empty, postmodern incoherence may appeal to some academics, a sizeable number of people outside academia are working frantically to create enduring meaning and coherence. Consider what two members of CoDA had to say:

> I recognize that, within me, there's a self—I prefer the term "inner child." And this child knows what's right for me to do, and this child has always been with me, but my codependency has boxed it in. In recovery, I'm trying to set that child free so that my life makes sense. I'll keep working the Program, and I'll see who I was supposed to be, and I'll be that person. (*woman, age forty*)

> All this time, because of codependency, I haven't been able to be myself. I didn't know it, though, until CoDA. Now I can see that there's been a purpose to that, so that I could find out who I am now. You know what they say at the meetings about becoming who you were meant to be, "precious and free"? Well, through working the Program and through sharing and listening to other people, I've learned who I really am, for the first time in my life. (*man, age thirty-nine*)

At CoDA meetings, one concern dominates all others. This is the idea of a "real" self that is solely and completely your own possession. On the surface of things, this seems "impulsively" oriented. The members talk, for example, of finding out who they are "supposed" to be by freeing the "inner child." However, while the "impulsive" self may be what CoDA members *say* they "have," their means of "having" it is wholly "institutional." At the meetings, they learn to piece together events of their lives using an institutionalized formula. Each meeting brings a new installment to the story. The narrator and the listeners situate the new information within the context of existing themes. With each telling, the narrators integrate new experiences and insights into an evolving "socio-biography" (Plummer 1983; Wuthnow 1994), which is a story about one's life and one's formative experiences that is created in a public setting. At each CoDA meeting, the narrators pick up the story where it left off, taking it in a new direction, and taking the story of the self in a new direction, as well. Over the long term, the narrator and the group remember these themes and, consequently, legitimate them as the narrator's identity. As Wuthnow explains, "What a person chooses to share in a group becomes ever more important to that person's identity. The group's affirmation of this identity reinforces and legitimates it" (302).

> I have a self now because, in CoDA, I've learned about why my life has taken its particular path. It's like I know who I am. These people here know me, the real me. *(man, forty-five)*

This is not to say that everyone in CoDA tells exactly the same story. To the contrary, they tell quite *different* stories—using the same formula. Much of the discourse's appeal no doubt stems from its ability to do both, to work at the somewhat universal level of a legitimate account of uncoupling and at the idiosyncratic level of a unique, personal history. At the universal level, codependency's core tenets echo popular beliefs about relationships and uncoupling. "Everybody knows," for example, that no one should have to sacrifice a sense of who he or she "is" for a relationship. Self-sacrifice fell out of favor with the arrival of the therapeutic ethos and the women's movement (see Cancian 1987). As a discourse, codependency legitimates the belief that relationships fail to work, in a universal sense, when people "give away" their "true" selves. Yet, it is not enough to say only that your relationship failed because you gave up the sense of who you "are." This may suffice for the most casual of acquaintances, but you must also have a more detailed explanation of the breakup that will satisfy yourself. Accounts of uncoupling must, therefore, be specific and idiosyncratic as well as universal. If a universal level of explanation would suffice, then people could attribute divorce to simple probability. But when the experience strikes home, statistical probability makes for a poor explanation. Most people never imagine that it will happen to them. Divorce rates may be predictable, but your *own* divorce is unique. Accounts of uncoupling must, therefore, follow cultural standards, but they must simultaneously accommodate individual lives. The codependency discourse's open quality allows people to use it to create accounts that do both. "Becoming" codependent involves an interaction between structure and culture, or between the circumstances of your life and the resources that you can draw upon to make sense of them. As codependency comes to include the variety of experiences that individuals see as problematic, its meaning expands and changes. This evolution represents the individual shaping of culture.

It also represents the institutional shaping of the self. This is best demonstrated in the segment of the meetings devoted to sharing.[12]

Sharing exemplifies a class of events and situations that Robert Zussman calls "autobiographical occasions" (1996). Autobiographical occasions require people to tell stories about themselves. Audiences for these occasions generate different standards for what constitutes a "good" story. The medical history given to a specialist would not satisfy a family member who simply wants to know how you feel (see Frank 1995). The story told during a job interview would not be the same one conveyed to a love interest. Likewise, the audience at CoDA meetings holds specific expectations about what constitutes a "good" story of codependency and recovery. By listening to hundreds of people share, I began to understand their expectations. I began to see the characteristic sequence through which believers in codependency order the events of their lives. This sequence, or "narrative formula," as I call it, follows a five-part chronology that produces a special type of life history.

Each speaker begins by describing the childhood circumstances that fostered his or her codependency. Next comes a recounting of the "dysfunction" that followed from that childhood. In the third part of the formula, the speaker gives a depiction of what is known in Twelve Step groups as "hitting bottom," the low point at which he or she recognized that something was wrong. In the fourth part, the speaker portrays how he or she is "working a Program," or what he or she is doing to "recover" from codependency. Fifth, and finally, the speaker redeems the past by describing the positive changes that have transpired since being in recovery. These five elements appeared in all the group sharing I observed and in every interview. Together, they create a "good" story of codependency. The *content* of each narrative differs among individuals, but the *order* is formulaic and provided by the codependency discourse.

The group attempts to ensure that speakers will share according to the formula, thereby giving members the "good" codependency stories that they expect to hear. The text read at every meeting suggests that only those who have spent "enough time in the Program to generally qualify" as "recovering" share in front of the entire group. By restricting the open sharing to more seasoned members, the group transmits a set of ideas about how recovery works. Moreover, because the more seasoned members tend to tell stories of success, newcomers learn not only *how* recovery works, but *that* it works.

At The House of Life, I learned just how important this is. A woman who seemed to be developmentally disabled began coming to meetings. "Beth" shared after attending only twice. She talked about a string of unrelated events, none of which kept to the chronological formula. She did not have enough time in recovery to inspire the others with tales of improvement. In addition, she volunteered to share two weeks in a row, pleading the need to talk about current crises that lacked any resemblance to a "good" story of codependency. After doing this a few times, the "glue" that normally held the meeting together would dissolve as soon as Beth started speaking. The others began quiet side conversations. They rolled their eyes. They glanced impatiently at their watches. Through their behavior, the others told her that the meeting had effectively ended, and some even left. On one particularly pathetic day, all the small groups had formed and individual sharing had begun, and Beth was left standing in the middle of the room, holding onto a chair and looking around helplessly. She eventually stopped coming to meetings, although I cannot say for sure why she did so. Beth nevertheless made something clear to me in the few times I saw her: While there are few explicit rules for sharing, there is a "correct" way of doing so.[13] Let me illustrate this systematically.

"ABUSIVE" CHILDHOODS AND THE ORIGINS OF CODEPENDENCY

Codependency, as the text read at each meeting explains, "is born out of our sometimes moderately, sometimes extremely dysfunctional family systems." Since all families are dysfunctional—either "moderately" or "extremely"—all manner of experiences become reframed to this end. In this view, families, by definition, "abuse" their children. As a result, any and everyone's family history becomes reconceptualized as "abusive." Those who do not come from families of addicts or alcoholics— and this includes most CoDA members—find other sorts of problems. I was struck by the ways that seemingly unexceptional childhoods became "dysfunctional." Even in the absence of any obvious family troubles, members went to great lengths to find or invent them. For example, I found that childhood "abuse" included general inadequacy, overwork, and Catholicism.

There's no drug addiction or alcoholism in my immediate family . . . Just a super codependent, shame-based family. I just never felt good enough. *(woman, age thirty-six)*

There was so much abuse in my family. Abuse and neglect. There was always food on the table, always a roof over our heads. But my parents were both working all the time and never there for us. It was so abusive emotionally. Really dysfunctional. *(man, age forty-one)*

Nobody in my family was alcoholic or into drugs. We were just guilt-ridden Catholics. *(woman, age thirty-eight)*

My father came from the old country, you know, where a man doesn't hug his kids. I never got a hug from my father. That's so abusive to a kid. *(man, age forty-two)*

Granted, some members of CoDA *did* give accounts of authentic-seeming physical and emotional mistreatment they endured as children. For the most part, however, I found that the term "abuse" was used indiscriminately. When a person cannot recall an instance of "abuse," it does not imply its absence, but its severity. The inability to recall "abuse" allegedly means that the "victim" has "denied" the experience in order to survive it. The "abuse" must have been so intense that the mind blocked it out as a survival mechanism. For example:

My upbringing was so dysfunctional that it's hard to remember. I shut down so much. *(woman, age forty-two)*

I can't remember anything before the age of 21, so I know it must have been pretty bad. My parents must have abused me so bad that I just shut down in order to survive it. *(man, age forty-five)*

As Rice (1992) puts it, "The canon CoDA members tap for their life stories systematically, however inadvertently, alters their lived experiences to fit neatly within its boundaries" (355). Thus, every childhood becomes an "abusive" childhood. Conversely, of course, this means that, "to 'explain' their lives using [codependency's rhetoric], members must sacrifice those aspects that lie beyond the outline of a 'good' theory of 'co-dependency'" (356). The possibility of "denial" makes this sacrifice less final.

It also raises the issue of the "truth" of the stories. Narratives of co-dependency—and narratives in general—do not correspond with any objective reality. That is not their point. Their point is to show how a particular "past came to be, and how, ultimately, it gave birth to the present" (McAdams 1993, 102). Audiences have standards for what constitutes a "good" story, and the person who shares in CoDA must adhere to them. The question is not whether any given item is true, but whether it makes for a "good" story. What is interesting about forgotten instances of childhood "abuse" is not their veracity. It is how they make particular kinds of stories possible, and so remake the lives of those who tell them. As Frank has written, "The stories we tell about our lives are not necessarily the lives as they were lived, but these stories become our experiences of those lives" (1995, 22). The person who begins a commitment to CoDA and its discourse enters a world in which all families are considered "abusive." Within the group, you can only legitimately tell stories that begin with "abuse." Were it not for the "abuse," your life would have turned out differently. Since you have ended up in CoDA, the "abuse" *must* have happened. Consequently, members develop stories about "abusive" childhoods, and those stories become their experience. Their histories gradually resemble what the formula for a "good" story of codependency prescribes. That this history may have only a weak resemblance to actual events is irrelevant, for the purpose is to "correct fortune by *remaking* history" (Berger 1963, 61, emphasis added).

EXCUSING "DYSFUNCTION"

The narrative continues with a description of how the "abusive" childhood set you up for "dysfunction." The chronology makes the present seem like the logical, and even inevitable, outcome of the past (Slavney and McHugh 1984). It attributes your recent past or present situation to undiagnosed codependency, which originated in childhood circumstances. By blaming relationship troubles on your unrecognized codependency in this way, the account reduces individual blame and its accompanying stigma.

As was the case with "abuse," what constitutes "dysfunction" varies widely. Within the discourse, any relationship or situation that has a less-than-satisfactory outcome qualifies as "dysfunctional." To be sure, someone occasionally described an appalling emotional or physical situation. But, often as not, the term described far less dramatic elements of dissatisfaction. Consider these examples from one small group:

> A man described a vague but troubling need to be "in control" of his relationship with his girlfriend. I say "vague" because he never got around

to explaining what he actually did to be controlling, but kept repeating phrases such as, "I've got to surrender my need to be in control. It's so 'dysfunctional,'" and "Having to be in control leads to a lot of 'dysfunction' in my life."

A woman described a falling-out with a friend who disapproved of the way she spent money. The woman speaking had planted a lot of flowers around her yard, and the friend questioned the expense. "We've got it [the money], and seeing the flowers makes me happy," she said. "I like to have my house looking a certain way and she shouldn't have anything to say about it." She "needed" to put in these flowers, she said, to have the kind of environment she wants. Her friend's disapproval is evidence of the friendship's "dysfunction"; she does not want to be around that kind of "unhealthiness."

A woman voiced concern about feeling resentment over her daughter-in-law's absence from a family gathering. She saw this as an attempt by the younger woman to ruin her day. "She shouldn't be able to control my feelings," the woman said. "This has taught me that I've got to detach. I won't be part of that 'dysfunction.'"

A woman expressed pride in her new ability to "take care of" herself by refusing to baby-sit for a family member who had asked her to do so on the spur of the moment. To do otherwise would have encouraged "dysfunction."

A man talked about a recent meal at a restaurant. The waitress had made an error in his order, and he did not bring it to her attention. He wondered what makes him "relate to people in such 'dysfunctional' ways."

A man described his general feelings of resentment and anger stemming from his "dysfunctional" relationship with his mother. She had recently recommended that he go to see the movie *Nell*, and he struggled to figure out why.

I offer these illustrations not to question their putative "dysfunction," but to highlight its role in the narrative. These were clearly instances that had not gone the way the speakers had hoped. By calling them "dysfunctional," the speakers could excuse their own role in the outcome. They could blame it on an intrinsic flaw, or "dysfunction," in the relationship, thereby relieving themselves of their share of the interactional responsibility. They could acknowledge that they acted badly, but disavow responsibility by claiming that, in light of such "dysfunction," things could not have gone otherwise. Things may have gone wrong, but through no fault of their own. In this way, "dysfunction" can excuse entire relationships, as well as discrete interactional instances:

> I married my father. I grew up thinking that he was what a husband should be like. So I went out and married a man just like him. What else did I know? My relationship with my husband brought out all the issues I had with my father. All I knew was dysfunction. *(woman, age thirty-six)*

> I realize now that I picked her because she repeated all that chaos from when I was growing up. It was hell—both the marriage and my child-hood. I did some really rotten things, I know, but it's because of the total dysfunction I saw as a kid. What I thought was love was really something else, some toxic stuff that went on at home. I acted the same way I saw my parents act. *(man, age thirty-nine)*

"HITTING BOTTOM"

The term is self-explanatory. Although the "bottom" differs among speakers, it is always an emotional low point.

> I hit my bottom around Christmas. I couldn't stop crying, and, being a man, you know, I wondered what was wrong with me! [he chuckles] But I just couldn't do anything else. It was miserable. Miserable. *(man, forty-nine)*

> When I was at my bottom, I went and bought a piece of hose, you know, to use in my exhaust pipe. I just wanted to have it around, to keep that option open. I was walking around feeling this dread, this constant feeling of dread. And in my more lucid moments I would say, "Geez, I've really got to do something or I'm going to end up dead." *(woman, age thirty-seven)*

The account of the "bottom" is an important aspect of the narrative. It foregrounds a self that has not only endured hardship and conflict, but one that has found an intriguing solution. The "bottom" brings richness and complexity to the self that will emerge from the story. As the narrative progresses, having survived the "bottom" will suggest a competence and maturity that help redeem the self from failure. More immediately, it introduces an optimistic tone to the narrative. Psychologists suggest that this better allows people to cope with adversity (see McAdams 1993). Sociologically speaking, optimism reveals the narrator's underlying faith in the belief that life can be good and that one is, to some extent, able to direct oneself toward that good life.

> You really do, you hit bottom and you say, "Look, I'm happy for the air that I'm breathing," and you start from there and everything else is a plus. *(man, age forty-five)*

> [The relationship] didn't serve me anymore. It was really devastating to realize that it didn't serve my growth. It brought me to a big dead end. And then I found CoDA, and it opened up a whole new avenue for me. *(woman, age thirty-six)*

WORKING A PROGRAM

This refers to how each speaker describes what he or she is doing to encourage recovery from codependency. Sometimes, particular meetings use particular Steps as points of discussion, and, in such cases, the leader asks the speaker to focus his or her sharing accordingly. One group I visited devoted the first meeting of each month to sharing about one of the Steps. Over the course of a year, the group addressed all Twelve Steps.

This is where, to use a Twelve Step phrase, you show that you can not only "talk the talk," but also "walk the walk." You demonstrate to yourself and to the group that you are serious about recovery. It is not simply something that you talk about once a week, but it is something that you "work on" the remaining six days, as well. Typically, speakers describe working through particular Steps or what they are doing to "get in touch with" themselves. The Steps, incidentally, involve a continuous process of self-assessment. You never "complete" the Twelve Steps. The "personal inventory" of Steps Four and Ten must be taken regularly. Consequently, the amends of Step Eight must be periodically made to those you have wronged. For example, in one depiction of working through Step Six, a striking, platinum blonde woman in her early forties described how she had become "entirely ready to have God remove all [her] defects of character." This Sixth Step assumes that you have already worked through the Fifth, which requires admitting "to God, to ourselves, and to another human being the exact nature of our wrongs." On this particular evening, the woman spoke of defensively clinging to one of her "defects of character," which was a hatred for her mother. She had finally become ready to give up that hatred, with the help of her Higher Power. She believed that she had been born to a mother who "abused" her, she said, in order to learn how to "take care" of herself emotionally. She had hated her mother for not loving her, but now saw that she had learned from the "abuse." For a long time, she had not known how to "take care" of herself, and although the details remained cloudy in her account, she said she had learned enough to begin to do so, and so, was ready to have her Higher Power eliminate her hatred for her mother.

What constitutes "working a Program" can vary widely, since each person alone knows best what he or she should do to foster recovery. It is difficult to fake—or at least it would have been for me. For this reason, I never spoke in front of the entire group. Because I was not "working a Program," I could not have given the group what they were expecting to hear, and if I had, I would have felt deceptive for doing so. In small group sharing, I could talk about other things. When I had to talk about "working a Program," I said things like "trying to figure out what's best for me."

My experience illustrates an important point: it is not enough to simply tell a story about yourself; you must also believe in your own story. Although I understood the formula for a narrative of codependency, I did not "become" codependent because I did not believe in that story as who I "am." I seem to have managed impressions successfully enough to have others attribute a codependent identity to me; no one ever called it into question, and, on several occasions, "my" codependency was even the subject of friendly teasing. But the impressions others had of me did not translate into my identifying myself in that way. Since a self "involves something internally felt as well as socially enacted, it cannot be constructed out of material the actor himself or herself believes to be untrue" (Vinitzky-Seroussi and Zussman 1996, 233). Although I could tell a story that convinced others that I belonged in the group, I never convinced myself, or even tried to.

Sometimes, convincing others is an important aspect of convincing yourself. I interviewed a woman who had come to CoDA because her grown son had alcohol and drug problems. She had nursed him through numerous rehabs, and her dedication had caused considerable friction with her husband. She eventually decided to "detach" from her son to preserve her marriage. Through reading numerous therapeutic books, she had begun to see her problem as one of codependency. But she had never said as much aloud, largely because she never had a sympathetic audience for her claim. She had withdrawn from friendships because she felt that her friends would not understand why she had banned her son from the house. "I felt like a failure," she said. What she claimed to appreciate about CoDA was having an arena in which she could say, "I am codependent. My son has drug and alcohol problems," without fear of a negative reaction from others. "For a long time," she told me, "I couldn't even bring myself to say it at a meeting. But there's no judgment here." Gradually, through practice in front of an audience that had heard it all before, she integrated "My son has drug and alcohol problems" into her narrative of the self. She can now speak of it without embarrassment; indeed, her embarrassment has been replaced by pride at what she has "overcome." It was not enough to be convinced of her codependency in private; saying it aloud among others who believed her was a turning point.

REDEEMING THE PAST

Here, the speaker talks about life in recovery. He or she recounts how codependency, though painful, was ultimately beneficial for personal "growth." The hardship it brought is portrayed as all for the best, thereby showing that he or she has indeed learned something through the misfortune. Consider the woman who said:

> I finally have come to the other side of the anger, the blaming, the bitterness, and finally have been truly able to see the benefits of it, that the characteristics that developed out of the abuse and dysfunction—I'm realizing that maybe if these things hadn't happened, I might not have the characteristics that I have today. (age forty-five)

Another had this to say:

> I think the pain was all worth it when I see what's happened for my growth. (age forty-six)

The redemptive quality of the accounts fits a pattern already observed among people attempting to make sense of loss. For example, Marris (1974) maintains that people demonstrate what he calls a "conservative impulse" in response to significant loss and change. In order to make new experiences manageable, people apply information from one situation to another and consolidate experiences into familiar categories. They depend on a "continuity of conceptions and experiences" to make sense of their lives. When an event disrupts your ability to find meaning in experience, as when an important relationship comes to an end, coming to terms with that experience "depends on restoring a sense that the lost attachment can still give meaning to the present" (149).

The experience of loss arouses contradictory reactions: return to the past, if possible; or forget it completely. Either of these would ultimately prove detrimental, since the former denies the reality of the present, and the latter denies "the experience on which the sense of self rests" (Marris 1974, 151). The resolution most people eventually reach reconciles both alternatives. People master grief, Marris claims, "by abstracting what was fundamentally important in the relationship and rehabilitating it" (34). Thus, bereaved family members often try to do what the deceased "would have wanted." This abstracts the intimacy once shared with the deceased and rehabilitates it in the lives of those who go on living. The process of abstraction and rehabilitation demonstrates the "conservative impulse." New, confusing information (the absence of the spouse) is integrated into an established framework (the spouse's preferences). In this way, the bereaved effectively restore the continuity of purpose that the death of a spouse disrupts. Likewise, codependents manifest a similar "conservative impulse" in their accounts. They abstract what had once been provided by their relationships—a coherent, reasonably optimistic story about their lives—and rehabilitate it in revised self-stories. Even the bad becomes part of a story about how your life is progressing in a manner in an order that is all for the best.

Good stories need satisfying endings. Since the lives of those telling the stories are still in progress, the endings must tolerate ambiguity. They must keep a number of alternatives open for the future, and they must have the flexibility to change as the tellers change. Yet, they must not have so much openness that they suggest immaturity and a lack of resolve. In sharing, ambiguity is accomplished through recovery clichés such as "Taking care of" or "Believing in myself" and "Getting in touch with my feelings." These and similarly vague phrases indicate a positive course of thought and action for the future without pinning you down to specifics. For example:

> The biggest help to me has been being honest with myself. CoDA has given me the courage to believe in myself and not believe all the lies from the past, from the way I was raised. *(woman, forty-five)*

> I'm more in touch with the power in the universe now. I pray and meditate every day. I read meditation books in the morning. I read spiritual books. I've been journaling. I've really been focusing on myself. I have

more of a sense of self now, and I have Program* to thank for that. *(man, age forty)*

Even if life had not yet taken a turn for the better, narrators seemed certain that things would improve in due time. They played up a sense of mastery over their lives—if tentative—as in "I'm not sure how this will end up, but I'll be fine as long as I keep doing what I've learned to do." For example:

> I've been in a real crummy spot, and it's been hard to try to do recovery and keep it all together. CoDA has made me realize that I have no control over what my wife decides to do. I can just take care of myself and know that, whatever happens, I'll get through it. *(man, age thirty-seven)*

With such endings—"Whatever happens, I'll get through it"—narrators affirm the "growth" of the self. They suggest the ability to reconcile the tough issues of adult life with their own capabilities and goals. This new skill at reconciliation is recognized as what was lacking in their lives before recovery.

The idea of a life in recovery raises a question. If people go to CoDA when a relationship ends, but continue to attend long after the sting of uncoupling has subsided, what, then, do they see themselves "recovering" *from?* I met people who had spent three, four, and even five years in the group. They came to CoDA on the heels of disruption and stayed. What were they *doing* there? Quite simply, they were "recovering" from codependency, but they never got a clean bill of health.

The discourse builds in large part on a medical metaphor: it portrays codependency as a *condition,* not an *injury.* You do not recover from a condition. It causes varying degrees of discomfort and inconvenience. It requires varying levels of intervention. But it forever affects the way you go about your life, and it never completely heals. Once people identify themselves as codependents, they can never fully "recover." [14] Even though the pain of a particular relationship may pass, the underlying condition that fostered the troublesome "dysfunction" does not. Your codependency may go into a remission of sorts as you begin to make "healthier" choices, but it will never go away. As a condition, it requires continuous monitoring, hence continued participation in CoDA. This subtly but effectively transforms your purpose for attending. People come to the group for support during uncoupling. In the course of re-

---

*CoDA members typically speak of "Program," omitting the definite article.

pairing that damage, they discover (or create) so many fundamental problems that they end up with a lifelong project. The loss starts the introspection, but it often continues long afterwards.[15]

Meanwhile, however, a more social phenomenon has also taken place, through the development of a socio-biography. By the time the crisis period ends, people feel little need to move on. They have "become" codependent—or at least they have in the sense that they see *themselves* that way. It is true that, as Wuthnow puts it, "people in groups do not simply tell stories—they become their stories" (1994, 301). But they must also find their own stories convincing. The existence of an established narrative formula of codependency does not reduce the experience of having a self to mastering a story. I am not proposing that narrators have established coherent identities if they have simply managed to use CoDA's rhetorical resources to their own advantage. If this were so, anyone who understood the conventions of a coherent narrative of self could speak one and, by doing so, could make it happen. Individual lives "could be improved with exercises in rhetoric" (Rosenwald 1992, 269), and I would have spent more time reading *Think and Grow Rich* than I did reading Sartre.

Because the narrative of the self is, as Gagnon (1992) put it, an "internal conversation," the experience of selfhood hinges as much or more on believing in your *own* stories than on getting *others* to believe them. The narrative accomplishment of selfhood is decidedly not analogous to the impression management that constitutes selfhood for Preedy at the Beach (see Goffman 1959, 4–6). Preedy carries a Spanish translation of Homer, others think him intelligent, and so he effectively is. Goffman claims that, "in so far as the others act as if the individual had conveyed a particular impression" (6), he or she has effectively done so. What I am describing is much more internal; it is impression management *directed at yourself* (see Vinitzky-Seroussi and Zussman 1996). As Hewitt explains, "much of the conversation in which we construct and reconstruct [our biographies] occurs within ourselves and not in interaction with others" (1989, 183). In short, we must not only "talk the talk," we must also "walk the walk."

The desire for integrity—whether phrased as an "internal conversation" or simply a feeling that we are "in some peculiarly subtle sense the same" (James 1910), seems in no danger of disappearing. Despite various claims that selfhood, in a permanent sense, has been irretrievably lost (and some would say, "Good riddance"), this seems not to be the case outside the ivory tower. If CoDA members are indicative of anything, they are indicative of the strength and ubiquity of the belief in the essential self, experienced as continuous and coherent. This continuity and coherence takes the form of a running story that people tell to themselves, as well as to other people. While the story has integrity, it also leaves room for a great deal of ambiguity, for it is not yet finished.

This does not mean that stories of the self are capriciously cobbled together; rather, they are grounded in institutions, which give life to the internal conversations. Neither does it mean that institutions simply provide set and setting for your narrative performances, only to fade away after the show. Rather, they remain long after the curtain falls. We cannot "do" selfhood alone, but it must work when we are alone if it is to work in front of others.

CHAPTER FOUR

THE INSTITUTION "LITE"

The institution that anchors self-stories in progress is itself built around ambiguity and ambivalence. The people who fill CoDA's meetings are thoroughly immersed in the therapeutic ethos. Yet, they often told me that they would be lost without the group. These "free agents" claimed to feel something lacking when they missed a meeting. They talked about feeling "at home" in CoDA, and of having a sense of "belonging" in the group. They spoke of it as the one place where they could "really be themselves." They spoke, too, of finding friends in the group, or at least finding something that felt like friendship. Some people became involved in the monthly business meetings and served on committees. I learned firsthand that CoDA picnics and social events were consistently well organized and well attended—by people who usually do not know one another's last names.

This both surprised and puzzled me. I had expected to find the "fatalistic, isolated individualism" that the discourse allegedly fosters (Mitchell-Norberg, Warren, and Zale 1995, 145). I had also expected to see an erosion of group loyalty (Lasch 1979) and "the weakening of traditional forms of life," including the tradition of mutual self-help (Bellah et al. 1985, 292). I envisioned finding people who had only loose connections to a group that they used mainly for selfish purposes. To be sure, CoDA has its share of "free riders." In some cases, people who claimed to feel a sense of "belonging" did little but attend a single weekly meeting. What is unique about CoDA, however, is the way that it can accommodate "free ridership" and simultaneously mitigate its worst consequences. Many of those who claim to appreciate the group's structure and security also worry that commitments and obligations can restrict personal "growth." They want "to be part of something bigger," as several people put it, but they do not want that "something" to demand obedience and sacrifice. CoDA responds to this ambivalence. Stability and latitude, ritual and informality, and structure and flexibility exist in dynamic tension at the meetings. This attests to CoDA's paradoxical status as an institution, but one that I call an institution "lite." It offers all the benefits of an institution, but with fewer obligations.

Consider Alex, whose experience illustrates the contradictory hopes and fears that people bring to the group. At age forty-two, he is a Keith Richards look-alike, and he is pleased when I say as much. He attended his first CoDA meeting at The House of Life one cold, grey, weekday morning in March. The weather matched his mood at the time. Some months before that, he had come home from work early one day to find his live-in fiancée in their bed with another man. He had had several serious relationships prior to this one, and thought this one would last. But after hours of fighting, they broke off the engagement and she moved out that very evening. Although this alone would push most people to the breaking point, it had happened the same week that Alex's much-beloved father died. Alex had fairly recently recaptured some closeness with his father after a long "free agent"–style estrangement, and he found the loss very painful. He had returned to work too soon after the funeral, he said, and had left early that particular day to try to rest. Little did he know.

Alex's thin face sagged as he recalled his thoughts:

> You really are alone, you know? You just can't depend on people. They betray you. They die. You can't blame them for dying, of course, but it reminded me that you can't get your sense of who you are from other people. You are alone. You've got to be your own person. It's all you've got.

Alex had languished for months when his sister, who had been attending CoDA in another part of the country for some time, suggested that he try it. He did not care for it. "I thought, 'This is nuts,'" he told me. "I'm out of here." Three months later, he went to another meeting. This time, it was a Friday night, also at The House. Friday night meetings at The House can get very large; forty or fifty people might attend, and many socialize afterwards. Alex felt intimidated by the size of the Friday night group. In addition, he occasionally plays guitar in rock bands, performing in local bars on weekends, so he wanted to keep his Friday evenings free for gigs. A few weeks passed. He went to a Tuesday night meeting at another location. He found that group "too cliquish."

He found the procedure "starchy," and the people "kind of selfish." The following Monday night, he tried another meeting at The House. The people there "were beautiful." He thought, "I can relate to this. I'll go back." That was four years ago. Since then, he has seldom missed a meeting.

"What made you keep trying?" I asked him. "Did you ever consider sticking with your original impression that CoDA just wasn't for you?" "I knew I needed it," he replied. "When I found out that [the meetings] were at The House, that made it even easier." Alex may have to sell his car to make ends meet. Since The House is within walking distance of his apartment, he can always get to meetings. Getting there was his main concern; I was curious about why he kept trying. I pressed him to explain what made him persist after the first disappointing meeting. Why not just go to a bar, I asked, or why not join a bowling league, or a church group? I knew fragments of Alex's "free agent" biography. He had told me about studying Buddhism and other Eastern philosophies. I knew he had studied yoga. He had also talked about drugs. Then, too, there was his music. Why not turn to one of these more familiar things that he could do on his own? He explained that he just "knew" he "needed" something else. I pressed him: "What was it about CoDA that you 'needed'?" "I like the affiliation," he told me,

> just the social affiliation with people my age. I'm forty-two. They've been divorced or are having mid-life crises or something, and I can associate with that. But, besides that, I like the order, the structure. A child without structure feels insecure. I know that.

He also claimed to "need" to be able to contribute to the group, but without feeling pressured to do so. "I like that I can do something, but not get tied into it forever. It makes me a lot more willing to do things," he said. Alex had recently decided to take responsibility for bringing his group's supply of CoDA literature to meetings. Some groups are able to use storage space at the facilities in which they hold meetings, but those who cannot must rely on members. A commitment like Alex's is known in Twelve Step circles as "service." "I want to give something back," Alex explained, "and it's time I started doing some service." If he has to sell his car, however, he will not be able to carry the cumbersome box of literature on foot. Alex knows that he can make the commitment now and give it up later without diminishing his standing in the group. Someone else would also be waiting for an opportunity to serve, and would take up where he left off. "I like that flexibility," he said.

You can do as much as you want there, you know? Some people just go to meetings, and that's it. That's all they have time for, or that's all they want, or whatever. Other people come early and hang out, and that's OK, too. Other people are always leading or setting up, and that's cool, too. Then, some people, like Jeff, I call him "Mr. Recovery." They do the meetings and the Step Studies and they're into service. But as much as you want to do, you can do—or as little.

Alex personifies the group's mix of ideological elements. CoDA appeals to people who appreciate the camaraderie but also see themselves as ultimately alone. It brings together people who claim to have "attempted to use others—our mates, friends, and even our children, as our sole source of identity" (CoDA 1995, iii). Yet, these same people who have allegedly *used* others believe that recovery *depends* on others. *The CoDA Book* explains that "the road to recovery is filled with fellowship . . . we see growth in people who work the program and look to the Fellowship of CoDA for support" (8). Then, too, the discourse denounces families as "sometimes moderately or sometimes extremely dysfunctional" (iii), while simultaneously asserting that membership in "the CoDA *family*" offers the possibility of "a life filled with peace and joy" (11, emphasis added). Although it is not surprising that a group would portray itself as an exception to a rule, what I found remarkable about CoDA were the ways that it indeed accommodates ambivalence among its members.

INSTITUTIONS — "LITE" AND OTHERWISE

The term "institution" is fundamental to sociology, yet it has numerous connotations. It generally refers to patterns of activities organized around a similar goal. From this point on, for simplicity's sake, I will distinguish this connotation by capitalizing the "I." The economy is an Institution, as is education, the family, religion, and other clusters of related activities. The term can also connote formal organizations, as in "this hallowed institution," when referring to a university, for example. From now on, I will distinguish this meaning with a lowercase "i." To make matters more complicated, institutions compose Institutions. An individual school, for example, is an institution that exists within the Institution of education.

The sociological sense of the term most often draws on its Institutional connotations. It refers mostly to practices and policies. When something has become "Institutionalized," it means that a practice or policy has become incorporated into the patterns of activities that come to constitute the taken-for-granted. One may speak of Institutionalized racism or sexism, for example, meaning that discrimination has become so thoroughly embedded in a given set of activities that it seems "normal," if not "natural." The practices and policies that constitute Institutions also "make" the people who come into contact with them, as when Kanter wrote that "jobs 'create' people" (1977, 3). This touches on the complicated connotations of the term, however, since what "creates" people are institutions, which are the mediators for Institutional forces. When Kanter said that "jobs 'create' people," she meant the Institution of large-scale bureaucracy, but she also meant that individual corporations—or institutions, with a lowercase "i"—"create" people. People cannot participate in Institutions directly; they are abstractions. The only contact people have with, say, the Institution of the economy is through individual institutions. They earn a paycheck at one, translate it into usable currency at another, and so on.

CoDA qualifies as an institution. It has by-laws, an incorporated Board of Trustees, and a formal organizational structure with local, state, national, and international levels. The group has existed for ten years on the basis of a model established nearly six decades ago. Each of its approximately four thousand groups meet regularly, for the same purpose. But CoDA also qualifies as an Institution, and it is this aspect that I emphasize here. If one thinks of Institutions as relatively permanent, organized patterns of activities and relationships that meet basic needs of a society, then CoDA also fulfills these requirements. CoDA participates in and maintains a set of ideas about selfhood. It diffuses and legitimates ideas about the self in the same sense that the economy legitimates ideas about bureaucratic capitalism. Most people are probably more conversant with codependency's psychospiritual discourse—self-consciously or not—than with the basics of large-scale capitalism.

Analysts of "real" Institutions would double over in laughter at this suggestion. Surely CoDA groups do not have half the importance of, say, the global economy. What "basic needs" of a society does CoDA provide? It produces none of the material requirements essential for human existence. It does not contribute to the economy. It creates no jobs. Its "organized patterns of activities" cannot compare to those that constitute the family or education. It provides none of those things one might consider "first order" societal necessities.

Or does it?

Institutions do much more than meet these sociologically orthodox "basic needs" of a society. They also provide something else considered absolutely essential in modern life: the self. As Randall Collins puts it, modern men and women "are not only allowed to be individuals, we are *expected* to be" (1982, 55, emphasis original). Institutions provide contexts for the "internal conversations" of the self. Their structures provide anchors for identity. They maintain and reproduce the norms that make behavior understandable and predictable. The sustained interaction that takes place within Institutions gives selfhood its continuity. Because they exist before you are born and continue to exist after your death, they create the sense that you are part of something bigger than yourself. These are the societal "needs" for which CoDA provides. As "real" Institutions such as marriage become increasingly less reliable as anchors for the self, CoDA and similar groups have emerged to provide alternatives. Institutions indeed create people, but when existing Institutions flounder, people also create Institutions.

Institutions also differ in *how* they create people. Lewis Coser has argued that, for the most part, modern Institutions "tend to make only limited demands on the person" (1974, 4). People can have multiple obligations and roles because no single set of relationships requires exclusive loyalty. Marriages coexist with careers, and both allow for other interests and commitments. A particular category of Institutions demands absolute devotion; Coser refers to these as "greedy." Greedy Institutions require that people weaken or even sever ties that might constitute competing claims for allegiance. Examples include the priesthood, which demands celibacy as a means of minimizing competing family obligations; monastic and utopian communities, whose clear boundaries between members and nonmembers secure the loyalty of the former; and the traditional family, which requires that wives, especially, cater to all its needs at all hours (see also Hochschild 1989). Coser calls these Institutions greedy "insofar as they seek exclusive and undivided loyalty and they attempt to reduce the claims of competing roles and status positions on those they wish to encompass within their boundaries. Their demands on the person are omnivorous" (4). Greedy Institutions require that their members "be so fully and totally committed to them that they become unavailable for alternative lines of action" (8).

While modern Institutions indeed "create" people, greedy Institutions concentrate their effort; they "encompass within their circle the whole personality" of those involved (Coser 1974, 4). In contrast, as an

Institution "lite," CoDA allows the personalities that come within its circle to determine how much of their lives it will encompass. To be sure, CoDA "creates" people. While it does, however, it also allows them to determine what their involvement means for them. Instead of demanding a prescribed or even minimal level of loyalty, CoDA "is there for you when you need it," to use the phrase that members themselves often use. CoDA supplies many of the benefits of an Institution, but, as an Institution "lite," it articulates with the "free agency" of its members. Even those who recognize that Institutions have their flaws also understand that avoiding them leads you from the frying pan into the fire. CoDA maintains a dynamic tension between criticizing Institutions and recognizing their necessity. It has accomplished this by Institutionalizing a respect for private sources of meaning. This is central to its "lite" character. Recovery is portrayed as "an individual growth process" (CoDA 1988), with each person growing at his or her own pace. Therefore, any given individual is always understood to be "right where he or she needs to be." But, according to the codependency discourse, being "right where you need to be" does not mean that you should run away from the world; the therapeutic ethos has proven that unworkable. Instead, you can allegedly best respond to your "true" self when surrounded by like-minded, "healthy" people.

Ironically, in CoDA, the respect for private meaning justifies remaining connected: the group is populated with people who collectively support the right to do what they individually believe is best. As a member told me, "You can't do Program alone. You can't read the books and do it yourself. You need the contact. You've got to get to a meeting, or it doesn't work." CoDA's ability to combine the respect for private meaning with the "need" for contact is a key to its success. It contains enough Institutional elements to keep the group running, but conceals and minimizes these intrinsically social obligations with the language of inner "needs."

STRUCTURE AND RELIABILITY, BUT NOT TOO MUCH

CoDA attracts people who appreciate structure and routine but have lost the basis for those elements in their lives. Alex couched his appreciation in somewhat vague language. "A child without structure feels insecure," he said. Another man is more explicit:

I used to hate to go home, especially at the beginning, when my wife first left. So I'd go to meetings every night. Two on my days off. I went just because it put some regularity into my life and gave me some contact with people like myself. *(age forty-seven)*

A woman echoes his sentiments:

When everything around you has fallen apart, you walk into a meeting and you find structure. You know how it's going to run. You know nobody's going to laugh at you or get mad or think you're crazy. It's so dependable. *(age forty-two)*

While members recognize the "need" for structure, not just any structure will do. They reserve the right to determine what they "need." While in many ways, when you have seen one CoDA meeting, you have seen them all, Alex's experience indicates that groups *do* differ from one another. I agree with him that the conviviality of Friday night meetings at The House of Life differs remarkably from the quiet of the other meetings held in the same room. I found that weekend meetings in Manhattan's East Village were consistently and markedly different from weekday morning meetings on Long Island. At the former, I heard people share about heroin use and homosexuality; at the latter, the sharing was relatively tame. Like all social environments, CoDA groups generate their own unique rules of conduct. The groups Institutionalize certain rules because they draw people who have similar expectations and feel similar obligations about deference and demeanor. Although the text read at CoDA meetings encourages members to "say anything you want, for you will not be blamed, judged, or punished," this is an exaggeration. More accurately, the group generates implicit standards. For example, a woman who attended meetings at The House of Life told me about learning what topics she could discuss:

I had to just listen a lot and almost like acclimate myself to the group and learn what was OK to say in the group and what was not, because I didn't want to turn people off and have them running away. I did that in the beginning. I used to say everything and people would just go "ooohh" [she cringes]. So I've learned what to say and what not to say. *(age forty)*

Members have the freedom to participate in maintaining a particular atmosphere or move to one they find more suitable, revealing just how "lite" the group really is. Since there are no membership or attendance records, no one will be chastised for skipping a meeting. The norms of anonymity mean that no one else will call attention to having seen someone in another group.

Although members are free to attend different groups, the informal rules of conduct largely determine the kind of person that you can "be" there. The extent to which a person can play by a particular set of rules determines his or her comfort level in the group. Goffman explains this as "the ritual game of having a self" (1967, 91). "If the individual is to play [the game]," he writes, "then the field must be suited to it" (91). Everyone has had the experience of entering a field and not being able to play the game; the rules may be unclear or may seem unfair or meaningless. In such instances, we often say that we cannot "be" ourselves, and long to get back to playing fields with more familiar, agreeable rules. The environments in which Goffman studied the rules of conduct— two wards of a mental hospital—did not grant those within them the freedom to inspect the field on which they would play the game. Members of CoDA have freedom that the patients of Wards A and B did not. They exercise it by visiting different groups until they find one suited to playing their particular version of the game. Recall that Alex tried several. At first, he thought, "This is nuts," but later found a group that made him think, "I can relate to this." In short, people select groups according to the ease with which they think they can "be"—or "become"—themselves. They know they "need" the group, but they also reserve the right to determine what kind of group they really "need." In this way, the "need" for the group—for connection to an Institution—is made more palatable by the freedom to select that group.

While this level of agency clearly appeals to people immersed in the therapeutic ethos, it also has its drawbacks. Because CoDA members do not go to the group to learn a specific doctrine, meetings can sometimes seem like the blind leading the blind. The benefits of CoDA, at least according to Twelve Step rhetoric, come through identifying with others who have a "common problem." But it is not simply *identification* that members value. More accurately, they value identification with certain others who respect similar rules about deference and demeanor. To the extent that it is possible, they select their small group "audiences" to increase the likelihood of getting a positive response. Despite the democratic, anonymous, confidential character of the groups, and despite the "common problem" that draws members together, people seek out particular others whose sharing they want to hear. Then, they incorporate aspects of those stories into those they tell about themselves. But it is never clear what criteria they use to determine what is worth incorporating. They appear to choose only what seems most useful for now. One man explains:

> Sometimes people just have the right things to say to you. Then I would, of course, want to be in the small group with them if these people generally had something to say that I needed to hear. *(age thirty-five)*

"How do you know who has 'the right things to say'?" I asked him. He explained that he had been very "controlling," always believing that he had the right way to do things. His recovery role model was a woman who had a very relaxed way about her. She struck me as someone who takes things in stride. Whenever possible, he got into a small group with her. The things he "needed" to hear from her allowed him to modify his own story along her more upbeat lines. "When I come out of here," he said, "I always look at things in a new way. I say, 'Well, she tried it that way. I'll see if it works.' And usually, it works, but the thing is, whatever it was, I got away from the way I'd naturally do it." In other words, *If I think it might be useful for me, it's what I "need."*

RELIABILITY WITHOUT OBLIGATIONS

Just as the members want structure, but not at any cost, they also want reliability, but without the obligations it may require. For example, the standardized meeting procedure has obvious benefits for those who move among groups. Its reliability also gives the group an egalitarian spirit because it allows anyone present to lead the meeting. At least one member explained that she liked knowing that, "even if nobody showed up to lead the thing, I could start the meeting." CoDA is, as the saying goes, "there when you need it," but it does not depend on particular people to be so.

The group maintains its balance between reliability and freedom with two related ideologies. One of these is the belief in "knowing" your own "needs." The other is the idea of service to the group as a part of your recovery. The emphasis on "knowing" their inner "needs" allows members to maintain the idea that they are not controlled by their obligations. At the same time, however, without members like Alex, willing to take on obligations, CoDA would cease to exist. CoDA is held together at every level by service. Volunteers staff the National Service Office, serve on committees, set up chairs, and lead meetings. Yet, the characteristics of codependency include a tendency to become so caught up in doing things for others that you neglect your own "needs." There-fore, no one can exert formal pressure on another to serve. Anyone who arrives early enough to set up chairs for a meeting may do so. Some may prefer to chat with others or to stand outside to smoke the cigarette that must last them the next ninety minutes. Reluctance to become more involved does not imply laziness or lack of consideration; it indi-cates a "need" to "take care of" yourself by limiting or changing your obligations. Other members must respect those "boundaries." Mean-while, the group's continued existence depends on those who feel the "need" to serve, or, in other words, who feel a sense of obligation to the group. CoDA's endurance suggests that its members are, for the most part, sufficiently immersed in norms of solidarity and obligation, although the rhetoric of individual "needs" conceals the social origins of their actions. People who do service make CoDA reliable and endur-ing, but depicting service as a thoroughly individual decision means that the endurance and reliability does not depend on designated people. According to Alex, this made him more willing to serve. I also had occa-sion to find this reassuring. Once, after I had signed up to lead a particu-lar meeting, I remembered another obligation that I had elsewhere on the same night. Not knowing what to do, I got out the phone list and called a long-time member. I told her I could not attend that night, and asked her advice. "Don't worry about it," she said. "Someone will always pick up the book." She even seemed mildly amused that someone would go to the trouble of seeing that the job would be covered.

The obvious drawback to keeping obligations "lite" is the "free rider" problem. CoDA's reliability does not depend on *formally* designated people, but it does depend on those consistently willing to serve. The same people typically arrive early enough to set up chairs at meetings. Those who dash in at the last minute also seem to have to dash out afterwards, without helping to restore the room to its original order. The same regular members cycle through the revolving door of leading the meetings. Because the group takes the obligation out of service— and it could not do otherwise without contradicting its internal logic— the burden of maintenance lies with those who feel the "need" to serve. Although this problem is common to voluntary groups, CoDA can do nothing to change it. Unlike voluntary groups that work for shared goals or causes, no one in CoDA can express frustration or give the others a spirited pep talk, for this would only be evidence of his or her codepen-dency.

Another drawback to linking service to "needs" is that, once someone decides to take on a responsibility, the group has no way to control how well it gets done or sanction those who do it badly. I suffered through meetings in which the leaders simply lacked the reading skills to follow the text. One woman consistently referred to the group as "Codependency Anonymous." She stumbled over the word "anonymity" and parsed sentences awkwardly. On several other occasions, I noticed that one particular long-term member characteristically led meetings in a casual, offhand manner. He was clearly willing to lead—this was no "free rider"—but his manner of leading made me wish he had not bothered. He tilted his chair back, ran his hand through his hair, and stifled yawns as he read. He often volunteered to speak on the same night that he led, so the group had to endure a double dose of his dreamy manner that I interpreted as carelessness.

Although no one confronts the careless or incompetent leader, at least some members clearly find such instances disturbing. They cast a tension over the entire group, made obvious by a restlessness that contrasted with the usual reverent demeanor. Nevertheless, the members excuse this with the same rhetoric they use for "free riders": the individual alone knows what he or she "needs." Someone who leads a meeting badly must have "needed" to lead nonetheless. My impatience with the careless or incompetent reader says something about me; I "need" to learn a lesson, perhaps about patience or tolerance. Once, after an evening of listening to the chair-tilter I just described, I talked to a member who had made rolling eye-contact with me during the meeting. "He's so nonchalant," he said of the man who led, "that I get pissed off and it ruins the meeting for me." But he saw his *own* attitude—and not the leader's delivery—as what had to change. "I know it's my problem that I let it ruin the meeting for me. I know I've got something to learn, no matter what the situation. John [the leader] *is right where he needs to be.*" Because members cannot challenge the group's norms even when they find something disagreeable, they cannot consider what may be right for the group, in some absolute sense. They have only two alternatives: they can leave, or they can ask *"what's in this for me?"* Most often, it seems, people tend to choose the latter option.

I saw many instances of this. In the previous chapter, I introduced Beth, a woman who was unable to grasp the formula for sharing. Although I lack specific knowledge of her background, her apparent developmental disability manifested itself as a lack of the social skills that others typically brought with them to the group. The group did not "work" for Beth because she could not understand what was going on and what was expected of her. This points out the importance of socialization in "mainstream" Institutions for getting along in a group that condemns those very skills as "dysfunctional." The reaction I got from others when I asked why they did not confront her, or at least explain to her how things work, points out the extent to which everything revolves around your private source of meaning: *"what's in this for me?"* Confrontation was to be avoided because it could only foster your own codependency. Why make trouble for yourself? As one woman explained:

> CoDA isn't about control. The Steps tell us that we are powerless over others. I can't change [anyone else]. And confronting would only feed into my belief that things should go my way, even the meetings, and I'm here to get away from that. *(age fifty)*

Paul, whom I introduce in a later chapter, had this to say:

> I have thought that, really, something should be done, you know, because it would be more beneficial for her and for the group for somebody to explain to [her] how it works. But I don't know if she could grasp it, either. Then, too, maybe somebody *has* spoken to her.

Paul's assumption that someone else has already done something is a classic example of the "diffusion of responsibility" (Latané and Darley 1970) in bystander behavior. When there are multiple witnesses to an event, people tend to ask themselves "why me?" While the unwillingness to get involved has its drawbacks—Paul admits it would be better if he did say something—it also alleviates obligation.

LIVE AND LET LIVE—OR LEAVE

Since the norm in CoDA is that people simply do what seems right to them most of the time, and since no one can challenge this norm directly, anyone who becomes uncomfortable must endure, join a different group, or leave altogether. For the most part, they seem to endure, although they couch it in terms of lessons to learn. It is impossible to know how many leave altogether. I did encounter several instances in which people violated a group's implicit norms and felt compelled to leave that group. Here, a woman describes how the inability to criticize another member's behavior prompted her to change groups:

> In college, I went through a period of a lot of drugs and sex. And so, I shared that. And then, what happened was, another woman in the group

stood up and started shouting at me. I mean she really attacked me. Pointed me out. Singled me right out of the group and said, "It's because of women like you that my boyfriend's not safe when he goes out." I switched meetings because I just didn't feel comfortable there anymore. So then I just found another meeting to go to. *(age thirty-seven)*

Although "crosstalk" is prohibited, and I saw little of it during my research, this woman's experience suggests that it does occur. What this instance illustrates is the weight of implicit norms over explicit ones. There are explicit norms against "crosstalk." Notice, however, that the woman who violated the *explicit* norm was not punished; she did what was "right" for her. The one who had to leave the group did so because she could not challenge the *implicit* norm that the other woman was indeed "right where she needed to be." There was no way of saying that her behavior was wrong, in an absolute sense.

The norm that allows people to determine what is "right" for them clearly allows tremendous freedom. At the same time, however, since that norm is the group's one absolute, the members never establish any collective sense of right and wrong, or better and worse. No precedent of "how things are done here" is ever established, except to say that you are free to believe whatever you want.

MEANINGFUL RITUAL: BRING YOUR OWN MEANING

You are free to believe whatever you want—as long as you believe in something. CoDA maintains that it "is not a religious program, but a spiritual one" (CoDA 1995, 11), which is the same claim made by AA. Six of the Twelve Steps refer to "a power greater than ourselves," or to "God." The Third Step makes this an open text, by adding the qualifier "as we understood God." As each meeting opens, the group observes a brief moment of silence followed by the Serenity Prayer: *"God grant me the serenity to accept the things I cannot change, the courage to change the things I can, and the wisdom to know the difference."*

To an outsider, this may make CoDA seem like a religion. The members and the organization alike steadfastly deny this, but they do so with the equivocation of "not religious, but spiritual." Few members maintained any association with organized religion, but "spirituality" was something they valued and cultivated.[1] For them, God had become "less of an external authority and more of an internal presence . . . more manageable, more serviceable in meeting individual needs" (Wuthnow 1994, 3–4). This was evident in their descriptions of their Higher Powers. Some believed in a traditional, white-bearded, Judeo-Christian patriarch. The traditional imagery usually ended with appearance, however, for this was not a punishing God. Although most had initially thought of God as a stern character waiting to catch them in the act and make them regret it, he had, over time, become more loving, like a kindly grandfather. Others held different images. Two women I interviewed had been influenced by Native American beliefs that incorporated male and female characteristics. At least one member found a Higher Power in music. One woman said, "It's just like an energy or a force or being that's out there that's loving and can take care of me."

The Higher Power concept can even accommodate atheism. Several people who did not believe in God told me they felt no discomfort in the group because of this. Nevertheless, they still believed in a Higher Power. One avowed atheist explains:

> For me, having a Higher Power means knowing that I can live through whatever life dishes out. I appeal to the knowledge that I might be in the deepest of emotional shit right now, but I'll survive. *(age thirty-five)*

A woman who had tremendous difficulty with the concept altogether describes "borrowing" another member's Higher Power:

> When I first got into recovery, I heard people talking about this concept of Higher Power, and it was, like—it was actually nauseating to me. It was like, give me a break! And, once, in a meeting—I'll never forget this woman as long as I live—she said to me, "Do you believe that I have a Higher Power?" And I said, "Yeah, I believe you do." She said, "If you believe I have a Higher Power, how would you like to borrow my Higher Power?" And just the fact that she presented it that way was really neat. And I went home that night and addressed her Higher Power in a form of prayer. *(age thirty-six)*

I was intrigued by the tenacity with which CoDA and its members maintain the ambiguity of "not religious, but spiritual." Others have noticed this in AA. Rudy and Greil point out that "AA is neither religious nor not-religious: it is quasi-religious. It is the 'sort of' quality that demands explanation" (1989, 47). If CoDA claims outright that it is not a religion, what accounts for the "sort of" quality? Why not simply have a therapeutic program for codependency and leave it at that?

This, of course, raises an underlying question: Is it *really* a religion?

The organization may deny that it is, but is it, for all practical purposes, a religion? Answering this particular question would only lead me to ally myself with one or another more or less useful definitions of "religion." The more interesting question, and one more relevant to the discussion of the Institution "lite," is why CoDA adopted and maintains an ideology in which religion and its denial coexist.

Initially, I understood the quasi-religious quality as a vestige of AA. Any history of AA lists the numerous influences on which Bill Wilson drew in founding the group (see, especially, Kurtz 1979). Wilson himself had only been able to achieve sobriety after a religious conversion. Early meetings of AA took place in conjunction with the Oxford Groups, the tenets of which formed the basis for the Twelve Steps (see AA 1957). But Wilson and his followers split off from the Oxford Groups within about a year. They emphasized that AA intended to offer therapy for alcoholism, not salvation, and no doubt recognized that alcoholics came from all faiths, as well as from no faith at all. Too much emphasis on religion would have hindered the group's therapeutic goals.

The tolerance built into Twelve Step ideology clearly allows the groups to assimilate individuals with divergent backgrounds. It makes good sense to avoid alienating any of those you aim to attract. But tolerance does not explain the continued emphasis on spirituality. Explaining why a group does not exclude anyone does not explain why it remains "a spiritual program" in which members need to depend on a "power greater than themselves." In CoDA's case, this is not simply a vestige of its lineage to AA. For why would this particular vestige survive in CoDA when so many others have not? Spirituality would have gone the route of "stinkin' thinkin'" and serving coffee at meetings if it did not somehow suit CoDA's goals.

The emphasis on spirituality endures because of what it accomplishes. CoDA is presented as a therapeutic program for recovering from codependency, but it is better understood as a program for rebuilding the self. While the "condition" of codependency and the state of lost selfhood are analytically distinct, members would no doubt see them as inseparable. In order to accomplish its stated goals, the group must have a way to be both a therapeutic program (explicitly) for codependency and (implicitly) an instrument of identity transformation. Its need to be both entails a need to be both religious and not-religious—or "not religious, but spiritual."

While CoDA claims not to be religious, its structural need for a level of commitment sufficient to transform identity leads members to experiences that they can only call "spiritual." Identity transformation hinges on commitment, which hinges on a feeling of "transcendence," or an Institutionalized "awe" (see Kanter 1972) for the power of the group. One member described it this way:

> What happens in "The Rooms" is powerful. No one in Program can do individually what the group can do. Something happens there, and that's my Higher Power. (*man, forty-five*)

As a culture, we seem to lack a language for depicting powerful emotional experiences shared with others. Perhaps more accurately, as Durkheim ([1915] 1961) pointed out, a sense of awe inspired by participation in the collectivity is generally expressed in religious terms. The language that we typically use for such experiences is superempirical, or "spiritual." To take the need for transcendent experience too far by prescribing a particular religious faith would compromise CoDA's explicitly therapeutic goals. Nevertheless, in order to be therapeutic, members must adopt the discourse wholeheartedly. To encourage them to do so, the group must Institutionalize the feeling of transcendence. This explains the emphasis on "spirituality." The ambiguity of the term originates in the need to appeal to a broad audience. The need for tolerance accounts for the claim that the group is not a religion. But the claim that it is instead *"spiritual"* comes from the simultaneous need to generate transcendence, which is most often expressed in superempirical terms, such as "spirituality."

The transcendent aspects of CoDA appear in the group's symbolic rituals and language. For example, the ritual of the Serenity Prayer turns an ordinary room into one of "The Rooms." This Twelve Step phrase makes a symbolic distinction between the sacred realm of the meetings and the everyday, or profane, world. In actuality, of course, "The Rooms" are simply community centers, church basements, and other places in which Twelve Step groups meet. After the Serenity Prayer, however, those places become a collective reality, loaded with significance. For CoDA members, the phrase "The Rooms" evokes personal transformation. They talk about what brought them to "The Rooms" with the same enthusiasm that Christians have when giving testimony about the born-again experience.

The sacred is also evident in the Twelve Steps and Traditions, both of which are read at every meeting. Together, the Steps and Traditions constitute something of a totem for the group, since "it is in connection with [them], that things are classified as sacred or profane" (Durkheim

[1915] 1961, 140). Without them, "The Rooms" lose their sanctity; after all, despite its departures from AA's original rhetoric, CoDA remains a *Twelve Step* group. The sanctity of the Steps and Traditions struck me on one particular occasion, when a member announced that CoDA's Service Office had proposed revising the Traditions to make them better suited to codependency, and had asked for member input in doing so. Several members expressed concern verging on outrage at this possibility. One woman said, "How can we just revise the Traditions? We *can't* revise the Traditions. They're the *Traditions*." In addition, like Durkheim's totemistic tribes, CoDA recognizes other members of the Twelve Step clan as sacred. The Preamble reads that "although separate entities, we should always cooperate with all twelve-step recovery programs" (CoDA 1988). In short, as Rice puts it, "CoDA meetings . . . are really more than 'meetings.' They are ritual enactments of a symbolic reality that saturates and permeates the members' interactions" (1996, 147).

This may not sound "lite" at all. Indeed, it may strike some as cult-like, but this is decidedly not the case. The religious movements popularly called cults are especially "greedy" Institutions. They eliminate all competing claims on new recruits. No group that meets once a week, has no dues or leaders, and keeps no attendance records could be an effective cult. Moreover, cults dictate the form of the divinity being worshipped and determine the obligations of the followers. Cults also police members' thoughts and behaviors to enforce conformity. In CoDA, each person creates a Higher Power that exists for his or her own fulfillment. Demanding unconditional obedience or a life of sacrifice would contradict the logic of the discourse.[2]

CoDA's emphasis on spirituality is "lite" because it makes the individual the measure of all things. It allows people to reap the benefits of superempirical experience without having to wrestle with questions of "truth" and understand the roots of an established doctrine of faith.[3] In any case, the diverse backgrounds of those in the group would make consensus on any one doctrine impossible. Their sole basis of agreement is that Higher Powers of one sort or another have worked in their lives— or can. Since no one is able to put anyone else's Higher Power to the test, they simply agree to respect one another's views. This agreement is implicit, preserved in the norms for sharing: No criticism; no feedback; no interruption; and so on. You are responsible only to a Higher Power of your own creation. Consequently, people who are trying out new ways of making sense of their lives may do so with minimal risk.

They are free to draw together disparate events and images without instigating laughter or questions. When threatened with any feeling of "divine" criticism or condemnation, they may revise their Higher Power to be more loving and less critical. This is the freedom of "liteness." It is largely possible, however, because the Institution secures respect for private sources of meaning through its norms.

THE INEVITABILITY OF INSTITUTIONS

CoDA offers a possibility that, by all accounts, should no longer exist. Judging by the argument presented in *Habits of the Heart,* Americans tend to "separate out" their ideas of self from Institutions. "Finding yourself" means breaking away from family, friends, and tradition. To be sure, an element of this exists in CoDA, and a one-sided reading of the evidence could lead to the conclusion that this is *all* that exists. But there is much more to the story. CoDA is not so much a group that attracts people who "separate out" their Institutional connections as it is a response to such separation. It is also an attempt to redefine those connections. Like other attempts at redefinition, it is an effort to make something more useful than what exists. It carries with it the best and worst of what it seeks to supplant. It is a product of our times.

"People do not join groups simply because their hearts tell them to." So writes Robert Wuthnow in his impressive study of small groups. They join, he claims, because the groups are available and because someone else encourages them to do so. While I would certainly agree with both latter points—and Alex is a good illustration of this—I would have to disagree with the former one; and here again, Alex is a good illustration. It is probably true that people do not join groups out of the blue. But on the face of evidence in CoDA, they are often driven to find replacements for Institutional attachments they have lost. While I cannot say that it is their *hearts* that tell them to do so, it may be something as close to the heart as this culture can get. Alex's case illustrates that *something* urges them to go, even when their experience suggests that "this is nuts." At a moment when questions of the meaning of the self arise, a vast number of people seek their answers through affiliation with a group that has an established structure and allows them access to the realm of the sacred. If Institutions had indeed lost their power to provide meaning, CoDA would be pointless. To the contrary, it would seem that Institutions remain so essential that even those who would be predisposed to reject attachments to them on ideological grounds will come to accommodate them. Despite operating on highly individualistic terms, collective respect for private meaning allows CoDA to offer the benefits of enduring structure without the burden of rules, assigned roles, and onerous obligations. In this way, CoDA offers the anchors for selfhood typically provided by Institutions. By keeping things "lite," however, CoDA makes them available—and acceptable—to a generation of free agents.

PART TWO

CODEPENDENCY AS NARRATIVE STRATEGY:
THE ROLE OF CULTURE

P ART ONE DEPICTED CODEPENDENCY as a discourse, or a
"ready-made way of thinking." Like all discourses, it has rules for
what you can and cannot say. All families are "dysfunctional," for
example. All children suffer "abuse"; adults who cannot recall instances
of it have "shut down" to protect themselves from its severity. Moreover,
everyone is codependent; some are in denial, and some have not yet
had to come to terms with the "condition." You cannot "be" codependent without agreeing with and making these claims. You cannot "be"
codependent, for example, and claim that your family was normal. Believing that all families are "dysfunctional" is one of the hallmarks of
subscribing to the discourse.

And yet, the discourse of codependency does not produce automa-
tons. The men and women of CoDA tell diverse stories, focusing on
diverse problems and articulating diverse concerns. How, then, does a
unified discourse, with its own vocabulary and truth rules, accommodate, even foster, difference? The answer can be found in culture.

There are many notions of culture, and the one I use here comes
from Ann Swidler (1986). She portrays culture as a "symbolic vehicle

of meaning, including beliefs, ritual practices, art forms, and ceremonies, as well as informal cultural practices such as language, gossip, stories, and rituals of daily life" (273). It influences action by creating a "tool kit" of habits, skills, competencies, preferences, relationships, and beliefs that people configure in various ways to solve the problems they encounter. In this view, culture is a means of constructing "strategies of action." This poses a contrast to the more traditional sociological concepts of culture-as-values, in which it shapes action by defining what people want and directing them toward those goals. Max Weber described this capability with the metaphor of "tracks" and "switchmen" ([1922–23] 1946). In this image, action is pushed along by the engine of interests, but the "tracks" have been determined by the "switchmen" of ideas. Thus, values become culture's central causal element, by defining the destination sought. Different courses of action are attributed to different values. In "culture of poverty" arguments, for example, the values of lower-class groups allegedly differ from those held by the middle classes. Lower-class values promote corresponding goals, which direct action away from steady jobs and deferred gratification. But, as Swidler explains, there is evidence that the underprivileged indeed share the values of the middle class; they *do* value steady jobs and financial security. What differs is the range of available skills, competencies, and habits. As Swidler explains,

> If one asked a slum youth why he did not take steps to pursue a middle-class path to success (or indeed asked oneself why one did not pursue a different life direction) the answer might well be not "I don't want that life," but instead, "Who, me?" One can hardly pursue success in a world where the accepted skills, style, and informal know-how are unfamiliar. One does better to look for a line of action for which one already has the cultural equipment. (275)

The inadequacy of the culture-as-values explanation also becomes apparent in the phenomenon of "culture shock." The discomfort you feel in an unfamiliar setting does not come from holding foreign values. It comes as a result of knowing that your conduct, habits, and preferences may differ from those commonly used in the unfamiliar setting, regardless of the fit or lack thereof between your own values and those that reign within the new setting.

The emphasis on values assumes that people "choose their actions one at a time . . . striving with each act to maximize a given outcome" (276). Action is not discrete, however, but continuous. It builds on established precedent and takes the form of an overall "strategy." The word is used here not to indicate a plan for reaching a specific goal, as an "economic strategy" would be used to reach monetary goals. Instead, it refers to "a general way of organizing action . . . that might allow one to reach several different life goals" (277). It indicates a way of linking together skills, relationship networks, habits, and preferences. "Culture influences action," Swidler argues, "through the shape and organization of those links, not by determining the ends to which they are put" (277). Thus, culture creates the "tool kit" or "repertoire" (Hannerz 1969) that people draw on to construct behavior.

The "tool kit" image of culture poses different causal questions than does the image of culture-as-values. In particular, if "values" are not steering the course of action, what keeps it on course? As Swidler points out, cultural explanations are typically invoked to account for "continuities of action in the face of structural changes" (277). "Culture" is often invoked to explain why immigrant groups maintain traditions in new countries. Culture can also change, though, sometimes independent of structural change. Societies characterized by mystical religion have constructed their own functional equivalents of the Protestant Ethic, independent of the modern economic structures found in the West. Swidler's distinction between "settled" and "unsettled" lives helps shed light on how both change and continuity can take place. In the former, culture explains continuities of action. In the latter, it explains the construction of new strategies.

The term "unsettled" refers to periods of structural upheaval on the social or individual level. In unsettled times, ideologies offer powerful means of organizing new courses of action, largely because they can answer the question of how one should now live. They make new strategies of action possible, and the structural opportunities for enacting them determine which will endure. In settled lives and periods, ideology plays less of a role. It becomes diversified through being adapted to varied life circumstances. Moreover, it "[goes] underground," as Swidler puts it, "so pervading ordinary experience as to blend imperceptibly into common-sense assumptions about what is true" (281). Settled cultures exhibit not so much the selection of new strategies of action, but the investment of those selected with meaning for specific life circumstances. Swidler explains that, "as certain cultural resources become more central in a given life, and become more fully invested with meaning, they anchor the strategies of action people have developed" (281).

Combining the images of settled and unsettled lives helps to create a picture of how people can draw on the discourse of codependency to construct diverse narrative strategies. Men and women come to CoDA during unsettled periods, when much of the structure has gone out of their lives. During this time, the ideological aspects of the discourse help to answer the big questions of Why? and What will I do now? In time, unsettled lives become settled again. The group puts structure, order, and affiliation back into their lives. New relationships develop, and life goes on. In this more settled period—and those I interviewed had each been in recovery for several years—members adapt the discourse of codependency to their own circumstances, incorporating it into the existing skills, habits, desires, and preferences they have in their "tool kits." Each person has a diversity of resources available. Some of these become more central to his or her life during recovery, and consequently, more heavily invested with meaning. This investment "anchors" the narrative strategy a person develops, making it his or her own.

The following chapters explore four different narrative strategies that I heard among members of CoDA. Each narrative reflects different cultural resources and responds to a different set of structural circumstances. Consequently, each one shapes action in a particular way. Chapter 5, for example, illustrates the use of codependency as a resource for making transitions between relationships. It provides the language and the justification for making such a change. Chapter 6 illustrates the use of codependency as a resource for emotion management. Chapter 7 presents a narrative used by members who believed that their attitudes about gender had created their troubles and, consequently, tried to change those attitudes. Finally, Chapter 8 explores the creation of a narrative of victimization and self-indulgence. It shows how codependency can respond to a complete failure of social structure, in which the emptiness of one's "tool kit" becomes a resource in itself.

This is perhaps an appropriate moment to restate that these four narratives are not the only ones I heard in my research. They by no means exhaust the possibilities. I have chosen to treat these four in depth because they represent topics that I heard repeatedly. In other words, they illustrate recurrent ways in which codependency becomes part of the cultural resources that shape narratives and that, consequently, shape the self.

CHAPTER FIVE

CODEPENDENCY AS A STRATEGY
OF TRANSITION

I t is not only *uncoupling* that shapes the self-stories of people in CoDA. It is also *recoupling*. Many of those who fill CoDA's rooms are moving from one relationship to another, and thus from one set of obligations to another. For about a quarter of those I interviewed, codependency serves as a strategy for making transitions of this kind. The discourse gives them access to a sense of self that reflects the fluidity of their lives and is capable of surviving transition. It also allows them to reconcile their new involvements with the concern that relationships have caused them to lose touch with who they really "are." Paul's is a case in point.

If a CoDA group can have a version of the "class clown," forty-one-year old Paul fits the bill. His self-deprecating style of sharing often had people rocking with laughter. He seemed capable—at least in hind-sight—of finding the hilarity in every situation. He made his life sound like a comedy of errors. He delivered his stories deadpan, too, which made them even funnier. He would lean forward with his elbows on his knees and "steeple" his finger tips together in front of him. He would stare at a spot on the floor in the middle of the room, keeping his head down but occasionally lifting his eyes to the group and peering out from under heavy eyebrows. This gave him a devilish look, which added to his whole presentation. He spoke in an Archie Bunker accent and a gravelly voice that sounded like it came from a man twenty years his senior. In the environment of the meeting, people would wonder, as I did at first, whether they should laugh at what he said. Before long, however, we had no choice.

The sense of humor, he told me, once had a sarcastic edge. "I could have cut you to shreds," he said, "without even changing my expression." He explained that, since recovery, he feels no need for sarcasm. These days, he directs his jokes at himself. The accent, he explained, came from growing up in one of the boroughs of New York. The voice came from years of heavy drinking and smoking. He gave up tobacco and alcohol eight years ago, though, and had recently given up caffeine and sugar, as well.

To see Paul on the street, he would not strike anyone as the type of man who worries about the effects of caffeine and sugar. With his stocky build and ruddy complexion, he looks like someone who starts each day with bottomless cups of coffee and ends with several beers. Once upon a time, he said, he did exactly that. But now, Paul takes his recovery very seriously. He believes he has an "addictive personality." He calls himself not only a codependent, but a severe alcoholic, a workaholic, and a carbohydrate addict, as well. Paul began his recovery in AA, which helped him quit drinking. He found CoDA two years ago through the Twelve Step grapevine. Along the way, he has also tried therapy and attended Step Study groups. He applies his efforts simultaneously to "body, mind, and spirit," he says. The "body" and "spirit" parts are self-explanatory. He wants to trim off some extra weight and "get in touch with" his Higher Power. In the arena of the "mind," however, he focuses not on intellectual pursuits, but on "knowing who he is."

Paul first came to CoDA at the end of a two-year relationship. It had been a "rebound thing," he said, that began immediately after the end of an eighteen-year marriage. He had married young, to "the first woman who paid attention" to him. They had four children very quickly. Although Paul now wonders whether he and his wife ever really got along, he marvels at how, after eighteen years, he had come to rely on the stability of the relationship—regardless of its quality. The divorce radically changed every aspect of his life, especially the character of fatherhood. Although he worked long hours and had a long commute to his job, Paul still managed to spend a lot of time with his children. "That's the role I was shown growing up," he said. "The father's supposed to be with his family, taking care of everybody, and to let go of that, and be in a separate household from that, was a big jolt to my system." When his next relationship ended, he felt a similar "jolt," though less intensely. After the two consecutive breakups, he began to believe that he had "relationship problems."

Paul tried to talk about the heartache of sequential breakups in his AA meetings, and met with a lot of "shaming." Although no one at AA spoke to him directly, the leaders of particular meetings would make blanket statements in the interest of "reminding everyone how things work here." Paul understood this as an attempt to rein in the discussion. Like several other CoDA members, Paul emphasized that AA "is really only about drinking." He heard about CoDA, which held meetings in the same location as his AA group, but on another night. He had no idea, at first, how his history of alcoholism would go over in CoDA. He thought that some of the members would shun him, particularly those with alcoholic spouses or partners. But he "was very accepted there," he said. He found that talking about alcoholism in CoDA created no problems, whereas he could not talk about anything *but* alcoholism in AA. He bridged the gap by attending both, and continued to do so when we met.

At the time that I interviewed him, Paul had been out of work on disability for about three years. For his entire adult life, he had worked as a carpenter, and had injured himself on the job several times. When he finally sought treatment for the injury, the doctor told him he might qualify as disabled. Initially, he found it difficult to live with that label. Now, he says, he takes advantage of the time. His days fill up, though he cannot say how. He goes to a lot of Twelve Step meetings, and was one of two or three male "regulars" in a mostly female weekday morning meeting of CoDA. "You know that old stigma that women went to the day meetings because they aren't doing anything all day, right?" he asked. "Now it's all the guys on disability at the day meetings."

Paul explained that, before his divorce, his work and his family had given him a life "full of labels."

> When I got into recovery, I was in a marriage. I was a commuter. I was a carpenter. I was a full-time father. I had all these labels. But who, really, was I? Now, it's all been stripped away from me. I'm divorced. I'm a single parent. I don't work. But I know a lot about me.

Like many people in CoDA, Paul makes sense of his loss by seeing it as an opportunity to know himself. I wanted to find out what he believed he knew about himself, and how he had come to know it. Learning about himself had come, he said, through managing "certain relationships."

After his divorce, Paul maintained a very close relationship with his children. He and his wife had complicated joint legal and physical custody arrangements, which meant that the children lived with him for one set period of time and with her for another. He said that over time, however, he began to feel that his involvement with and availability to his children jeopardized his emerging sense of selfhood:

Even when they were living with her, I would, initially, always be on call for them. Just call me up, and I'd run out the door and take them somewhere. I'd change my plans for them. I was a cab service for them. It was like bending over backwards. But I was raised to believe that the kids always came first, even before yourself, and that's what I practiced. The kids have got to come first. But the thing that was missing from me was not having a self.

I asked Paul how he knew he did not have a sense of self. Since this is allegedly a key indicator of codependency, I wanted to know how someone might recognize it. He knew that he lacked a self, he said, because he had no idea of what he wanted. For Paul, as for others in CoDA, a set of inner wants and desires indicated who he truly "was." Paul claims that, before recovery, he had no indication of what his wants really were. "I would always lean towards what [others] want," he explained. "I wasn't in touch with my desires at all." When I asked how he knew he had a sense of self now, he gave a circular argument: *I know what I am like, therefore I am.*

I have a sense of self now because I'm more in touch with what I want. . . . I'm compassionate and caring. I'm a sensitive person.

I pressed Paul to tell me what he had done to gain this sense of self. He shifted between, or attempted to integrate, two accounts of his behavior. One expressed a somewhat "internal" motivation. "What did I do to get a sense of self?" he said. "I started to say 'no.' I wasn't taking care of myself. I was doing things to make people love me, not because I love myself." Another account, however, or another facet of it, revealed a more "external" motivation. When I pressed him to elaborate on what he actually did to "take care" of himself, he talked about his commitments to recovery and to the woman he now planned to marry. "I made my meetings primary in my life," he said, "and I started to put my relationship with my fiancée number one in my life."

Paul admitted that his fiancée resented the attention he paid to his children. It caused a lot of "stress" and "conflict" in the relationship, he said. In one particularly clear example, he said that he used to carry a beeper so that his children could contact him at all times. But they beeped him constantly, and for all sorts of reasons that did not require his immediate attention: to mediate minor squabbles, for example, or to get permission to have Cheerios instead of Rice Krispies. His fiancée understandably found this intrusive. She told him it was "really ridiculous," and he stopped carrying the beeper. They had fewer conflicts, he said, once he started "taking care" of himself. I asked him what this had involved. He said, rather straightforwardly, that he began to refuse his children's requests. He curtailed his involvement in their lives and limited his availability to them. He began to see being "on call" for them as "over-responsibility." The more detached manner in which he loves them now, he believes, benefits them as well as him. "I found out through CoDA that the only one I can really make happy is myself," he explains. "And, the paradox is that the more I can let go of my kids the better off they are." He continues:

> I know I can be a lot better parent to my kids when I have a sense of self than I could ever be before. What I'm modeling to them now is more important than what I used to model to them before. I smothered them with being over-responsible in what I labeled "love" then. And now I'm teaching them that it's important to have a life.

Whatever benefits Paul's detachment from his obligations to his children provided in terms of personal growth—theirs as well as his—it also eased the transition to a new partner and new obligations. He justifies his detachment from his children by claiming that it allows him to be a better father. It may do that, but it also justifies his shift to a new relationship. He claims to have taught his children the importance of "having a life" and a sense of self. What does this involve? In a nutshell, it means acting on his wants: "Making my recovery a priority in my life," he told me, "and making my relationship with my fiancée a priority in my life." When he was "on call" for his children around the clock, he had no life and no sense of self. Now that he has drawn a limit to the demands they can make on him, that has changed. Moreover, what he used to see as love, he now calls over-responsibility. And what of his relationship with his ex-wife? Evidently, that was not love either. In recovery, he claims, he "has learned how to love, for real, for the first time."

For Paul, having "a life" and a sense of self comes through *attachments* to others, not through *disengagement* from them. When one set of attachments loses its pull, another set replaces them. Disengagement exists only to facilitate transition. Paul claims to have gained a sense of self within the security of courtship, eventual marriage, and the Twelve Step culture surrounding AA and CoDA. This stands in contrast to the idea, so popular in the therapeutic ethos, that finding your "true" self comes from rejecting these potential sources of "dysfunction." For Paul, and others, too, a coherent story of the self depends on relationships and obligations—as long as he gets to choose them. Selfhood becomes a sacred concept that justifies leaving some obligations behind in favor of new ones. Ironically, the quest for selfhood began with the end of a relationship; now, it necessitates ending other relationships, as well.

In typical CoDA fashion, Paul uses the idea of an "emerging" self to rationalize the end of, first, his marriage, and then, the relationship that followed it. Paul sees his life as a series of necessary stages. If the divorce and the next breakup had not happened, he would not have come to the point where he knew he "needed" CoDA, and would not have realized that "what was missing from [him] was a sense of self." In this sense, Paul gives a formulaic story of codependency. His losses make sense when the pursuit of the self provides a thread of continuity.

For Paul, though, making sense of loss is only half of the story. He also has to make sense of a new relationship. Paul's version of recovery—of gaining a self—is a story of transition. He does not tell a story of rejecting all obligations in favor of self-absorption. He tells one of moving from old obligations to new ones. The way that he does so addresses two related issues of selfhood. It suggests that the notion that contemporary men and women have become less willing to define themselves in terms of roles and obligations is too simple. It also suggests that acquiring a new identity is not just a matter of switching labels.

On the surface, Paul appears to hold two contradictory beliefs about the self. These are perhaps best phrased in question form: How can someone who believes that relationships can inhibit your sense of who you really "are" rationalize having relationships at all? It is easy to understand how a recovering alcoholic would stay out of bars, and how a recovering gambler would avoid casinos. But, apart from a few legendary hermits, people cannot avoid relationships. In any case, seclusion is neither a requirement nor a suggestion for recovery from codependency. Some people who have been badly stung by a relationship may avoid commitment for a time, but many—like Paul—have new ties immediately available to them. Some have old ties that they cannot or prefer not to completely sever; others want to start new relationships. Paul's case illustrates how the discourse of codependency can justify having relationships while simultaneously encouraging an exclusively personal sense of who you really "are."

Paul claimed not to have had a sense of self when he was married, working, and being a full-time father. When I asked him what he had done to gain a sense of self, he used two related vocabularies that CoDA makes available. One of these manifested what I refer to as an "internal" motivation. This suggests Paul's belief in an "essential" self. At this level, Paul talks about the importance of knowing what he wants, in a deep, inner sense. He said, "I have a sense of self now because I'm more in touch with what I want." His codependency had pushed him to do things that other people wanted, and to think that this would trickle down and make him happy as a result. Because he had no idea of what he wanted, though, he depended on the reactions of other people, which were undependable for a number of reasons. He considers his wants indicative of who he "truly" is, at some essential, reliable level. He talks about qualities and characteristics in the same way, describing himself as "compassionate and caring . . . a sensitive person." He despaired of the extent to which the labels he acquired through marriage, fatherhood, and work prevented him from knowing who he "really was." He talks as if, once free of the labels, he could find out. Through divorce and disability, Paul lost all his traditional labels.

Labels have not disappeared entirely from Paul's life. But today he uses labels that reflect what he believes to be permanent, underlying qualities, not ones that exist within relationships that can be dissolved. For example, he describes himself as a recovering alcoholic, codependent, workaholic, and carbohydrate addict. He does not consider these fleeting traits, useful only as long as he is attached to particular other people. He considers them permanent dimensions of his character. "I know I have this addictive side of me," he said, "and it will always be there. I can choose not to give in to it, one day at a time, but it will always be there."

Paul has not simply rejected his more traditional labels—along with their attendant obligations—because he finds it convenient to do so. He lost them through the trauma of divorce and disability. It makes sense that someone in his position would want to anchor his sense of self to something that cannot dissolve so easily. In the same vein, a woman I call Cindy told me about her dislike of the labels that came with her roles and relationships:

> I used to be so worried about being the perfect wife, the perfect mother, the perfect daughter-in-law, the perfect neighbor, whatever. I drove myself crazy with all that. I got divorced and, hey, guess what? I must not be the perfect wife after all. I'm nobody's daughter-in-law. Neighbors come and go. Kids grow up. So now I say don't label me, because as soon as you label me, or I label myself, I'm going to put all my eggs in that basket and when I drop it, where will I be? *(age forty-five)*

Cindy, like Paul, speaks from the standpoint of someone who fears losing the sense of who she truly "is" to a relationship. The sense of self that she feels she gained from her relationships was only temporary. As she said, she got divorced, neighbors moved away, and children grew up. If Cindy and Paul ground their sense of who they are in qualities and wants, instead of labels, they can call it their own, in some essential, inviolable way. The belief in the essential self helps them adapt to their loss. Their sense of self does not depend on being attached to particular others. At the same time, however, if they are sufficiently convinced of this "essential" self, they can have relationships without the fear that they will again lose the sense of who they "are."

In order to reconcile the fear of relationships with their necessity—especially among those who have new attachments waiting in the wings—the discourse provides a second vocabulary. This is the one I refer to as "external." Underlying, or adjacent to, the "internal," or "essentialist," vocabulary of wants is a language of "healthy" relationships and obligations. It allows people who believe that obligations have inhibited their personal "growth" to justify new obligations. For example, as long as Paul is able to maintain the idea that he is "in touch with" what he wants, he feels able to have relationships and obligations. Indeed, within CoDA, a secure sense of self is seen as a prerequisite for having "healthy" relationships. Paul does not reject relationships altogether, he simply wants to *choose* which ones will have weight in his life. For example, he is creating a new relationship with the woman he plans to marry, and chooses to give that relationship priority. Two failed relationships no doubt give him cause for concern. If he believes that he is in some essential sense the same—regardless of his relationships—he can risk involvement. Meanwhile, he reduced some of the friction that was fueling his concern by "detaching" from his children. He can justify having done so by saying that he can be an even better father to them now that he has a sense of self.

In social-psychological terms, Paul is engaged in resolving "role conflict." He is rearranging identities within a "hierarchy of salience" (Stryker 1980; see also Hewitt 1994).[1] Social psychologists claim that each person has a complement of identities, corresponding to the number of roles or social positions he or she occupies—or would like to. Identities often overlap, and some situations draw on more than one identity, which may be compatible or incompatible. Sometimes, two or more roles come into conflict. One role might demand a level of commitment that makes it difficult to enact another. People resolve this "role conflict" by withdrawing from the relationships that cause it. They sort and rearrange identities within the salience hierarchy, giving priority to those they find particularly gratifying, and investing less in those that cause friction. They do what Paul did. His identity as a single father began to cause friction in his relationship with his fiancée. He found that new relationship increasingly rewarding, and his relationship with his children less so. Consequently, he moved his relationship with his children to a lower rung of the hierarchy. He gave his involvement in CoDA priority, and also made his relationship with his fiancée "number one." In short, what social psychologists call resolving "role conflict" is known in CoDA as "detachment." The relationships that social psychologists would call "salient" are known in CoDA as "healthy."

The idea of shifting identities within a hierarchy is a useful illustration, but it also makes the achievement of selfhood seem as simple as rotating shelf stock. Although Paul is clearly rearranging his hierarchy of identities, he is also doing something far more complex. In many ways, his life before recovery consisted of a self-conscious shifting of identities—and he considers this a problem. What he is engaged in now is a process in which identities are indeed being shifted, but he is undergirding them with what he believes cannot be shifted or subject to detachment. Of course, he is giving more priority to his identity as a fiancé than as a single father, but apart from this, he is convinced that he knows who he "really" is. Whether he really *does* know is unimportant. What is important is what the belief allows him to do. He can now go on to have new relationships without feeling as though he is simply rotating shelf stock. He believes that he has an underlying sense of who he "is"— *I'm more in touch with what I want. . . . I'm compassionate and caring. I'm a sensitive person*—and this keeps him from resenting his obligations to relationships.

The qualities that Paul now emphasizes as his "true" self—the "essential" traits he found after losing his labels—have not *replaced* his obligations. He is not abandoning his children, for instance, while claiming to be compassionate and caring. To the contrary, he uses his "essential" traits to reshape his obligations as father, and, now, as fiancé. In claiming that, while he may have less involvement with his children, he has become a better father to them, he redeems his "detachment" from them. Simultaneously, his "detachment" allows him to make his relationship with his fiancée "number one," which hinges on his believing that he has learned how to love "for real."

Likewise, Cindy uses essentialist language largely to reshape her relationships. Having heard her bemoan the need to be a perfect wife, mother, daughter-in-law, I wondered how she would describe herself today. While she lists essential qualities, she does so in the context of relationships. The kind of self she believes she "is" today conveys her fear of the negative side of involvements. She does not want to avoid relationships altogether, but she is clearly on guard:

> I believe that I do good things. I do good things for people, and I want good things back. I have a lot of repressed anger. I want to be less naive than I have in the past, so I can avoid being taken advantage of.

Other members of CoDA spoke in similar terms. One woman I interviewed told me that, when she started attending, she "didn't have [her] own identity." After a year in CoDA, she says, "I'm an individual. I have my own identity." How did she get to this point? "I got involved in CoDA," she said. "I listened to other people. I looked to people who had time in the Program." She developed an identity by modeling her stories after those she heard in the group. Her previous relationship and her family-of-origin only "messed her up." But the group—a set of relationships to which she now gives priority—gave her what other people could not. Another woman told me that she liked CoDA because it helped her focus on herself. "The thing I got from CoDA," she said, "is myself." When I asked her to elaborate, she explained that she got "herself" through developing relationships with people who would provide her with a "reality check." She began talking to people after meetings, getting their feedback on things that went on in her life. She also began to use CoDA's phone network in between meetings. She saw herself as making an effort to see things the way others saw them—as long as she was able to choose which "others."

In weaving together the layers of selfhood, the practice of sharing is crucial. I have already suggested that your stories must not only convince *others* that you have a coherent identity, they must also convince *yourself*. Although the telling of a narrative is not sufficient for making it convincing, it is necessary. Everyday life provides few settings in which a man such as Paul can say, "I'm compassionate and caring," and also talk about "detaching" from his children. In CoDA, however, he may freely do so. But he does not believe that he is compassionate and caring simply *because* he has said it. He believes it—or wants to—and saying it helps make it so because it involves integrating it into his accounts of himself. It fits with other narrative strands and story lines, such as his need for "detachment." This coherence, not the mere repetition, gradually makes the narrative accomplishment of selfhood convincing.

In view of all the claims that have depicted contemporary Americans as less grounded in Institutional obligations, the narrative of transition presents a very different image of selfhood. The idea that there are two irreconcilable, polar modes of selfhood is an oversimplification. While the members of CoDA may shy away from the *idea* of a self rooted in roles and relationships, they cannot, in *practice,* escape using these Institutional reference points. To be sure, they want to choose those that will have an impact on them, but they continue to use them as a sign of who they are. This is especially true for members who are beginning new commitments. Like Paul, they "detach" from or reshape relationships that cause friction within those they find rewarding, or consider "healthy." But it is not relationships *alone* that create their image of who they are. Having lost relationships before, they are on the alert. CoDA's "essentialist" vocabulary of wants allows them to be cautious, while still recognizing the necessity of relationships in their lives.

It is not surprising that a society in which adulthood is characterized by dramatic transitions has generated CoDA as a response. It does seem surprising that the discourse of codependency has been portrayed as a cause of such transitions, not a remedy or response to them. Consider what Bellah and his research team have to say about "therapeutic modes of relating." They admit that, among the contemporary middle classes, people can take few sources of social support for granted. Instead, they place a great deal of weight on inner feelings. In their professional and economic lives, people are immersed in a "managerial" style that has led them to subject their inner, or "expressive individualist" concerns to a utilitarian calculus. This has allegedly put Americans more "in touch with their feelings" and better able to seek what they want in relationships (139). The drawback, however, is that "psychological sophistication" has come at the price of "moral impoverishment" (139).

This argument assumes that Americans were, for the most part, comfortably situated in traditional relationships until the advent of the therapeutic ethos. Then they jumped ship, as it were, and devoted themselves to lives of self-absorption. This assumption is misguided. Paul does not simply tell a tale of transition because he finds it more appealing to do so; he has actually made several transitions. In reality, he *is* divorced and disabled. He *is* no longer the same kind of father he once was. He tells a particular kind of story *because* he has changed. The change triggers the need to account for it. Moreover, accounting for change in a particular way reshapes the way he looks at his situation, thereby calling for additional change.

The kind of selfhood generated by and expressed in a story such as Paul's is clearly and necessarily different from one characterized by less disruption. When Paul says "I have a sense of self now," he means something quite different from what that phrase would have meant in the past. Whether he realizes it or not, "selfhood" means something over which he has considerable control. His essential characteristics are traits that he has chosen, rather than ones that might have been assigned to him by a set of prefabricated roles. To be sure, this tendency has been observed outside of CoDA as well. It is suggested in the shift to "impulse" and toward particular categories of responses to the Twenty Statements Test. But to suggest that this is all that is going on is to miss the rest of the picture.

The narrative of transition indeed reflects changes in the process of defining the self. As relationships have become less reliable for anchoring a sense of who they are, people have created new definitions. Paul's story makes two stronger points, however. The first is that these new definitions do not rule out relationships and obligations. They are not grounded exclusively in "impulse." Rather, they offer an "essential" self that can survive the disruption of uncoupling and the transition to a new spouse. This can be illustrated by imagining a fictional world in which there is no belief in an essential self, apart from one's relational ties. In such a world, people would hold ever tighter to relationships for a meaningful sense of themselves. This "meaning" would, however, be available only to those who did not suffer divorce, abandonment, bereavement, job loss, or geographic mobility. The less fortunate would have nowhere to turn. One can imagine that, in such a world, the loss of self would be unredeemable. Today, the existence—indeed, the prevalence—of a belief in an essential self means that people can move on after loss. As Paul's story suggests, that belief has not necessarily come at the price of relationships. It is a more portable image of the self that can be carried into relationships, but can survive them, as well.

The second point that Paul's story makes is that these new definitions also reinforce the very trends they reflect. In this sense, Bellah and other critics of the therapeutic ethos are on the mark. The image of selfhood offered in the narrative of transition allows people to adapt to disruption such as uncoupling, but it may also make it easier for them to dissolve their relationships. CoDA offers selfhood to people who have lost their

Institutional anchors, but it is not doing so by insisting that people stay together. CoDA is responding to a social need not by serving as a corrective to what has been lost, but by allowing people to adapt to the loss. It helps them develop a sense of self that is readily adaptable to the kind of world in which they live. They cannot return to a golden age of extended families and tightly knit communities. They need a sense of self attuned to complex, fluid, rootless lives. This may enable them to become even more mobile, but it will also help them to do so more comfortably.

This does not mean that CoDA does its members a disservice by offering a narrative of transition instead of initiating social change. Neither does it mean that the group somehow meets unmet needs. Rather, it means that CoDA helps people to develop self narratives that are adequate to the task of making adjustments and meeting new challenges. To expect something else is to expect more than CoDA can provide. Indeed, to expect something else is to expect more than *any* Institution can provide. Institutions seldom initiate radical social change; they help people adapt to existing conditions. In this case, "existing conditions" involve a great deal of personal disruption and upheaval. The person who claims to have found a sense of self that can survive it is better off for having done so.

"EVEN BETTER THAN THE REAL THING":
CODEPENDENCY AS A STRATEGY
OF EMOTION MANAGEMENT

One of the most challenging aspects of this research was deciphering what people in CoDA meant when they shared about
"getting in touch with" their emotions. Very early in the research, I realized that it was important, judging by the frequency with which I heard
it spoken of and the knowing nods the phrase elicited from those who
heard it. Yet, because its meaning was taken so thoroughly for granted,
no one explained what it meant to "get in touch with" their feelings. I
was often reminded of the Harley-Davidson bumper sticker I have seen
that reads, "If you have to ask, you wouldn't understand."

Taken literally, "getting in touch with" the emotions presupposes that
feelings are a sort of instinct, capable of prompting action consistent
with the "true" self.[1] People who are "in touch with" their feelings would
presumably want to act on their impulses because they would offer the
most reliable guides to behavior that is consistent with who they "really"
are. Being "in touch with" your feelings would probably mean expressing
anger freely and loving unabashedly. It would also mean acting quickly
on what you feel, wasting little time on reflection that might contaminate
the impulse. To do anything else would deny the value of the emotions
as indicators of who you "truly" are. It would also, by extension, deny
the value of the "true" self.

But expressing feelings intensely and acting on them immediately is
not what I saw going on publicly in CoDA. Nor is it what people claimed
to do privately in working the Program. This does not mean that they
did not use emotions to make claims to an authentic self, for they did
exactly this. However, "authentic" feelings are seldom what they seem
to be. The members of CoDA indeed proclaimed authenticity through

claims to emotion, but not by "getting in touch with" emotions at some raw, instinctual level. Instead, they used a careful process of emotion management that was masked by rhetoric about the value of free expression and depth of feeling. Their efforts meant that the self to which they laid claim, and the emotions that allowed them to do so, were, in the words of U2, "Even better than the real thing." Meet Susan, who will illustrate how this is done.

SUSAN'S STORY

Around eight o'clock one wintry Thursday evening, I drove along the streets of the development where Susan lives with her young son and daughter. It is a neighborhood full of working families. The modest, colonial-style houses sit close together. Most have at least two vehicles in the drive. In many cases, the second vehicle is a truck or van emblazoned with the logo of a building trade. Small boats, trailered and wrapped in plastic for the winter, appear in a few side yards. The developers seem to have named the streets after their own children. I pass Laura Lane, Jennifer Drive, and Michael Street before I reach Susan's address. Her nine-year-old son answers the door and calls to her. As she comes to greet me, she explains that she has just finished washing the dinner dishes. Her son rejoins his sister in front of the TV, and Susan shows me to the kitchen table, where I set up my tape recorder and we begin to talk.

Susan has just turned forty. She is slender and has blonde highlights in the Farrah Fawcett hairstyle that she has probably worn since high school. Currently, she has a part-time job and goes to school full-time, working towards a master's degree. Despite her schedule, the house looks tidy: lived-in, but very presentable. The children seem to get along well. In the few times they interrupt us, they do so politely. Susan explained that she gets child support from her ex-husband, which pays for a sitter while she works. "Most of the time, they don't really need a sitter," she admitted. "It's more for my own peace of mind." Understandably, she has some doubts about the wisdom of leaving her son, at age nine, in charge of his six-year-old sister.

At the time of our interview, Susan had attended CoDA for four years. She visited different Twelve Step groups at the recommendation of her therapist. "It was a backup for what my therapist was saying and doing, more support," she explained. She has since stopped seeing the therapist, but "felt right at home" in CoDA. "I really got the feeling that the people in CoDA cared about me," she said, "which had never happened before in my life." She also attends the occasional Al-Anon meeting, mostly when her schedule prevents her from going to CoDA.

Four years ago, Susan's husband left her. Initially, she felt relieved that years of fighting would finally end. They had tried marriage counseling and a trial separation. Once they agreed to end it, she told "anyone who would listen" that she was getting divorced. During the first Christmas that she and the children spent alone, however, she "hit bottom." "I was in shock," she told me. "I couldn't believe he wasn't going to come back. . . . I was desperate to change anything and everything in my life." What has changed, she said, is that now she feels she "has a self." I asked her how she knew this. "I'm so much more in touch with my feelings now," she explained, "so I know when I'm being true to myself."

For Susan, codependency has to do with emotions. She has ample Institutional anchors in her children, her work, and her studies. Her recovery focuses on "getting in touch with" feelings that she believes she had buried somewhere. Before recovery, she was "out of touch" with her feelings. She knew she *had* them, she said, but had no access to them. According to the discourse, codependency can allegedly cause people to lose touch with their own feelings in their concern for pleasing others. This is a problem because it renders them unable to "take care" of themselves. As one expert explains, "Co-dependents cannot do what they want to do because they have grown so out of touch with their feelings that they cannot determine what it is they even want" (Schaef 1986, 58). Susan makes a characteristic distinction between *having* emotions and being "in touch with" them. "For me," she explained, "being codependent is not being in touch with my own feelings. I just knew I must be feeling more than I was. I just was totally numbed out." When she first started therapy, her therapist asked about her emotional state and she had nothing to say. "The therapist would say, 'How does that make you feel?' and I wouldn't even know. My feelings were, like, frozen." I asked her if she thought this might have been a normal response to the divorce. She had, after all, felt as if she was in shock. Perhaps "frozen" feelings were part of that, I said. Susan disagreed. She did not associate the trauma of divorce with her emotional state at the time. Instead, she believes that her codependency had put her "out of touch" with her feelings long before. In her view, the divorce forced her to seek help for a problem that had existed for some time. If a therapist were to ask her the same question today, she knows how she would answer:

> I would say that I have a lot more feelings than I used to. I used to not feel at all. I was very rational about everything. I just thought I could intellectualize it all. Now, I listen to my feelings more than I used to. In any given instance, I can identify what I'm feeling.

I asked her for an example. What was she feeling *right then,* for instance? She paused for a moment, and said, "I'm not really feeling anything. I feel fine. I've got my serenity." I asked what that would tell her about her *self.* How could she listen to her feelings if she felt nothing? Evidently, feeling nothing was itself an ideal emotional state. "When I feel like this," she explained, "when I've got my serenity, then I know I'm being true to myself. I *have* to be, or else I wouldn't have serenity. If I don't have my serenity, then I check out my emotions." As if anticipating my next question, she added, "Maybe it's mainly the really strong emotions I listen to." I pressed her for an example of one. She answered immediately: "anger."

Before recovery, Susan would have "stuffed" her anger, she told me, or kept it bottled up. Then, it would have come out at inappropriate times.

> I think for me, really strong emotions, like anger, I just can't stuff them anymore. I have more control over the emotions than I did before [recovery], I think. Before, I used to just stuff them, so I had no control over them, but they used to come out wherever, whenever. I never knew.

LI: And now?

> Now, when they come out, I can usually trace the source sooner and they don't interfere with my life as much as they used to.

On the one hand, emotions allegedly let Susan know when she is being "true" to herself. On the other, she speaks of not letting an emotion such as anger "interfere" with her life. Before recovery, she explained, an angry episode would have distracted her from doing things she really needed to do, such as cooking dinner or helping her son with his homework. Now, she believes she can control her anger so that it does not interfere with things she must do.

> In recovery, I can get some relief from the emotional things and not let them carry over into the rest of my life. Before recovery, I definitely would have taken [my anger] out on the kids. I would have been a basket

case. I would have been screaming at them, or irritable, or not be able
to concentrate, and I don't do that too often anymore.

For Susan, having control over her anger does not mean stifling or ignor-
ing the emotion. Rather, it means acknowledging that she feels angry,
but not acting on it. She might talk about her anger to a CoDA friend
on the phone.

> I don't stuff [my emotions]. I talk about them with people on the phone.
> Sometimes I just need to do that repeatedly, because whatever the emo-
> tion is, I know it will dissipate with repeated yakking about it.

Or she might divert it into something nonemotional. She refers to this
as "making anger her friend," a phrase I heard from time to time in
CoDA.

When Susan wants to "make anger her friend," she starts to do something that requires mental concentration or physical exertion. She sees
no conflict between believing that anger interferes with what she really
needs to do, and believing that she can concentrate while angry. Appar-
ently, "making anger her friend" involves purposely taking time out to
do mental or physical things, such as writing in a journal, jogging, or
organizing her desk. She explained that, if she had just tried to go on
with her life, her anger would have interfered. If she takes on a new
task, however, it does not interfere. In either case, she does anything
but express anger as anger.

> Making anger my friend means putting it to work for me. Every time I
> felt angry, I'd, like, really dig in to something I had to do. It made me
> feel less angry, and I knew I had finally gotten in touch with it. If I can
> make anger work for me, like make it help me, say, then I'm really in
> touch with it. It's like my friend.

For Susan, making anger her "friend" means feeling less of it, which,
in turn, means being "in touch" with it.

Both of Susan's strategies achieve the same end: through talk or physical activity, she ultimately feels less anger. She equates this dissipation
with "being in touch with" the emotion. She believes that, when she
used to "stuff" her anger, she had no control over it. Anger would burst
out "wherever, whenever." Now, since she has stopped "stuffing" it, she
feels she has *more* control over it, and it does not "interfere" with her
life.

If an emotion dissipates, I asked her, how can it give her any insights
into the self? She explained again that being "true" to herself essentially

means achieving a feeling of serenity, meaning a more or less neutral emotional state. Strong emotions, such as anger, were not "really" her. She had to let them dissipate in order to get back to who she really was. Otherwise, she would just keep them bottled up inside and they would burst forth in ways that were not the "real" Susan.

Susan did not strike me as a person who flew into angry rages. I mentioned this to her, and she laughed. I should have seen her five years ago, she said. "In CoDA," she explained, "I've learned not to act on every feeling that I have. Some of my feelings used to be very large and inappropriate. I've learned how to get them under control." I asked for some other examples. She thought for a moment and named guilt as one.

Like anger, guilt receives a lot of discussion in CoDA. Susan spoke of it in terms by then familiar to me from meetings. Most members of CoDA distinguish between two types of guilt: that which they "own," and another kind that they call "garbage" guilt. The distinction depends on responsibility. They feel responsible for the behavior that brought on guilt they "own." "Garbage" guilt usually results from a failure to act on beliefs they now see as dysfunctional. Susan explained:

> If I break somebody's anonymity in Program, say, then I feel guilty. I own that guilt. I did it, and I knew better, and now I have to deal with it. But if I sit around thinking like, "Oh, I should be earning more money. I should be a success at my age. I'm a failure," and so on, that's garbage guilt. I don't own that.

Susan tries to "deal with" both forms of guilt as soon as she recognizes them. When she "owns" the guilt, she tries to make amends for what she did to bring it on. If she jeopardized someone's anonymity, for example, she would go to the person and apologize, if possible. If she could not apologize, she would talk about her mistake to her Higher Power, which for her means prayer, and probably talk about her feelings in group without revealing any names. This is "doing Step Five," which reads "Admitted to God, to ourselves, and to another human being the exact nature of our wrongs." The group qualifies as "another human being." The optimal solution is the apology, especially if the person forgives her. If Susan cannot apologize, she will have to live with the guilt, which, in her view, means that she was meant to learn a lesson about breaking anonymity. Either way, the experience teaches her something. If she can apologize, then she "needed" to learn a lesson, perhaps about humility. If she cannot apologize, then she was meant to learn about something else. Susan believes that this is how feelings help her be true to herself. "It doesn't mean I should beat myself up about [guilt that she 'owns']," she explained, "but I should learn from it. It tells me I have a weakness somewhere, and I need to work on it."

In contrast, "garbage" guilt has no analogous solution, nor does it teach any lessons. It is the emotional vestige of the "dysfunction" that codependents learn from their families and society. "Garbage guilt comes from all the things we've been told about what we should *do*," Susan explained. "It tells us nothing about who we should *become*." I said that, from her example, I thought that "garbage" guilt was telling her to be a success, in economic terms. "Right," she said, "because that's how this society defines success. But, for me, it means being a good mother, a good friend, getting through school, and enjoying life. But those old tapes keep playing, telling me I'm a failure for taking this route." In CoDA, the "old tapes" refer to messages from before recovery that occasionally replay in one's mind. "Old tapes" are always associated with "garbage" guilt; one hears nothing positive on them.

When the "garbage" guilt creeps in, "you just have to put it out of your mind," Susan explained. She tries to stop thinking about the messages playing on the "old tapes." If she starts to feel guilty—to "beat herself up"—she takes that as a cue to do things to contradict the feeling. However, guilt does not receive the focused physical or mental treatment that anger receives. "When you start beating yourself up, that means you're not taking care of yourself," she explained. "You need to do something nice for yourself then." For Susan, this could mean taking a bath, reading something for pleasure instead of for school, or calling an old friend on the phone. And what would happen then, I asked? "You get your serenity back. You're at peace with yourself." "Garbage" guilt, then, while certainly an emotion, has nothing valuable to reveal. Only serenity, which assures Susan that she is "right where she needs to be," offers any insights in that direction.

EMOTIONS AND THE "TRUE" SELF

One need not go to CoDA meetings to hear the emotions equated with instinct, capable of revealing your most authentic desires and intentions. Hochschild claims that, "as a culture, we have begun to place an unprecedented value on spontaneous, 'natural' feeling. We are intrigued by the unmanaged heart and what it can tell us" (1983, 190). The singular quality of emotions makes them especially useful for the process of self-definition. Jürgen Gerhards calls emotion "the modern *a priori;* it is the principle that does not fail when all other principles do" (1989, 749). As with other highly subjective experiences—religious faith, for example, or claiming to have a headache—claims to emotions must be taken as truth. They do not require any kind of verification. "Emotions can claim authenticity," Gerhards writes, "since any actor can personally attest that he or she has them, without others being able to refute the claim" (749). In other words, *I feel, therefore I am.*

One need not go to CoDA, either, to hear that some feelings are more equal than others. Despite a curiosity about what Hochschild calls the "unmanaged heart," middle-class Americans live in an increasingly "cautious" emotional culture.[2] Over the course of the twentieth century, the American middle class gradually rejected Victorian intensity in favor of a more moderate emotional style that signifies "a uniformly cool, controlled personality" (Stearns 1994, 263).[3] It is as if to say, *I feel OK, therefore I am OK.* Although emotions are indeed respected as instinctual, some are simultaneously considered dangerous, especially when intense, because they jeopardize your "cool." The expression of intense emotions, like anger, is sanctioned, and nonemotional activities of the sort Susan describes serve as functional equivalents. Other strong emotions, like guilt, are thought to have damaging psychological consequences. The obvious but unstated preference is for a moderate emotional display that suggests that you have everything under control. Studies have documented similar shifts toward emotional restraint and the sanctioning of intensity in several industrialized Western nations (see de Swaan 1981; Gerhards 1989; Wouters 1991), but the United States leads overall (see Sommers 1984).[4] The emotional culture of self-restraint is concealed by admiration for the "natural" quality of emotions.

When Susan and other CoDA members talk about "getting in touch with" their feelings, they are making a uniquely contemporary claim to authentic selfhood. They believe that the "unmanaged heart" offers access to what mainstream society has suppressed. In this sense, they focus on the capacity of emotions to serve as signals (see Hochschild 1983, 17, 22, 221–22). The signal function, first set out in Freud's work (1959) and later elaborated by Hochschild (1983), refers to the way that emotions help shape your perceptions of the world. Beattie says as much when she refers to feelings as "indicators" (1987, 131). Likewise, Wegscheider-Cruse and Cruse write that "our emotions may be our *sixth sense* and possibly our closest link to reality. They need to be responded to every bit as much as our other five senses" (1990, 38).

Emotions indeed convey information about the world; this much the codependency experts have right. However, no one has access to raw, uninterpreted emotion. Instead, emotions function as signals in conjunction with expectations. Hochschild explains:

> When an emotion signals a message of danger or safety to us, it involves a reality newly grasped *on the template of prior expectations.* A signal involves a juxtaposition of what we see with what we expect to see. . . . The message "danger" takes on its meaning of "danger" only in relation to what we expect (221, emphasis original).

To be sure, emotions involve a very direct, physical experience. But whether a racing pulse and butterflies in the stomach signal life-threatening danger or the presence of a potential new love depends largely on what you expect from and know about the situation. The signaling capacity of emotions thus involves more than the simple relaying of unprocessed information. What an emotion signals depends on your understanding of the context in which it occurs.[5] We human beings have no access to raw, uninterpreted emotion. The emotion that we feel is already mediated by culture. In this sense, our emotions are less real than reality, in the usual sense of the word. We know what we know about feelings through culture, not through direct contact with something "real" called "feeling." There is no such thing as emotional reality (in the usual sense of the word), and the emotions that people feel are, therefore, *less real.* This does not render the emotions powerless, however. To the contrary, emotions have *more* influence on selfhood precisely because they *are* less real. They help to produce a self that is mediated by culture and, thus, more real than real. The self is remade along lines that ensure that what you "get in touch with" will have been worth the effort. Let me make this point with an illustration.

I often listen to a program on National Public Radio called *This American Life.* One week, the program was titled "Simulated Worlds." A segment of this particular show featured people who reenact Civil War battles. These are not the paid employees that one might find at Gettysburg, although some of them might well make a living that way. Rather, these are people who devote themselves to the minutiae of nineteenth-century military life and warfare purely for fun. One of the reenactors claimed to be a more authentic period character than most because he had even gone to the trouble of researching nineteenth-century eyewear, and his own corrective lenses resembled as closely as possible those that would have been worn by a soldier in the Civil War. He claimed to be a better—meaning more "real"—reenactor than those who wore contemporary wire-rim glasses. He proved—to himself, primarily—that he was "really" what he said he was, but he did so on the basis of things that were less real. He did not have "real" nineteenth century glasses. His glasses were a simulation. They were made of modern materials, but made to look old. They were, therefore, less real. In being so, they were, simultaneously, "even better than the real thing." Even if the reenactor could locate a truly authentic pair of Civil War–era glasses, they would be useless to him. In the unlikely event that they matched his prescription, their optics would be vastly inferior to today's standards, and the lenses would probably be in such bad condition that he could not wear them. The simulated glasses were, therefore, more real than real.[6]

In much the same way, the codependent's emotional life is "even better than the real thing," which would be painfully intense and so raw as to offer nothing in the way of practical guidance for behavior. The CoDA member, like the Civil War reenactor, uses a set of techniques that yield a product that is better than authentic. For the Civil War reenactor, the "real" glasses either do not exist or, if they do, are worthless. For the codependent, "real," uninterpreted emotion, if it does exist, is inaccessible, and, therefore, worthless. Still, in both cases, claims to worth are based largely on authenticity. Moreover, in both cases, it is the person making the claim who craves the authenticity, not the audience. Verification is not something that others demand, but something that you require as a means of proving to yourself that you are "really" who and what you purport to be.

To explain why this has become necessary, it may help to retrace a bit of history. The self, as an idea, gained great strength during the Romantic movement of the late eighteenth and early nineteenth centuries. Romantics affirmed the possession of a self through activities that demonstrated their estrangement from conventional society (see Gagnon 1984). Just as Calvinists could seek assurance of salvation in the next world through particular behaviors in this one, Romantics sought assurance of a unique self through adventure travel, isolation, and artistic or literary innovations that set them apart from the mainstream. The ability of behaviors to verify selfhood depended on "their inaccessibility and unacceptability to the other" (Gagnon 1984, 97). You could prove that you were a unique, differentiated individual only by doing things that others neither understood nor found agreeable. Over the course of the nineteenth and twentieth centuries, Romantic innovations that had begun within a small group of elites were co-opted into and assimilated by conventional society—including the innovation of the self. Today, the self is "a sort of birthright" (103). It is not necessary to affirm the possession of a self in front of others who are also assumed to possess selves. In any case, many of the behaviors and activities that constituted Romantic innovation are now commonplace and, therefore, inadequate to the task. As Gagnon puts it, the success of the Romantic program meant its failure. There is virtually nothing left to do that would demonstrate your possession of a unique self, and, indeed, little need to do so. Nevertheless, there is still a need to demonstrate authenticity and integrity *to yourself.* One way to do this, and perhaps the only remaining way, is to justify your decisions on the basis of the unique character of emotional experience. Before an audience of assumed selves, the only experience that can form the basis for authenticity is that of feeling. This applies even when—indeed, especially when—the audience consists of yourself alone. It also applies when that audience, however constituted, is busy convincing itself of that selfhood, as is the case in CoDA. Others may neither understand your decisions nor find them acceptable, but they cannot dispute their justification in the emotions. The "unmanaged heart" is above reproach.

Although this irreproachability would seem to be attributed to the "natural," instinctual quality of the emotions, this is not really the case. A person who acts on the basis of ungoverned emotions would be considered irrational, immature, and unpredictable. He or she would not appear to be "in touch with" the emotions, but at the mercy of them. The emotions have the respect that they do not when they are unpredictable and capricious. Rather, they have it when the person who feels them is able to keep them in check. The quality of authenticity is seldom ascribed to those who are subject to tantrums, passion, and jealousy, but to those who remain calm and self-controlled, epitomizing what has become CoDA's standard of "serenity." At a deeper level, then, what appears to be thoroughly "unmanaged" must be carefully cultivated. Like the reenactor's glasses, the emotions that form the basis for authenticity come through understanding how best to present yourself. In some cases, this goal is explicit, as it was for the reenactor, who self-consciously researched nineteenth-century eyewear in order to be more authentic. In other cases, it is less obvious, as it is for the members of CoDA, who would see an intentional effort to manipulate one's presentation as "dysfunctional." Instead, they believe they are actually "getting in touch with" their authentic selves. But by making a conscious effort to be authentic, they are engaging in something far more complex than what the phrase "getting in touch" conveys.

NAME IT AND CLAIM IT

When codependency's popularizers talk about "losing touch" with the emotions, they connote the loss of the signal function, though they do not use this language. Considering the events that lead most people to CoDA, a loss of the ability to make sense of emotion is understandable. During uncoupling, "the template of prior expectations" becomes unreliable or altogether useless. The process of uncoupling not only disrupts the familiar structures of your life, it also evokes intense feelings of anger, grief, betrayal, guilt, disappointment, and, often, relief. In addition, those feelings now appear in opposition to their familiar contexts. You now feel angry at and betrayed by a person you once loved; what you *thought* was love is not what you expected; and so on. The mixture could hardly provide a reliable guide to thought or action. Feeling anger one minute, guilt the next, alternating with a combination of relief and fear, you could easily conclude that you have "lost touch" with the emotions. In this state, advice to "get in touch" with your feelings seems on target. You can then allegedly think and act in ways consistent with your "true" self. But as Hochschild explains, trying to "get in touch with" feelings "makes the thing we get in touch with . . . *into* a feeling or emotion. In managing feeling, we contribute to the creation of it" (Hochschild 1983, 18, emphasis original). What takes place in CoDA is far more cognitive and less visceral than "getting in touch" suggests. It is emotion management that creates emotions themselves. In so doing, it makes them comprehensible, and therefore useful in self-definition.

The task begins with naming, and CoDA offers a characteristic language with which to label experience. The vocabulary produces five emotions: anger, guilt, love, serenity, and pain, sometimes called devastation.[7] With the exception of serenity, a kind of calm acceptance, all the emotions in CoDA's vocabulary are intense. Anger is considered dangerous, and therefore best avoided. Guilt and love are potentially so, and receive more selective treatment. These emotions come later, however, and "pain" and "devastation" are the starting points. They provide good examples of how an experience can be transformed by naming. As Hochschild explains, "The names we give emotions refer to the way we apprehend a given situation—the aspect of it we focus on—and what our prior expectations about it are" (223).

"Pain" and "devastation" are the names given to what might be commonly called heartache. By labeling the emotions of uncoupling with these particular terms, the experience becomes both temporary and constructive. As one woman told me, "Pain goes away. You know that saying, 'What doesn't kill you makes you stronger?' You heal. You don't even remember how much something hurt, so you can go on." Naming the situation helps to minimize the intensity because it portrays it as fleeting. It also helps to alleviate some of the fear that the experience entails, since, mercifully, we never recall pain with any of its original severity. Pain is also portrayed as constructive, since it motivates people to seek out CoDA. One man told me that, if not for his pain, he would not have come to CoDA, which he believes has changed his life. "I think pain is probably the best motivator," he said. "It's only when we get into a lot of pain that we really self-doubt." Likewise, for devastation. A woman explained how thinking of her emotional state in this way made her optimistic.

> I was a complete wreck during the divorce. I didn't know whether I was coming or going. I cried, I pitched fits, I did everything. I think it was at my second meeting when I heard the speaker share about "devastation." I thought, "That's what I feel. I'm devastated." To me, even though it meant total ruin, it made me almost optimistic because it meant starting over. It gave me a new way to interpret my feelings. It gave me a direction: forward. *(age forty)*

Because people hear others "share" about surviving "devastation," they learn to interpret their experience as unpleasant, but temporary, and even constructive.

Even with a positive spin on them, however, pain and devastation both imply considerable intensity. In CoDA, this is moderated with time and talk, and the more talk, the less time. Many people told me that, in the early stages of uncoupling, they went to meetings as often as possible, even every day. Many could not bring themselves to talk much at first, but only cried.

> At the beginning, I used to go every day, even twice a day sometimes. I couldn't even stay more than five minutes by myself. So I went to meetings. Constant meetings. I would start to talk, and after two or three

words, I would just break down and cry. And [the other members] were very sympathetic, you know, they didn't criticize me for the fact that I was crying, especially as a man. Gradually, it got better. I could talk more and cry less. *(age forty-five)*

I heard versions of this over and over again: "After a while, I could talk more and cry less." Also, most people simply had no other place to take their feelings, no place where crying would not raise an eyebrow. In CoDA, even men may cry with impunity, and men and women alike talked about how the ability to cry without criticism lightened their emotional load. Then, when able to talk, they gradually began to feel less pain. Although it is perfectly acceptable to cry at meetings, the eventual point is to talk. Putting your emotions into words and constructing an account of the circumstances surrounding the emotion provides some distance from the firsthand experience of those feelings. Saying "I felt hurt," "I felt betrayed," and so on, already demonstrates some mastery over the initial state of "devastation."

Talking also breaks the inchoate experience of uncoupling into the more identifiable emotional components of CoDA's vocabulary. Then, the recovering person can manage specific feelings using strategies to suit. In the case of anger, the emotion is acknowledged but channeled into other activities, for anger has no redeeming qualities *qua* anger. The abstract emotional energy can, however, serve more constructive purposes. Anger can "be your friend," as illustrated by Susan's narrative. CoDA members portray anger with a "hydraulic" metaphor that gives it the ability to build up and then flood into your life at unexpected and potentially embarrassing moments. Susan, for example, said her anger "used to come out wherever, whenever. I never knew." One member told me that he used to "have a lot of anger towards family members that [he] just took out on everybody. . . . There was a lot of anger that was *oozing out.*" Codependents claim to need to pay particular attention to the hazards of "stuffing" your anger. They claim to be particularly vulnerable to its ability to cause stress-related physical ailments, as well as its unpredictability. In time, Beattie explains in "hydraulic" language, anger "may one day come roaring out. . . . We may lose control" (1987, 144).

In "The Rooms," and from experts such as Beattie, the members of CoDA learn that *feeling* anger is not wrong. *Expressing* it is a problem, however. "We have every right to *feel* anger," Beattie writes. "But we also have a responsibility—primarily to ourselves—to deal with our anger appropriately" (1987, 145). Echoing this logic, a member explained that "I try to understand that it's not a wrong feeling. It's not a bad feeling to be angry. I should have a right to be angry. But what I do with it is my choice." Susan has described some of the techniques that she uses to "deal with" anger. Of the thirteen suggestions Beattie makes for doing so, none include expressing it directly. Instead, she recommends thinking and talking about it, writing letters you do not intend to mail, and burning off the "anger energy" through physical activity.

Why the concern about expressing a little anger once in a while? There are at least three reasons why it is problematic. First, if you subscribe to the "hydraulic" metaphor, the expression of anger suggests a concealed part of the self with which you are not "in touch." Talking about feeling anger implies having some awareness that pressure is building within, which in turn calls for techniques to "deal with" it before it "bursts" out. Expressing anger, however, suggests a lack of sensitivity to your inner states, as well as a shortage of techniques for "making anger your friend." Second, and related to this, expressing anger indicates a lack of trust that you are always "right where you need to be." Anger clouds your ability to see what you "need" to learn. For example, a man I call Gary described a potentially angry moment on the road. He had been late for an appointment, and the car ahead was going slower than he would have liked. Gary started honking his horn, tailgating, and swearing to himself. When the other driver got ready to make a left turn, Gary told him what he thought of him. He motioned for Gary to pull over, as if to fight it out. Gary said, "I really wanted to, and a few years ago, I would have pulled right over. But I asked my Higher Power what was really going on, and I realized that I was frustrated with myself, not with this guy, so I drove on by." Gary believes that he "needed" to learn a lesson about the better use of time so that he will not be so rushed on the road. In Gary's view, he was "right where he needed to be" in order to learn that lesson, and his Higher Power prevented him from going to extremes. "If I had pulled over," he said, "who knows what would have happened. But I wouldn't have seen that it was really my problem, and not his." In seeing anger as "his problem," and not the other driver's, Gary highlights a third problem with expressing anger. It may cost you the approval of others, and, consequently, your self-approval. Anger suggests that you are intolerant. Just as it prevents you from seeing that you are "right where you need to be," it indicates an inability to recognize that others, too, are so positioned.

Love, another intense emotion, receives a more selective treatment than anger. Expressing anger is never considered appropriate; not so with love. Love is treated as if it has a "minimum requirement." If you feel that your need for unconditional love has been met, then the emotional "overflow" can be positive. If that need goes unfulfilled, however, then the shortage produces an "unhealthy" search to fulfill it. Under those circumstances, love is supposedly not *really* love, but codependency. Once you start "taking care" of yourself, then love can spill over to others in "healthy" ways. For example:

> Now, after five years in CoDA, I have enough to fill me up and the rest can flow over. I could have people coming [to my house] because they have nowhere else to go. I could pick up a person who needs a ride to a meeting. I want to be that way in the world. It's only when you've got that good stuff and people are taking advantage of you, ripping your lungs out. That's codependency. *(woman, age forty-five)*

> I'm just learning how to love myself. Once I do that, I can think about having someone in my life because then I'll have enough to let it flow to someone else. *(man, age thirty-nine)*

In practice, the distinction between "healthy" and "unhealthy" love depends entirely on how one interprets a given relationship. Only the individual can judge. Recall that Paul believed that he had not *really* loved his children, only "smothered them with being over-responsible in what [he] labeled 'love' then." In reality, he wanted to decrease his investment in his identity as a dad in order to smooth things out in his relationship with his fiancée. Now, after sorting out his priorities, he believes that he can show his children what it "really" means to love. He believes he has "learned how to love, for real, for the first time." He portrayed this with a "minimum requirement" metaphor: "The more I have of [*sic*] a sense of self and I love myself," he said, "the more I can give it away."

Overall, expressing intense emotions such as anger and love places you at considerable risk. Emotional outbursts, depending on their form, demonstrate either childishness or vulnerability. Overwhelming emotion—still considered irrational—exposes a part of the self that is somehow not the "real" person. Thus, intensity, left unchecked, sends potentially discrediting messages about the self—to yourself as well as to others. After all, the self that you seek to "get in touch with" must not disappoint. When it does, however, CoDA even offers a set of techniques for eliminating the ensuing feelings of guilt.

As Susan explained, guilt, like love, receives a selective treatment. It is considered "garbage" when it comes from violating the rules enforced by people you now consider "unhealthy." This is contrasted to the guilt that you "own." Members of CoDA echoed Susan in describing the difference:

> There's guilt that you own and then there's garbage guilt. . . . If I'm just being negative with my kids or something, I know that's wrong, and I own that guilt. Garbage guilt is really kind of inflicted upon you. You know, if I didn't shovel Aunt Millie's driveway when I was younger, I was made to feel guilty. That, to me, is garbage. That's not mine. It's not deserved. *(man, age thirty-eight)*

> Say if I ate too much or smoked too many cigarettes, I feel guilty. But I'm not going to beat myself up about it. . . . I can learn from it and change [the behavior] and not let it happen again. But the other guilt that I experienced with my family, that was placed on me and it doesn't even belong to me. It wasn't even my stuff. *(woman, age thirty-six)*

Beattie explains that "some [guilt] is earned; some of it isn't. By working the Steps, we learn to tell the difference so we can deal with it appropriately. Amends and forgiveness of self and others is the remedy for real guilt. Unearned guilt can be banished with self-love and realistic thinking" (1990, 224).

When codependents talk of "unearned" or "garbage" guilt, they refer to what John Carroll (1985) calls "dispositional" guilt. This guilt "is deeply embedded in character" (10). Dispositional guilt produces an anxiety that "cannot be traced back to some specific act or thought that aroused the conscience. It has no specific cause, a fact however that in no way inhibits the need of someone suffering from it to find one" (10). Carroll poses Hamlet as the ideal-typical sufferer of dispositional guilt: "he has committed no crime, he has breached no moral code, and yet he is paralysed by guilt" (11). Likewise, codependents "feel at fault for everything" (Beattie 1990, 224). "If my relationship falls apart," a woman in CoDA told me, "I blame myself. If AIDS exists in the world, I blame myself. I take it all on." Dispositional guilt offers no hope of remission, only a nagging sense of culpability.

Because of its unremitting intensity, "unearned" or "garbage guilt" is sanctioned altogether and replaced with the less emotional substitute of "taking care" of yourself. Anyone who experiences "garbage" guilt, must "let go" of it, to use the recovery language. This is the "realistic thinking" to which Beattie refers. The source of the emotion is delegitimized, and the emotion therefore becomes unnecessary. Because the parents, ex-spouses or partners, or the conventions that instilled the guilt can be considered "unhealthy," their values become "garbage," something to be discarded.

Other feelings of guilt may be constructive, however, if they arise from standards for behavior that the person now respects. This guilt that you "own" is a more situational form that Carroll calls "moral" guilt. Moral guilt "is tied directly with a breach of morality" (9). Moral guilt therefore holds the possibility of remission, and it can prompt you to change, eliminating the emotion as a consequence. The woman who ate too much or smoked too many cigarettes "owns" her guilt because she can atone for her sins and move on. The man who was "negative" to his children also "owns" his guilt because he can apologize and treat them differently in the future. Not so with dispositional guilt.

CoDA sanctions dispositional, or "garbage" guilt, precisely because it has no hope of remission. Its intensity cannot be moderated, and no one can "make amends," to use the Twelve Step term, for "garbage" guilt. If recovery involves reinventing yourself along the lines of what you want to become, you cannot easily embark on this task carrying a heavy existential burden. Without hope of remission, the possibility of "recovery" vanishes, as well. It makes pragmatic sense to dismiss the experience and its sources as "unhealthy," and to say, therefore, that they have no part in your new life.

The problem codependents have with dispositional guilt, and with unpleasant or intense emotions altogether, is that they interfere with the ideal state of serenity. It is perhaps ironic that, in a program that poses "getting in touch with" the emotions as one of its goals, the pinnacle should be a state characterized by *freedom from* emotions. Yet, if we consider that emotions provide information about yourself, serenity means that all is well. *I feel OK, therefore I am OK.*

EMOTION MANAGEMENT, SELFHOOD, AND MORALITY

CoDA's selective treatment of the emotions offers insight into the group's solipsistic brand of morality. In CoDA, each person acts as his or her own moral agent. All judgments as to exactly how to "take care" of yourself are considered expressions of preference, perspective, or feeling; no impersonal criteria for decision-making exist. The highest good is knowing what you need and "taking care" of yourself, and this brings its own rewards of emotional serenity. The emotion management skills offered in CoDA allow people to manipulate the relationship between what they do and feel so that they can, in theory, feel serenity about almost *anything*. I talked with one member of CoDA about how this works.

> I guess when I know in my heart that I'm doing the right thing, and I ask my Higher Power about my motives, then I know it's the right thing to do.

> *LI: What do you mean by "knowing in your heart"?*

> When something just feels right, you know, when it feels good or I have peace about it.

> *LI: What do you do when you don't feel good about something?*

> Well, usually, if something doesn't feel good, it's not right for me to do. If I feel lousy about something I've done, then I see if I can do anything to make up for it, you know, to make amends. If I can, I do. If there's nothing I can do about it, then I just let it go. There's nothing I can do.

> *LI: You just let it go? Do you ever feel guilty?*

> Yeah, but if I can't make amends for it, it's guilt that I don't own. So I just start taking care of myself more. Like I felt guilty because I didn't go to this family picnic. I just didn't show up. But I realized that those people are so unhealthy for me to be around, I shouldn't feel guilty if I don't do something with them. It wouldn't be taking care of myself to be around them. That guilt, I don't own. That came from my family and it's sick.

> *LI: What about right and wrong? How do you tell the difference?*

> I have my own sense of right and wrong, and it's different from the one I grew up with. If something works for me, it's right. It might not be right for somebody else, but it works for me. I have no hard and fast rules.

Robert Bellah and colleagues (1985), puzzling over the apparent lack of moral grounding for the "therapeutic attitude," could have had this man's sense of morality in mind when they asked:

> If the self is defined by its ability to choose its own values, on what grounds are those choices themselves based? . . . each self constitutes its own moral universe, and there is finally no way to reconcile conflicting claims about what is good in itself. . . . In the absence of any objectifiable

criteria of right and wrong, good or evil, the self and its feelings become our only moral guide (75–76).

Bellah et al. address a fundamental shift in morality. Though their tone conveys disapproval, I would argue instead that the self and its feelings constitute a perfectly legitimate basis for morality, given the concerns that CoDA addresses. Within a context in which many people believe that they "exist wholly by the laws of [their] own being" (Trilling 1972), a moral system built around subjective standards makes sense. To be sure, it lacks the "objectifiable criteria" for which the authors of *Habits of the Heart* express obvious nostalgia. Instead of wishing that CoDA were something it is not, however, why not focus on what it is and ask what it can do as a result? It is absolutely true that CoDA offers no moral absolutes. Since this is so, what does its subjective, emotional-moral system accomplish?

First, the absence of objectifiable moral principles means that the group can appeal to people of various moral persuasions. This works in much the same way that CoDA's claim that it is "not religious, but spiritual" ensures that no one will be excluded on the basis of belief. A member who reveres the Ten Commandments has access to the same resources as the nihilist. In appealing to people with varying moral persuasions, CoDA spreads middle-class emotional standards and ideals of selfhood to the more marginal segments of the middle class.

Second, just as there is more to "spirituality" than simply tolerance, there is more to CoDA's system of morality, as well. The subjective basis for morality one finds in CoDA prepares members for fluid lives with increasingly fewer absolutes. Something that was once solid has, in many cases, melted into air, and CoDA is decidedly not challenging the loss. It is not countering the lack of objectifiable moral criteria; it is helping people adapt to it. The members of CoDA—and the rest of us, for that matter—are likely to continue to face situations for which a uniform system of morality would provide only inadequate answers. The absence of objectifiable moral principles means that the group can appeal to people who, by and large, have been disappointed by traditional institutions. There is no reason that they *should* be attracted to moral absolutes that, in all probability, have already failed them in one way or another. The emotions, the "modern *a priori*," can serve as a portable gauge that works in unfamiliar situations.

Third, it is decidedly not the case that a subjective basis for morality is equivalent to no basis for morality. When a person is engaged in answering the question of who he or she "really" is, that person is always doing so within particular moral frameworks. To have an answer is to know where you stand morally (see Taylor 1989). The person without moral frameworks cannot answer the question of who he or she is, because defining who you are always involves questions of what you hold as good and true. Within a setting like CoDA, it is easy to see how serenity becomes a thoroughly rational choice. A person who believes that he or she possesses a naturally good, "inner" self would also believe that such a self would tend toward happiness and stability, or serenity. It makes sense to choose serenity over the estrangement of intense, turbulent emotions. In this context, using the subjective experience of serenity as a moral framework is rational. It not only assures the person of existence *(I feel, therefore I am)*, it also offers assurance that his or her choices are authentic *(If I feel good, I must be in touch with who I really am)*.

What Bellah and his colleagues lament—the choosing of values on grounds they consider capricious—does not represent the erosion of morality altogether. It represents the appearance of a system of morality suited to a culture steeped in the value of the "unmanaged heart." Those who see their task as one of "getting in touch with" their feelings necessarily, albeit inadvertently, manipulate those feelings in their efforts. Their claims to authenticity mask this manipulation. Perhaps, more accurately, they make it irrelevant, since the end result is "even better than the real thing."

CHAPTER SEVEN

GENDER TROUBLES: CODEPENDENCY AS A NARRATIVE OF EQUALITY AND RESPECT

What goes into a "healthy" relationship? I was surprised by the extent to which the answers to this question referred to gender politics. To be sure, most of the members of CoDA do not use the language of academic feminism. Nevertheless, many of them understood that the problems in their relationships had stemmed from traditional beliefs about how men and women should behave toward each other. Because they now equate those beliefs with "dysfunction" in their lives and in society, they recognize the need to change them in order to have "healthy" relationships. As a result, a number of their narratives focused on a renegotiation of gender relations. Specifically, the tellers had acquired in CoDA an egalitarian concept of mutual respect that echoes the claims made by feminism. Members used the discourse of codependency, not the language of politics, to resist repeating oppressive arrangements of the past.[1]

Sometimes a degree of change that seems resolved at the level of culture comes late to the level of the individual. In an era that is often referred to as "postfeminist," it is easy to underestimate the durability of traditional, stereotypical gender behavior. One can easily get the impression that Americans who came of age after 1970 automatically formed relationships characterized by what Cancian (1987) calls "interdependence." As gender roles have become less restrictive, relationships have allegedly become more androgynous in their divisions of labor. Men are no longer the sole breadwinners, and women are not solely responsible for creating a "haven in a heartless world." The increasing number of women in the workforce, the greater acceptability of cohabitation among young middle-class adults, access to birth control and abortion, and the popularity of the therapeutic ethos contributed to new ideas about what relationships should be and do.[2] The image of the married couple that springs most readily to mind is closer to Paul and Jamie Buchman, of *Mad About You,* than to Ozzie and Harriet Nelson. The most pressing concern that most couples seem to face is learning to communicate their way through any problems that arise.

One can, however, read this history differently. In many ways, gender politics continue to pose an intractable problem. While gender-based divisions of labor vary among couples, studies such as *The Second Shift* (Hochschild 1989) and *The 50/50 Marriage* (Kimball 1983) suggest that they have by no means disappeared, and most couples continue to divide domestic labor on the basis of gender. The edges of the separate spheres may have softened over time, but the separation still exists.[3] For many couples, androgynous roles have largely failed to materialize. Meanwhile, ambiguous concerns about "communication" mask the conflict that continues to stem from gender arrangements.

The evidence I saw among the members of CoDA substantiates this "alternative" reading of the history of relationships. While the accepted version would have most Baby Boomers creating egalitarian relationships, many of the men and women in CoDA had had very traditional first marriages that replicated what they had seen their parents do. They expressed surprise at the ease with which they fell into traditional patterns of behavior. For example, a thirty-six-year-old woman described how her husband would have gone hungry before he cooked, because cooking was her job.

> I left my first marriage because I realized that my husband was completely dependent on me, and that if I didn't come home at night by a certain time, he would actually go without food and then be angry with me because he couldn't feed himself.

Another woman, thirty-eight, divorced, and recently uncoupled from a live-in relationship, shook her head and rolled her eyes when she recounted leaving college at twenty-one—though a dean's list student with only one semester to finish—because she had met the man she wanted to marry.

Women were not alone in having subscribed to stereotypical, traditional views. Thirty-seven-year-old Richard, who appears again in the next chapter, described the beliefs he once held:

> I felt back then that it was my job to financially secure the family, and it was her job to hold things together at home. I was your typical breadwinner: "No wife of mine will go out and work."

Eric, also thirty-seven, and estranged from his second wife, said, "I used to think that relationships were like businesses. Somebody had to have the bottom line, and that had to be the man."

For many of the members of CoDA, the event of uncoupling becomes a time not just to shop for another partner, but to seriously assess the beliefs and expectations they hold about relationships.[4] This often leads to a critique of the beliefs and expectations they hold about gender. For example, *The CoDA Book* urges readers to "explore our definitions of what we've been taught about relationships. We look at our roles within them as well as our expectations of the other person's roles" (116). The critiques that emerge from this invariably reveal the discourse's debt to family systems theory, as well as the influence of the therapeutic ethos. The "dysfunction" of your past is attributed to your family, which, by virtue of history, was characterized by traditional gender roles. By extension, these arrangements are also considered "dysfunctional." For example, Eric explained that he learned his "man is the boss" expectations from his father. "I was brought up by a father who thinks he's in control," he said, "and I thought I was, too. That led to a lot of dysfunction in my life." Likewise, the woman whose husband would not cook said that "I learned that women did [certain things] and men did other things. And that's pretty codependent, don't you think?"

Once this critique has begun, the group then offers support for the behavioral changes to accompany it. Having denounced traditional gender roles and expectations as "dysfunctional," members strive not to just "talk the talk," but also to "walk the walk." The norms and values of the group, combined with the presence of others who have made similar changes, reinforce more egalitarian behaviors. Let me first introduce Liz, and then Tom, to illustrate.

LIZ'S STORY

At fifty-two, Liz is just over the cusp of the official Baby Boom. It is perhaps understandable then that her first marriage would have followed an older, more traditional model. By the same logic, however, it is also impressive that she has rejected that older, familiar model in favor of an egalitarian one she learned through CoDA.

Liz married a "very possessive, very controlling man" when she was in her late teens. They had two daughters, and Liz did not work outside the home. While domestic life itself limited her range of interests, her husband dominated her social life, even to the extent of monitoring her interaction with mutual friends. He never allowed her into situations in which she might have contact with other men in his absence. "Even if we went to a wedding," she explained, "the other husbands and wives could go to the bar, but I couldn't sit at the bar, because I might talk to someone. I couldn't do whatever everybody else did just normally."

Shortly after their thirteenth wedding anniversary, Liz learned of an ongoing affair between her husband and her best friend. In the ensuing confrontation, her husband became violent. "The whole thing blew up, big time," she said. "It wasn't a little thing. It was a big time police thing." She wanted to leave him, but had no idea how she would survive outside the marriage.

> I was devastated, but I had nowhere to go, because I'm an only child, and I have a mother who threw me out of the house at sixteen, so I didn't have a mother to go to. And my father was remarried and it was an embarrassment for me to ask him if he would take me in with the children. So I stayed in the marriage, and I stayed in it hoping that we could get close together again. But that broke my whole trust in him.

She endured the continuing infidelity and episodic violence by moving out of the bedroom and into the den. That arrangement lasted for ten years. "It was no life," she admits. "There was no closeness. There was no marriage." After twenty-three years together, the last decade living separately in the same house, she and her husband divorced.

I knew from Liz's sharing that she had "taken a soaking," as she put it, in the settlement. During the interview, she explained that she had given up so much to her husband that her lawyer had her sign a release form certifying that she had done so against his advice. "That's the co-dependent part of me," she said. "Whatever you want to give me, you give me, and if you don't, it's OK. But I realize now that sometimes it's not OK." Today, she believes that she "deserves" better. A person "who does good in this world deserves good things," she now thinks.

Liz has had her share of financial concerns. At the time of her divorce, she had never worked outside the home. Even now, she has virtually no marketable job skills. She mostly works "under the table," doing cleaning, catering, or other things that promise immediate cash. Remarkably, she has managed to buy a house with an attached apartment, the rent from which pays the mortgage. She explained that, however burdensome her financial worries have been, they have always paled in comparison to the major problem she had to conquer in leaving her marriage: her fear of living alone.

> I was scared to death of being by myself. Biggest fear of my life. The hardest thing about leaving my marriage was to be by myself. But the marriage got so bad that I said, "I'm going to have to do something, even if I die." Last-ditch effort: "even if I die." That's what I said. "I have to get out of here, and I will do whatever I have to do. Whatever happens, happens."

What happened was that, within a week, she had begun another relationship that would last for the next seven years. She described this partner as another "very controlling man." He was suspicious of her every move, to the point of following her around while she did errands or met with women friends. He also became violent with her. She felt as if she had jumped from the frying pan into the fire; she had left a marriage that allowed her no life, only to enter a relationship that did not allow her one, either.

Initially, she was determined to make the relationship a success. In retrospect, she thinks that she wanted to make up for the failure of her marriage.

> He was the first person I dated right out of my marriage. My first Friday night out, I met him. And I just took up where I left off. It had nothing to do with finances, because we had nothing financial together. We had no home together. We had no children together. It had everything to do with, "I'm going to make this work. Boy, this is going to work." It was all tied in to that.

As the years went by, she realized that she wanted to break up. But this would not happen easily. "Every time I wanted to leave the relationship," she recounts, "I felt like I would be nonexistent, as though, when I would leave his apartment and go to my car and get in my car, I'd be gone forever. Like I would disappear. I guess he gave me an identity."

Liz started reading self-help books. She wanted to understand why she allowed herself to endure the treatment to which her ex-husband, and now this other man, had subjected her. Eventually, she found *Women Who Love Too Much* (Norwood 1986). Shortly after that, she saw an ad for a meeting of Codependents Anonymous in a local pennysaver.

> I didn't know why this was happening, why I allowed myself to be treated the way I was being treated, because I didn't deserve it. I really felt—

and I still feel—that I'm a kind, compassionate person. And why would somebody take such advantage of that and be so rude and cruel? That's what I was experiencing. That's what made me get the book. And that's what made me go to The Rooms.

Liz felt comfortable in CoDA right from the start. She had no difficulty telling her troubles to strangers and found that what she heard from the other members struck a resonant chord. "I heard myself in their sharing," she recalls. "I said to myself, 'OK, I'm going to give it those five or six weeks, because they're talking about my life.'" She took one of CoDA's pamphlets on the Twelve Steps, and wrote down the date whenever she attended a meeting. "It was so important to me to start seeing meetings building up," she explains, "almost as though the more I had, I would already know I had a foot on getting better or understanding more."

At first, Liz's boyfriend encouraged her interest in CoDA. He saw it as something she would do for a while, and then quit once she reached some elusive goal. Gradually, however, he began to resent it. He antagonized her about the books she read and the amount of time she spent at meetings. His reaction, she claims, was fueled by her new ability to rebuff him. "I started to gain independence through the Program," she explains, "and I was starting to become myself and I was starting not to listen to all of his verbal stuff. I was answering back. In fact, I started being relentless." A woman in her CoDA group suggested that she look into a support group for battered women, and she attended both for a few months. She listened to the stories of women who, despite physical abuse, could not leave their husbands or boyfriends because of money. In contrast, Liz had no financial motivation for staying. Her motivation—equally powerful—came from her desire to make the relationship work so as not to lose her sense of identity.

She kept trying to make it work for two more years, until the time that her boyfriend came looking for her after a CoDA meeting. He knew that she and her friends from the group gathered for coffee at a local diner, and he showed up there one night. He was suspicious of their conversations and the time that Liz spent away from him, and he wanted to find out for himself what went on. That was "the last straw," she said. Although it embarrassed her to make a scene at the diner, having her CoDA friends around gave her the courage to end the relationship once and for all. They had heard her sharing for two years. They knew she had already tried to end the relationship several times. They agreed that he had acted inappropriately by looking for her at the diner. Since they had survived breakups themselves, they offered her proof that she would not "disappear" if she left him. "It gave me the courage," she says. "I walked away from it and never went back."[5]

Three years after that incident, Liz marvels at having gone from being scared to death of living by herself to having little concern about whether she has a relationship. Although she had just started seeing someone when we talked, she had remained single for several of her five years in recovery.

> If I have a relationship, great. If not, I know that I have made a life for myself. And all the self-esteem I got from going to CoDA has made me see that this is a pretty decent life. It's up to me to make it as full as I want it or as sparse as I want it. I will not wait for someone to knock on my door and make life happen.

Today, Liz makes an effort to avoid situations where other people, especially the men she dates, can control her. I was especially interested to learn how, given her history, she had reshaped her expectations of the give-and-take. For example, how would she safeguard the freedom she now had? Would she inadvertently repeat the familiar pattern that would, ultimately, leave her dependent on another man who might take advantage of her? Liz's primary strategy is to date only men who respect her. "No relationship can work if one person is completely vulnerable to the other, like I was," she explains. "I'm not going to date guys who have to put themselves above me. Before, I thought it was normal for the man to be above me. Now I know that's not right." Not letting men "put themselves above" her translates into gender equity. For example, Liz will only date men who "have their heads on straight" about sharing household labor. The man she currently dates often cooks dinner, and when he does, she cleans up, and *vice versa*. He wipes up the bathroom sink after he shaves, and she appreciates that he does not take her for a maid. The equity extends to the economic realm, as well. She shies away from dating wealthy men because their expenditures make her feel obligated to them. She prefers men who, like her, have little disposable income. She insists on paying half of the dinner check when she and her current boyfriend go to a restaurant, or else she will pay the entire check the next time. Sometimes the two of them arrange it so that one buys the groceries and the other cooks. She insists on equitable emotional arrangements, as well. She recognizes that, in the past, she has tended to be "a doormat." She tolerated jealousy, infidelity, and violence because she believed she could somehow turn things around. Now, she sees no need to tolerate men who do not respect her emotional "boundaries." "I'll have empathy for another person's feelings," she explained, "but I want that back . . . and if not, well, it's easier said than done, but I would say 'Get out of here.' I'm willing to give it, but I want it back. And that's what I've learned from CoDA: that I deserve to have it back."

FEMINISM'S UNFINISHED BUSINESS

Liz has clearly changed her life for the better, thanks to CoDA. Some might add, however, that, also thanks to CoDA, she has done nothing to change the world. Feminist critics of codependency often point out that the discourse does not orchestrate change at the political level. For them, its greatest fault lies in its transformation of political problems into personal ones. A paradigmatic indictment claims that codependency "can be seen as an attempt to replace women's developing political analysis of female oppression with a personalized and pathologized alternative" (McKay 1995, 235). Others echo this, accusing codependency of offering "a false sense of empowerment while taking energy away from political solutions to political problems" (Lodl 1995, 215).[6] It is true that codependency is not a political movement. However, stories like Liz's convinced me that the analysis it evokes or the empowerment it produces is not somehow false as a result. There is more to it than this.

First, it is insufficient to see CoDA and other forms of self-help as having agendas that are flawed inasmuch as they are personal instead of political. This dichotomy is not very useful, since social change always contains an effort to liberate subjectivity. For example, the events of the 1960s and '70s, including feminism, the black civil-rights and student movements, the New Left, and the surge of therapeutic techniques, can be seen as variations on a central quest for the "democratization of personhood" (Clecak 1983). During that era, millions of Americans gained "the resources—cultural and personal, and, to a lesser extent, political and economic—to pursue self-fulfillment on a scale hitherto unknown" (226). Granted, these resources were unevenly distributed. The point, however, is that, over the two decades, a significant number of Americans could aspire to "a satisfactory synthesis of the main elements of fulfillment" (7). These "elements" consist of "salvation" of the self from a number of conditions and "a piece of social justice" for one's own group. In practice, salvation and social justice mix, so that the quest for fulfillment can have multiple dimensions: religious and secular, spiritual and therapeutic. In overtly political activism, the therapeutic current is immersed in the larger theme of political good works. Nevertheless, Peter Clecak explains that, "although it often takes political detours, the logic of dissent . . . begins and ends with expanded claims in behalf of the self" (161). Consequently, Gloria Steinem could speak of feminism as "a gift" that "gave her life" (Obst 1977, 285), and Carl Davidson and Greg Calvert, leaders of SDS, could say that "no individual, no group, no class is genuinely engaged in a revolutionary movement unless their struggle is a struggle for their own liberation" (Teodori 1969, 414). In short, even the leaders of overtly political movements expressed personal concerns in therapeutic terms. The distinctions between the personal and the political become less relevant once one considers the larger outcome of opportunities for fulfillment.

From this perspective, codependency is a therapeutic continuation of feminism's overtly political battles. They exist as part of the same trend, with the former carrying out some of the "unfinished business" of the latter. Both represent dimensions of a larger, continuous, and essentially coherent, struggle for the "democratization of personhood." [7] Both are openly critical of dominant social Institutions and norms. Both are especially critical of arrangements that perpetuate dependence. Both use forms of "consciousness raising" to help people understand that their problems are not purely idiosyncratic. Although CoDA does not share feminism's emphasis on collective action, it does not prohibit members from engaging in such efforts on their own. Moreover, CoDA has implicit political elements in its Twelve Step norms. Respect for the pace of another's "growth" and "boundaries" is not a politics of "me first" or "me only." Rather, it is a politics of intersubjectivity, which democratizes the experience of selfhood. Likewise, Liz's language of "deserving" applies to the personal realm, but it originates in wider ideas of justice. She asks for equitable treatment, not privilege, and is willing to give back what she gets. CoDA did not teach her that the self is the *only* thing that needs to change, merely the *first* thing.

Second, and related to this, is the issue that a CoDA member summed up as "Not in my lifetime!" "If things have to be just right in the world before I can have a relationship," she said, "I might as well forget it." In other words, while debates over the personal versus the political continue, millions of women—and men—go about the business of trying to have satisfying intimate relationships with each other. For some, like Liz, that means ending relationships that are irredeemable. For others, however, it means making changes within relationships that they have no desire to end. For example, one member told me that her husband had never given her much companionship. They had married young, had a very traditional marriage, and, with children to look after, she had scarcely had time to notice her husband's detachment. However, their youngest had recently started college, and she felt a lack that she had not felt before. As it became more serious, she thought about divorce, but dreaded the thought of losing a lifetime together. She began attending CoDA and found that she appreciated having somewhere to go on a particular day and at a particular time. "CoDA is something just for me," she told me. "Never in my life have I done anything just for me. It makes me feel special, that I have a special place to go." She attended a weekday morning meeting that caused no friction in her marriage; she maintained her routine of having breakfast with her husband and spending evenings at home. She enacted no tangible changes in her life, but used CoDA to "live peacefully," in her own words. I would not offer this as the ideal solution under all circumstances, but neither would I underestimate the value of coming to terms with your circumstances, when the alternative might have taken a less comfortable direction.

Third, as Liz's story illustrates, CoDA can encourage behavioral change that, while not openly aligned with feminism, nevertheless advances similar goals. To my knowledge, the definition of feminism has not been fully resolved. Regardless of what they call their behavior, women like Liz are effectively challenging the Institutional status quo. Because the feminist critics often see power as a top-down arrangement, they overlook how presumably "oppressive" aspects of culture can often serve progressive purposes.[8] The political scientist James Scott points out that "most acts of power from below, even when they are protests— implicitly or explicitly—will largely observe the 'rules' even if their objective is to undermine them" (1990, 93). Women may strike bargains that appear to acquiesce to male privilege, but surely not at all times and under all circumstances. Even so, their acquiescence does not necessarily imply acceptance or approval. They may just as often resist, and their resistance may take a multiplicity of forms. Observers may not see many acts of resistance if they expect them to take overtly "revolutionary" forms. Liz, for example, came to CoDA after reading *Women Who Love Too Much*, a book that has been accused of portraying women as "dependent snivelers, reluctant to give up the security of protected life"

(Simonds 1992, 199). But instead of "sniveling" and clinging to her "protected life," Liz faced her biggest fear. CoDA gave her the resources to leave a relationship that, although abusive, provided her with an identity.

Fourth, although I have often read that codependency is a Band-Aid solution to a larger social problem, no one has, to my knowledge, proposed the preferable solution. What *is* the social or political answer to the multidimensional problem of feeling as though you have no sense of self? Dismantling patriarchy? A daunting task, indeed. Moreover, who gets to define the problem? Who gets to say what the answer is? In this sense, CoDA represents a distinctly political move: *I get to say.* The individual diagnoses his or her own problem and decides how to remedy it. While this is undoubtedly not the way to start a social movement, it was never intended to be. Codependency is understood as a problem of the self, and selves, at least in American culture, are considered deeply subjective. Even if they are seen as products of interaction, they remain private property. The possessor of the self is usually assumed to have privileged knowledge of its requirements. It is at this level that change would have to occur in order to make codependency less appealing, and American individualism is not likely to become any less robust very soon.

The objection could be raised that, while codependency may bring about some feminist goals, it still holds women responsible for orchestrating the change. To be sure, using meeting attendance as a measure, women are slightly more likely than men to identify with codependency. But the focus on women ignores or trivializes the many men who also identify with the phenomenon. Men account for roughly 40 percent of those in CoDA meetings. A comprehensive examination of codependency must take their presence into consideration. If codependency pathologizes the situation of women under patriarchy, what does it do for men? If recovery has to do with improving the quality of your relationships—something in which men allegedly take little active interest—why, then, do they attend CoDA?[9]

"YOU HAVE TO BE OPEN"

When I first realized that men attended CoDA in such numbers, I expected them to differ from the women in the group and from other men in some way. In a sense, it would have made my research much easier if they had. Instead, the men in CoDA talked about the same topics the women did.[10] They looked like any men that one would see outside of CoDA. When I discussed gender in interviews with men, they said that the men in CoDA *were* different from most others; they were open to self-criticism and change. I discussed the topic of "openness" at some length with a man I call Tom.

"Face it," he said, "the average guy won't even ask for directions. How's he going to admit that he might have blown his relationship?" When we talked, Tom and his ex-wife had nearly finalized their divorce. He had attended CoDA for about a year and a half. His wife started going to CoDA when they first began having serious difficulties. She brought home some literature, and he looked it over. He responded in what he calls a "typical male" way. "My first reaction was good because I looked at the Steps, and I guess when I read about making amends, I thought, 'Wow! This is great! She'll realize the error of her ways.'" She did not, however, or at least not in the way he had expected. He now understands that the Program may have helped his wife decide in favor of divorce. More to the point, however, he sees his initial reaction as characteristic of the kind of man he once was. "I had the typical man's way of dealing with problems in relationships," he said. "I thought there really *was* no problem because she'd come around to my way of seeing things eventually." They would sit down to have a discussion and end up in an argument, he said, because he "was incapable of seeing her side of things."

Once Tom and his wife separated, he started attending meetings to help him "go through the period of grief and devastation." He believes that most men experience some of the same intensity during the breakup of an important relationship. The difference between those who end up in CoDA and most other men, he claims, is the willingness to "admit that you messed up, and that now you've got nothing."

> Most guys, you know, they work on a project, and it might be over their heads, really, but they insist that they can do it. Anything. Plumbing. Electrical. Automotive. We can do it. When we screw up, we can fix it. If we can't, we get mad. That's the way most of us look at relationships. But when your marriage falls apart, you can't stay mad forever. In the middle of the night, you know you're at fault for at least 50 percent of the problem. You realize that nothing's going to change unless *you* do. My salvation was what I call the "humility angle" in CoDA, where you really do hit bottom and you say, "Look, I'm happy for the air that I'm breathing," and you start from there and everything else is a plus.

Tom appreciated many of the same things about CoDA that Alex claimed to like. He appreciated the company of people who had felt similar "grief and devastation." They showed him that he, too, could survive the experience. He found that the Twelve Step focus on "one day at a time" kept things in perspective. But more to the point, going to CoDA pushed him to think about how he behaved in his marriage, and how he will behave in future relationships. The "humility angle" helped him assess his behavior and his expectations, and other aspects of the group helped him do so without becoming overwhelmed.

Tom now attributes most of his negative behaviors to "typical male ways of doing things." His careers in the Navy, the defense industry, and in sales have given him plenty of exposure to "typical male ways." One of these was the belief that he had a solution for everything.

> . . . and that's another male thing. I never even really thought about feelings. I was "Mr. Fixit." I would always have a solution ready. Once I realized I couldn't fix my own marriage, I felt like a failure. In CoDA, I basically realized that having a solution ready was all about making myself feel superior to somebody else.

In CoDA, Tom began to see that, in his rush to find a solution, he often did not fully understand the problem. He believes that the norms of sharing—having to listen without commenting—have made him a better listener. "I know now that I never let my wife finish what she was saying," he told me. "I was answering the question before she even asked it. Now that I know that I have that tendency, I can change it. I *have* changed it. I don't feel threatened now if I'm not in charge of the conversation. I intend to listen better next time around." The rule to "talk only about yourself" instead of talking about other people has forced him to articulate his feelings. Through doing so, he has found that many of the things he did, such as jumping to a solution before he understood the problem, were "all about making [him]self feel good."

> I never really talked about how I felt. In CoDA, I realized that life's not a competition. I don't have to prove that I'm better than anybody else. It made me feel ashamed for not giving my wife the respect she deserved. Then, I realized I probably didn't give *anybody* the respect they deserved.

Thinking about feelings has "opened up a whole new dimension," Tom says. Although he does not "go around spilling his guts to everyone," he believes that he now weighs the emotional consequences of his actions more carefully than he ever had before recovery. He no longer believes that "it's my way, or the highway," to use his expression. Now he asks himself, "Where am I coming from, emotionally, in this?" or "Is this about trying to make myself feel good?" Moreover, CoDA's norm of respect for others has become key. "I have learned to respect others right where they are. I may not *like* where they are, but I have to respect it. I can't change it."

Careful listening, respect, and reflection—admirable qualities, but not ones readily associated with "typical male behavior." Tom claims that, by providing an environment of acceptance, CoDA encouraged him to try to do things differently. He admits, however, that he had to be ready to do so. "You have to be open," he said again. "Any man who comes to The Rooms and is not open to the possibility of change will not stick around."

CoDA AND MASCULINITY

Tom's suggestion that "openness" makes the men in CoDA somehow different is more than just self-congratulation. He makes an important point about masculinity, and about the alternatives that CoDA makes available. If the "average man" will seldom ask for directions, then the man who seeks out a group such as CoDA risks appearing less than manly. If the "typical male" has a solution to every problem, then the experience of "hitting bottom" and what Tom calls the "humility angle" would surely make a man wonder whether he measures up to the "typical" standard.

Because codependency offers no gendered symptoms or cures, men as well as women can tap into the discourse as a means of accounting for the events of their lives. And because it offers believers a "democratized personhood," some of the men who come to identify with it have used it to create an image of manhood that opposes that of the "typical male."

Over the course of American history, masculinity has taken many forms. Race, class, ethnicity, sexual preference, income, education, and geography all generate differences among men. Nevertheless, despite considerable variety there is, as Michael Kimmel (1996) points out, "a singular vision of masculinity, a particular definition that is held up as the model against which [men] all measure [them]selves" (5). This "singular vision" is the Self-Made Man. Born during the era of the separate spheres, this standard "carries with it the constant burdens of proof" (x). The history of manhood in America, Kimmel writes, is a history of relentless tests. Men must prove—mostly to other men—that they are contenders, whether in feats of physical or sexual prowess or economic superiority. They must, therefore, have the self-control to condition themselves for the test. At the same time, men have also tried to limit the competition by excluding others from the playing field. Thus, the *real* Self-Made Man is native-born and white. If the risk of failure seems too great, one solution is escape. In the face of diminishing manhood, men have often run away—to the sea, to the frontier, or to the men's club—to seek new challenges and avoid old ones. Kimmel argues that, although manhood has had many different meanings throughout American history, self-control, exclusion, and escape constitute prevailing themes.

The men I encountered in CoDA came to the group having failed a significant test of adulthood, and by extension, of masculinity. They had failed at maintaining a relationship. They were unable to find a solution, and consequently, found themselves broken as well. Many of these men used the opportunity to rebel against the competition, in principle. They did not escape to repair their ability to prove their manhood once again, but they rebelled against the idea of having to pass a relentless series of tests. Some, like Tom, found in CoDA's "democratization of personhood" a way to become men who stand up for equality and mutual respect. Tom claims to have "realized that life's not a competition." He and others have come to accept the responsibility for having learned a particular pattern of behavior—"the typical male way"—but see that abandoning that pattern might prevent them from repeating past mistakes. They believe that "typical" manhood has limited their emotional lives, and they search for the "tools" that can enrich them. They engage in "quiet daily struggles . . . to free themselves from the burden of proof" (Kimmel 1996, 334).

This is not to say that every man in CoDA enters The Rooms as a "typical male" and emerges profeminist. Nor is it to suggest that CoDA offers the best or the only alternative masculinity available today. It is simply to say that, in the group, some men reevaluate what being a man means to them, and reject much of it in favor of new definitions. The definition that appeals to any particular man depends on his resources and circumstances. CoDA does not impose a standard of masculinity on its members; as in most areas, the group can accommodate a range of variation. Nevertheless, the group does have norms. Members must respect others and treat them as equals. As one man put it, "The Program gets to you one way or another if you hang around long enough."

Men, as well as women, learn the collective respect for others that makes "democratized personhood" possible. Thus, both men and women can use the discourse for progressive ends.

The point remains that, while CoDA and other alternative forms of masculinity allow men to "live peacefully" with each other and with women, they do nothing to change inequality. This echoes much of the criticism aimed at recovery for women. While individual resistance makes individual lives more livable, it does not change the inequality between men and women. Each man and each woman has to work out the terms of his or her resistance. Unfortunately, as the members of CoDA demonstrate, this sometimes requires learning things the hard way.

I recognize the importance of calling attention to those aspects of inequality for which codependency offers no recovery. For example, economic inequality has given women particularly pressing reasons to invest themselves in relationships with men. The majority of women depend on the incomes of male partners because their earning power alone does not provide a tolerable standard of living, especially when children enter the picture. Because of their inequality in the economic realm, women have developed skills in the emotional realm that they exchange for economic support from men. As Hochschild puts it, "Women make a resource out of feeling and offer it to men in return for the more material resources they lack" (1983, 163). This constitutes something more complex than the personal troubles of codependency. The feminist criticism does well to remind us of this. It also does well to remind us that, by calling almost every behavior that a person finds unacceptable "abuse," codependency trivializes the very real violence that many women and children experience at the hands of men. The critics rightly point out that codependency does not hold men, as a group, accountable for their behavior towards women.

Still, the critical attention paid to women has left open the question, "What about the men?" Surely men have not won a zero-sum game. As Kimmel explains, men *as a group* may have power over women, but men as *individuals* have little feeling of empowerment. The image of the Self-Made Man has limited the range of emotions that men may feel and express. It has deprived them of active roles in child rearing and homemaking. Because the Self-Made Man is diminished by participation in these "feminized" realms, he has turned his efforts elsewhere. As a consequence, men are judged mainly by "the size of their biceps or their wallets" (Kimmel 1996, 333). A man who fails to measure up must preserve the shreds of his masculinity by escaping or by excluding those who pose the threat. Both of these "solutions" ultimately preserve the terms of the contest over manhood; at some point, failure occurs. In short, men, as well as women, have borne human costs as a consequence of the social and economic inequality between the sexes. Men's disadvantage may take different forms, but I would be loath to decide which is worse.

Ultimately, I feel uneasy about dismissing "living peacefully" as the lesser achievement. The men and women in CoDA recognize the social sources of inequality. They are not ignorant of the impact of Institutionalized sexism. At the same time, however, they—like the majority of people—continue to want intimate relationships, marriages, and families. With its critical perspective on all arrangements between men and women, feminism offers no answer to the question of how to construct a "politically correct" relationship. In the absence of such information, CoDA offers a strategy for both men and women to work out potentially egalitarian arrangements—*in the present.* As one woman put it, "Eliminating codependency would mean changing the sex roles in this society. But I've learned that I can't change other people. I can change the way I treat men, and I can insist that they treat me as an equal. I can raise my kids to do the same. I can only do so much." For people who want to build equitable relationships *in their lifetimes,* CoDA offers a practical means of doing so.

CHAPTER EIGHT

CODEPENDENCY AS A NARRATIVE OF VICTIMIZATION

S ome people in CoDA personify what the "middlebrow" critics fear most. For them, codependency produces a narrative of victimization. They focus on the harm that various people, and life in general, have inflicted on them. The "abuses" they have endured now justify the self-indulgence they "deserve" in recovery. "Taking care" of themselves entails shirking responsibilities and obligations to others. This is a narrative that few people in CoDA use. It nevertheless embodies aspects of culture that, when taken to extremes, allow codependency to take the form of self-indulgence writ large. Meet thirty-seven-year-old Richard.

I first interviewed Richard soon after he and his wife had separated. At the time, he looked about fifty pounds overweight. He drove a battered old van. He always turned up at meetings in well-worn clothing and old sneakers. His eyeglasses had tape on them. Over the course of the next six months or so, he began to lose weight. He never became slender, but he slimmed down noticeably. He started showing up at meetings in new clothes and sneakers. He got more stylish glasses. As summer came around, he got a tan. He began to talk about working out and in-line skating. The New Richard, I thought. People often change their physical appearances after a breakup. But I also knew that Richard lived on the economic margins, off of the erratic, unreported income generated from a small business that he ran out of his home. Having some idea of the cost of clothing, shoes, skates, and eyeglasses, I began to wonder.

Richard really aroused my curiosity when he arrived at the second interview in a brand-new four-wheel-drive sport utility vehicle. As the interview progressed, I worked my way around to asking him how he had managed to buy it. He told me he paid for it, as well as the new clothes and other things, with the money from the sale of his house. I knew he had a stormy relationship with his estranged wife, and I asked how they had managed the details of the sale. He explained that, since he had owned the house before they married, it was not marital property. Therefore, she had no right to anything from the sale of it. She had moved out, and he lived there for a while by himself. Then, he decided he could use the money, so he sold the house. Initially, he planned to use some of what he made to get a divorce, but decided to spend it all before their divorce went to court. Besides, he said, his wife had a serious relationship with another man. If things "heated up," she might initiate the divorce—and incur the expenses—herself.

> Whatever money I got, I spent it right away before somebody else spends it. You know, between the state and her and lawyers, they're all going to spend my money, so I spent it.

I asked Richard about his wife's financial situation. She did "fairly well," he said, pointing out that she had full insurance coverage while he had none. He had injured his knee and probably needed surgery, but could not even consider it without insurance. He wanted to see a therapist, too, but could not without insurance. In contrast, his wife saw a therapist and took their children to a dentist. "She's actually doing fairly well," he reiterated. I wondered how she managed to do so, and asked what kind of job she had. She did not have a job, he told me. She got insurance "through the government." During the next few minutes, as I worked to conceal my anger, he explained that his wife supported their two children on what he called "social services." As it turns out, they lived on welfare while he spent the proceeds from the sale of the house as fast as he could.

Although Richard's actions fell within the legal limits of property law, I steered him towards a discussion of their moral dimensions. He justified what he had done by portraying himself as "deserving." He told me about the suffering he had allegedly endured up to then. He saw his newly cultivated selfishness as essential to his recovery:

> I've always put everybody else first, you know, their feelings first, and it's just today, putting myself first. I don't want to walk around with holes in my sneakers anymore. The kids used to have nice clothes, nice shoes, nice sneakers, and everything else, and I used to walk around with holes. I don't do that anymore. It's like being true to myself, you know, not being in an abusive situation, not allowing anybody to abuse me, and stuff like that. I'm an important person.

"Putting himself first" consists, he said, of doing whatever he wants to do. He sees his children two afternoons each week and on alternating weekends—an obligation he fulfills without fail. He attends meetings of three Twelve Step groups—CoDA, Overeaters Anonymous, and Parents Anonymous—which occupy as many as four mornings and several evenings each week. He often goes out for coffee after these meetings, extending his commitments for at least another hour. He belongs to a gym and works out every day. He does errands. In short, he fills his days with "things that [he] wants to do."

His wife had recently asked him to agree to look after their children for some additional time during the summer so that she could register for vocational training. He refused to make the commitment in advance, making it impossible, in turn, for *her* to commit to the course. "Basically, I have no problem with it," he told me, explaining that he would probably end up doing it anyway. I asked him why he did not simply tell her so. He explained that he "has a problem" with other people asking him to make a commitment. He seemed to resent her ability, diminished though it was, to make a claim to his time.

> I just don't want to make a commitment, OK? And in talking with other people, and being validated that, you know, that it's OK not to want to make a commitment, I just really know in my heart that I'm doing the right thing.

He discussed his decision with friends from CoDA—really, the only friends he has anymore—and they had seen things his way. He often talks to CoDA friends about important decisions and events in his life. Although he sees them as reliable "reality checks," they share the same CoDA reality and are predisposed to be sympathetic to his point of view. They "validated" his decision to put her off, on the basis that he should never agree to things that do not feel right to him. His wife, however, saw the situation in a different light. She became angry at his reluctance to make the commitment; lacking reliable plans for child care, she had no assurance that she could register for the course that might help her get a decent job. He saw her as intentionally standing in the way of his recovery. He reminded me of his history of putting others first, and said that, in doing so, he had always "squashed" his own "needs." His wife resented the "growth" he had experienced in his recovery, he told me. During their last heated phone conversation, she had become angry, allegedly because he was "taking care" of himself.

I told Richard that someone who looked at his life might call it a little self-indulgent. I asked him what he would say in his defense. "I wouldn't feel I have to defend [his actions]," he said. "It works for me. They haven't lived my life, you know?" He began to tell me about the "pain" he had endured.

> They weren't there when I was sitting at a desk with a loaded gun, trying to give myself a reason not to blow my head off because the pain was so great. They're not there in the mornings when I wake up and I can't move my leg. They're not there every three times a week when I've got to drop off my kids and see what that's like.

He reminded me that, two months before his wife "decided she wanted out," he lost his business through a fire. "To me," he said, "it was more than a business. It was my everything." He took a job, but quit after his boss failed to give him a raise. "It was an abusive situation," he said. When I asked him what this meant, he told me that "promises were made that didn't come true. Promises of more money, more benefits, and stuff like that." His boss had not kept those promises. Richard saw this as "abuse," and quit. Evidently, this was the last in a series of "abusive" jobs. Prior to owning his own business, he had worked for a family member for ten years. "I stayed in that dysfunctional, abusive job out of fear of getting out," he said. The experience had made him determined not to remain "stuck in situations that I [don't] enjoy."

When Richard's wife left with their children, the remaining structure of his life disappeared. He referred several times to "the loss of that dream," and "the pain of all that loss." He had found it "just unbearable." Although the theme of loss comes up often in accounts of uncoupling, Richard continues to wear his losses like a badge of honor. He organizes his life around them, or at least around "recovering" from the behaviors that he now believes contributed to his losses. He sees only problems in the way his life had once revolved around his family, his business, "and doing everything for everybody else so they would like me." In retrospect, Richard sees himself as having been "so codependent that I didn't have a life." He sees his devotion to his business as "workaholism," which he blames for the failure of his marriage. Because he used to believe that his primary task in his marriage was to bring home a paycheck, he claims to have worked to the point of neglecting his family. When he asks himself why his wife left, he fixes on his devotion to work. He learned "workaholism" from his family, he claims. (He started working with his brothers in his early teens and never took a vacation.) Nobody ever told him he was good, or smart, or important, he said, so he worked hard, for years, without vacations, in order to feel as if he had those qualities. Eventually, it backfired on him.

In addition to his "workaholism," Richard now sees other evidence of codependency in his family. His widowed mother and his brothers "have a lot of denial going on." To avoid exposure to the circumstances that can bring out his codependent tendencies, he has virtually no contact with his family. In the case of his mother, she "doesn't hear what I have to say," he explained, "so why bother?" His brothers have criticized the extent of his involvement in CoDA. One told him that "you people in recovery think that a hug is going to cure everything." When I asked how he responded to such comments, he said that he felt no desire to respond at all. He believes that the brother who made this comment also resented his "growth." Instead of responding, Richard avoids his family as much as possible. Instead, he associates primarily with friends from CoDA. He has only limited interaction with people outside that realm. He refers to this, as do many members of CoDA, as "having healthy people in my life," where "health" means seeing things from his point of view. "We can either work dysfunction in our life," he explained to me, "or we can do it the other way."

> I choose to have Program, you know, recovery people, and stuff like that. I'd rather have the message on the answering machine that says, "Hi, how are you doing? I hope everything's going all right," than the one like I had from my cousin today about, "Come and get this freaking thing out of here!" You know, I'd rather have the other conversation.

The "recovery people" Richard has in his life are mostly women. This is not because he wants another relationship, however. His female CoDA friends simply make him feel safe, he says. He hesitates to make friends with other men in recovery, although he has become fairly close to one. He explains that, as the youngest in a family of four boys, "men were either dying or leaving in my life." Once again, he says, "Why bother?" Richard told me that he does not feel "ready" for another relationship with a woman. When I asked him what his idea of a good relationship might involve, he spoke of "unconditional love," as did many other members of CoDA. For Richard, this does not mean loving another person unconditionally, but of being loved in that way. "I don't know if anybody ever loved me unconditionally," he told me. He seemed to feel that he deserved unconditional love, merely by virtue of his existence.

Although Richard's marriage ended nearly three years before our second interview, he clearly continues to use it as a means of organizing his life. More accurately, he organizes his life around "recovering" from the loss. For him, this requires complete focus on things that he wants to do, in order to avoid having others push him into "dysfunctional" or "abusive" situations. "Today," he told me, "I worry about Richard first. I just work my program, and that's basically it. My life consists of doing what I want to do." I asked him if this was what it meant to "take care" of himself. "Yeah," he answered without hesitation, "yeah, it is."

"THE OBLIGATION TO DO WHAT YOU WANT TO DO"

Among the members of CoDA, I did not find Richard's behavior exceptional, nor did I find it a characteristically "male" version of "taking care" of yourself. I interviewed a woman whose version of "care" meant quitting her job, living off her savings as long as she could, and spending her days watching soap operas and writing letters to herself. "I'm too wounded to do anything else," she told me. "I've got to take care of myself for a while." Rice (1996) gives an account of a woman who "took care" of herself by reneging at the last minute on a promise to help her brother move (195). I heard men and women alike justify buying everything from clothing to cars by saying that they "deserved" those things because of the "abuse" they had suffered. In many cases, the buyers complained about their debts in the very next breath.

Some codependents seem to feel strongly what Daniel Yankelovich (1981) calls the "obligation to do what you want to do." Yankelovich describes a set of contemporary norms that justify the belief in "a moral duty to yield to [your] impulses" (86). The discourse of codependency takes this to an extreme, and some who identify with codependency push this extreme to its utmost. The discourse turns the sense of *obligation* into an urgency. It transforms what you *want* into what you *need*. Codependents do not talk about finding out who they are; they talk of finding out what they need. They assume that a good person waits underneath it all, and indulgence can encourage that goodness to flourish.

In logic that by now sounds very familiar, the obligation to do what you want to do is compelled by growing up in "dysfunctional" families. As children, codependent adults were deprived of love that they deserved unconditionally, and they tried to win that love by pleasing others. As a result, they developed codependent selves based on trying to gain the love and acceptance of those around them. If they had instead been assured of being loved, they would have been free to develop abilities and interests that come with a "healthy" childhood. They have no idea what kind of people they might have become had they received the love they needed. What they *did* become resulted from childhood messages that they were somehow not good enough, or did not deserve love. For example:

> I'm still that scared, shy little kid, trying to figure out what the hell I need to do to make my parents love me. In every relationship I've ever had, until recently, I would think, "Geez, this relationship sucks," but I never thought I deserved anything else because I thought I was so unlovable. *(woman, thirty-eight)*

> I'm the youngest of a long string of kids. A change-of-life baby. My parents had had it with raising kids. The thrill was gone, you know, so I was forced out of childhood without ever having had one. I became a little adult. I didn't get any of the nurturing that I needed. My codependency came from just trying to get love in that environment. *(man, forty-one)*

In order to recover from the effects of their "abusive" childhoods, codependents must accept that they *are* good enough, just as they are. Beattie, for example, advises her readers to believe that "we are the greatest thing we've got going for ourselves" (1987, 113). Codependents must fulfill their own need for love by learning to love themselves "just as they are." They must also fulfill some of the wants and desires that went ignored through abuse and dysfunction. Since these wants and desires may provide keys to the development of a healthy self, they become elevated to the status of "needs." Loving yourself and discovering and providing for your "needs" constitute "taking care" of the self. Recovery from codependency revolves around perfecting this skill. Each person must discover and cultivate things that he or she really wants to do. These vary from person to person, and only the individual can know his or her own "needs."

Initially, I had tremendous difficulty thinking analytically about this self-indulgent version of recovery. I became angry and distracted just listening to it. Even when the behavior *itself* did not seem inordinately selfish, the endless deliberation and discussion surrounding it made it so. I began to think that perhaps the cultural critics had it right, and the venerable American preoccupation with the self had truly gone beyond acceptable limits (see Rieff 1966; Bell 1976, 1980; Lasch 1979). Even if this were the case, however, the question remains: how does this kind of self-indulgence serve as a strategy within the context of the lives of those who engage in it?

In some ways, Richard's story has much in common with the one I heard from Liz. Both use CoDA's rhetoric of "taking care" of themselves to resist obligations they find oppressive. Both feel compelled to do whatever they want to do. Their behavior, however, has very different moral meanings. Liz's personal history justifies her harmless indulgences. She spoke of a life so closely monitored that first her husband and then her boyfriend scarcely let her out of their sight. In addition, both men punished her physically for doing things that "normal" people did. But even in the absence of this history, Liz's version of "taking care" of herself does not offend because her actions do not come from a politics of victimization. She has oriented herself towards reestablishing a self without dwelling on mistreatment she received at the hands of others. Although she can use the vocabulary of "abuse" and "dysfunction," her narrative focuses on constructive change. She portrays herself more as a survivor than a victim.

To be sure, elements of victimization appear in many accounts of codependency. In what I observed at CoDA, however, victimhood usually exists as a transitional status. Most people do not take it on as a permanent organizing principle for their lives. Instead, they make new attachments or find new goals to strive for. Although they believe they suffered harm in their "dysfunctional" families, they move beyond blaming and focus their efforts on change. Liz, for example, cultivates her independence, and Tom watches out for "typical male" behavior. Alex looks for his niche in "service" to CoDA. Susan has found CoDA's responses to emotions more constructive than those she had been using on her own. Paul has begun a new relationship. Each of these cases illustrates how new Institutional ties gradually come to substitute for those no longer available.

In some cases, however, victimhood becomes a more permanent status. New attachments become improbable as the victim's suffering takes center stage. Alternative Institutional ties wither and disappear due to the victim's dismissive negativism. As the victim continues to try to meet his or her "needs," those very "needs" continue to change, exhausting the resources of all but the independently wealthy. Meanwhile, the victim persists in attributing each frustration or defeat to "abuse" and "dysfunction." This, in turn, opens up a new horizon of suffering and the required compensation. Granted, Richard may have made a transition since I last spoke with him. Nevertheless, during two interviews nearly a year apart, he talked of having settled into victimhood quite comfortably. Other "victims" told similar stories. Their "sharing" dwelled on the power that past "abuses" had to limit present and future courses of action. While everyone in CoDA touched on these elements, most moved on to talk of present successes or things they wished to change. The "victims," in contrast, remained bitter and resentful, hemmed in, even in mid-life, by the failures of their parents. In short, while I have no basis to argue that Richard, and others like him, will remain victims forever, victimhood represents one of several narrative strategies that codependency can serve. It constitutes an extreme version, however, even an abuse (in the literal sense), of a more general process that one might otherwise treat more sympathetically.

VICTIMIZATION AS RESPONSE

The narrative of victimization seems to respond to two factors. First, those who portray themselves as victims typically are in the position of having been left during the uncoupling. They were "dumped," or left behind as a spouse or lover moved out or ended the relationship. Thus, victimization responds to your position with regard to "leave-taking" in the relationship. Second, and related to this, "victims" usually have few social-structural resources available to them for telling a coherent story of the self independent of the relationship. They are more likely to be unemployed, for example, or to lack commitments to family or to service in CoDA. For reasons having to do with uncoupling and with the victimization narrative itself, social structure has failed the "victims." Ultimately, the victimization narrative both responds to and intensifies these social-structural losses. The way into that double bind, however, starts with uncoupling.

In Vaughan's study of the process, she claims "that the role taken in the leavetaking is the primary determinant of how separation will be borne" (127). The one who initiates the breakup has more and better preparation for the transition than does the partner who is left behind.[1] This is the case regardless of other contributing factors, such as sex, age, occupation, social class, income, social networks, and duration of the relationship. The initiator has advantages that the partner does not. He or she has undertaken some advance planning, or at least some thinking, about life after uncoupling. Initiators can, for example, organize resources in advance, save some money, or find a place to live. Most importantly, the initiator's discontent has already motivated him or her to begin to locate the self in alternatives outside the relationship. For initiators, "alienation from self began before the actual end of their marriage" (Weiss 1975, 70). They begin to anchor their notions of selfhood in alternative sources, such as work, hobbies, interests, or another love relationship. Often, the alternatives bring new networks of friends who know the initiator independent of his or her relationship. This provides still more support for an independent self. Meanwhile, because the partner carries on unaware of the initiator's dissatisfaction, the initiator can delay making the break until he or she has garnered the necessary resources. According to Vaughan, initiators usually cover up their discontent until they have the material and emotional preparation to leave. Although the relationship continues, "the initiator already has left in a number of ways" (60). They "take whatever time they need to overcome the obstacles they face; when the break comes, they've prepared to try it without the partner" (129).

In contrast, partners have a very different experience. While the initiator accumulates resources to negotiate the transition out of the relationship, the partner continues to use the relationship as a central anchor for identity. Partners "often report that they were unaware, or only remotely aware, even at the point of separation, that their relationship was deteriorating," Vaughan writes (1986, 62). Because they have not had the opportunity to develop alternative sources of identity, the end strikes partners particularly hard. Indeed, they experience a double hardship; they feel betrayed by an initiator who clearly has planned his or her escape, and they lack the resources to respond to the initiator's action with either grace or acceptance. They "have been the recipients of traumatic rejection," Weiss explains, "with what may seem to have been inadequate opportunity to retaliate" (Weiss 1975, 64). Vaughan found that partners often resort to drastic, yet temporary substitutes. They abuse drugs or drink to excess more frequently than initiators. When they begin new relationships, they often take up with lovers who have no interest in a long-term relationship, thereby protecting themselves against another uncoupling while also depriving themselves of an anchor for selfhood. Some partners move back home to live with parents. Others turn to religion.[2]

In most cases, that "first refuge" after the breakup, whether religion, alcohol, or living with mom and dad, is merely temporary. A partner may go through a spell of heavy drinking, for example, but will eventually reorganize his or her identity around something more rewarding. For some partners, however, victimhood becomes a more permanent role. They "come to believe they deserve to be left," Vaughan writes (160). They organize their identities around rejection. They feel "misused," Weiss adds, "not only by the one man or woman who ended the marriage to them but by the entire human race" (1975, 65). Many partners have mental breakdowns or become physically ill, "focus[ing] their disordered life around their loss and the routine of professional care, either incorporated into their regular daily activities or administered within an institutional setting" (Vaughan 1986, 162).

Many of the "victims" I encountered in CoDA were partners, having been left instead of doing the leaving. Of the thirty-six people I interviewed, a quarter of them were partners. All nine stories had elements of the narrative of victimization; four took the rather strong form illustrated by Richard. Some of them gave accounts of illness—particularly mental breakdowns—at the end of their relationships. While most people go through a time of intense emotional distress during uncoupling, the "victims" do not seem to improve. Some had taken antidepressant drugs for a number of years. Others, like Richard, considered or attempted suicide. On the whole, partners often take comfort in the "sick role" (Parsons 1951, 1978)—with modifications. Customarily, an ill person may step into the "sick role" by seeking competent professional help for the illness and demonstrating a desire to get well. Having satisfied these two conditions, the ill person is not held responsible for his or her sickness. Moreover, he or she is granted exemption from routine duties and responsibilities in order to get well. For example, most people do not expect someone with the flu to keep up the kind of schedule that he or she maintains when well. The flu constitutes sufficient excuse for not doing some things that a person would ordinarily do, if healthy. These exemptions hold provided that the sick person seems to want to get well and actively seeks to do so. Anything less begins to suggest hypochondria or malingering.

Codependents modify the established obligations of the sick role in two ways. First, no obvious source of "competent professional help" exists for codependency. While some CoDA members have seen, and continue to see, therapists, therapy is not the primary means through which the majority come to identify themselves as codependents. More commonly, they diagnose themselves—and treat themselves, as well—in CoDA. The very language of "taking care" of yourself suggests this capability. In addition, Twelve Step groups historically equate working the

Steps with seeking help (see Conrad and Schneider 1992, chapter 4). The third of the Twelve Steps involves "[making] a decision to turn our will and our lives over to the care of God as we understood God." The chairman of the board of AA once wrote that "this turning over of self direction is akin perhaps to the acceptance of a regimen prescribed by a physician for a disease" (Norris 1970, 740). *The CoDA Book* discusses the "healing" involved in this Step, and provides an accompanying prayer that uses language such as "heal my wounds" (1995, 37). Thus, the "competent help" sought in codependency consists of some combination of yourself and your Higher Power. This is consistent with CoDA's logical system, in which only the individual—along with a Higher Power—knows what works best for him or her.

Second, seeking help in this loosely construed manner does not mean that codependents necessarily want to get well. Granted, they claim to want to put an end to the "unmanageability" of their lives. This, however, does not translate into getting well. Indeed, the casting of codependency as a condition rules out the possibility of a full recovery. *The CoDA Book* cautions against holding this hope. It lists a series of "Frequently Asked Questions" about codependency. In answer to the question, "Am I ever recovered from codependency?" the book states, "We can become very disappointed if we believe we can stop all of our codependent behaviors" (107). The "hope and miracles of recovery" consist of "a life progressively filled with serenity, acceptance, and love," but not a full recovery. In short, the rhetoric of codependency makes it impossible for the individual to fully recover, and advises against even wishing to do so.

These modifications to the requirements of the sick role do not prevent codependents from claiming its benefits. They begin to disavow blame for their "condition," blaming instead a "dysfunctional" family and society. Moreover, they elaborate a vast network of nearly universal symptoms and causes, connecting almost any behavior with codependency, and excusing it as a consequence. Again, Richard provides an illustration.

Richard believes that he was largely responsible for the breakup of his marriage, a breakup that he did not want to happen. He can enumerate things he did and things he wants to change in future relationships. Yet the responsibility that he appears to take does not lie squarely on his shoulders. In his view, his contribution to the failure of his marriage did not come from him directly, but from codependency. He readily admits that he worked too much and failed to hear his wife's side of things. He sees neither of these behaviors as his fault, however. Each stemmed, in different ways, from his codependency.

To further complicate things, not only does Richard see his "worka-holism" and his failure to listen to his wife as codependency-related problems, he also sees his self-blame as a manifestation of his "disease." In other words, he believes he played a major role in the failure of his marriage, but blames codependency for making him act in those ways. In addition, he believes that codependency has *also* made him self-critical, and that criticism *itself* constitutes a symptom. Through co-dependency, he says, "we've become our own worst enemies. . . . I'm really beginning to see why it is classified as a disease." Ultimately, it is impossible to recover from codependency, and codependency comes to include an ever-expanding number of behaviors and thought patterns. Although the individual does the acting and thinking, he or she only does so at the mercy of codependency.

Having disavowed blame for their "condition," victims also claim ex-emption from routine responsibilities on account of their vulnerability. While I know of no instances in which people explicitly used the term 'codependency' to get out of work or school responsibilities, they did construe their wish for exemption in terms that noncodependents would honor. In particular, "taking care" of yourself was often used success-fully, perhaps because the need to do so seems so subjective that it is beyond question. For example, one woman told me about how she took time off from work:

> I told them that I couldn't give them a hundred percent anymore. . . .
> I really needed to put more focus on myself and to work out a lot of stuff
> that was, at that time in my life, more important. *(age thirty-seven)*

In another example, a woman who enrolled at a local university became overwhelmed by the work. She did not complete the courses, and justi-fied her failure to do so by saying that her schoolwork did not leave her time to "take care" of herself.

More commonly, "taking care" of yourself exempts you from obliga-tions to significant others. Richard's narrative provides several examples of this, as does Rice's (1996) brief account of the woman who backed out on a promise to help her brother move. Paul's narrative illustrates the use of this as a strategy to disengage from particular relationships altogether.

In sum, partners who organize their lives around the loss of their relationship often capitalize on codependency's links to illness, and, therefore, to the sick role—with some modifications to Parsons's classic formulation. If the sick role worked as it does in theory, this strategy would have certain advantages. In particular, it would allow the victim time out to adjust to his or her new status. In practice, however, codependency's sick role often becomes an ever-expanding lens through which to view the events of your life. A strong form of the victim narrative, such as the one given by Richard, makes it nearly impossible to move into a new, separate identity.

VICTIMIZATION AS A NARRATIVE OF THE SELF

Taking on the narrative of victimization as a self-story means that the partner may never catch up, as it were, to the initiator's advantages. The partner's focus on the victim role reduces potential sources of support for a self, making the victimization more encompassing. A person who feels wronged by uncoupling continues to focus on the relationship, excluding opportunities to develop alternative Institutional ties. Such a person may hold out hope for reconciliation, ruling out other possible relationships along the way. He or she may choose to remain in the home once shared with the initiator, "prolong[ing] the sense of belonging to that other person and perpetuat[ing] the coupled identity" (Vaughan 1986, 163). While this may seem comforting at first, it ultimately slows the transition to a separate identity. Friends in the neighborhood know the partner as half of a couple, making it difficult for him or her to create a life apart from the past. In short, the victim role helps the partner to maintain a focus on the failed relationship, while overlooking alternative sources of identity. Vaughan points out that, "as these alternatives atrophy, these partners, by default, invest increased energy in the victim role, intensifying their focus on the relationship and their loss" (163). Such is the case, I suggest, with Richard—and with others like him.

Richard has faced several kinds of failure. His means of coping with it—the victim role—has ruled out the possibility of taking advantage of social-structural resources for establishing a new identity. His status as a partner, and not an initiator, for example, represents a failure of a major test of adulthood (see Vaughan 1986; Weiss 1975). In playing the victim, however, he has not taken legal steps towards divorce, but remains separated, hoping that his wife will initiate the divorce. By main-

taining his semi-attachment to his wife, he complicates any new relationships that may appear on the horizon. In addition, he portrays himself
as "unhealthy" and "not ready" for another relationship. He remains
married yet resentful of his wife, and unprepared to move into a new
attachment should one present itself. His choice of the victim role has
ruled out a major source of adult identity: another relationship.

Richard's victimization extends into the realm of same-sex friendship,
as well. His belief that men "were always dying or leaving" in his life
has minimized the likelihood of friendships with other men. He remains
protective of his vulnerability to men, thus choosing, indirectly, not to
take advantage of the resources of friendship.

He has also eliminated the resources of family. Partners usually have
the support of sympathetic family members and friends who recognize
his or her vulnerability and offer comfort. But those who take on the
permanent role of victim eventually alienate even "these well-meaning
others, who tire of the seemingly endless introspection, anger, and negativism" (Vaughan 1986, 164). Richard's account implies this, although
he colors it differently; he blames the "dysfunction" in his family. His
mother, for instance, cannot "hear what I have to say." He sees this as
her problem, however, having nothing to do with the content of what
he may say. Eventually, he asks himself, "Why bother?" Recall that
other family members have criticized his involvement in recovery, and
he claims that they are just out to hurt him, as they have in the past.
He prefers to stay away from his family and minimize the conflict. His
decision eliminates the possibility of drawing on their support, as well.

As if ruling out relationships, friendships, and family were not
enough, Richard has also failed at work. While a job could offer an alternative source of identity, Richard's status as a victim has ruled out the
possibility of working. According to Vaughan, many partners strengthen
a damaged sense of self by investing more in their jobs. Richard, however, sees himself as so badly in need of recovery that it requires his
full-time attention. Moreover, he sees mainly "abuse" and "dysfunction"
in the jobs he has held. When he and I discussed what might happen
when the money from the house ran out, he again played the victim.
He explained that, by growing up in "this society," he had learned such
low self-esteem that he feels unprepared for most jobs. He has no education beyond high school. He can think of no job in which he might
do well. "If you grew up in a judgmental family where you never did
anything right," he explained, "you can achieve so much, but it's never
ever going to be enough." He adds that his bad knee—a consequence

of other "neglect" he has endured—could also keep him from working. From his perspective, even if he were to get a job, he would find a deck already stacked against him. Again, why bother?

VICTIMIZATION AND THE FAILURE
OF SOCIAL STRUCTURE

Ultimately, the victim narrative both responds to and intensifies the failure of social structure. At best, Richard has only limited access to Institutional anchors for selfhood. Without education or skills, he has few opportunities for employment. With his wife and children gone but still in his life, he continues to have obligations to them but cannot really draw on them for a sense of self. He lacks even the resources of close family and friends, which could provide the basis for a coherent self-story grounded in history. The victim narrative responds to these very real circumstances. Richard truly does not have many social anchors for his identity. In this sense, he *is* a victim. He is not to blame for his limited education, nor is he at fault for his wife's departure. The narrative of codependency responds to these circumstances by shouldering some of the blame for them. If social structure seems too vague a factor to blame, perhaps because it seems impossible to change, codependency makes the culprit seem more accessible—at least initially. But codependency comes to take on such a vast variety and number of attributes that it eventually becomes less tangible than social structure itself. Still, the label brings the problem home, in a manner of speaking, convincing the self-identified codependent that he or she can solve it. Since real solutions to problems such as Richard's do not exist, any salient cause can seem compelling.

Unfortunately, CoDA's narrative of victimization also makes Richard and others accomplices to their continued misfortune. By encouraging Richard to believe that he "is enough, just as he is," the rhetoric leads him to make choices that will only result in further alienation. For example, Richard believes that he can get along without work, or a relationship, or other people. He "doesn't need those things to make [him] feel worthwhile." He wants to get away from those "false" senses of the self. He believes that he is an "important person," just as he is, without Institutional anchors.

This much is a common theme in CoDA; believers see themselves as good, valuable, important people, *in and of themselves.* The narrative of victimization adds the idea that victims are too wounded, too weak, too badly "abused" to do anything but focus on themselves. If your relationship was "unhealthy," better avoid relationships for a while. If your job was "abusive," better avoid work, too. If your family is "dysfunctional," better avoid associating with them, as well. Victims gradually devalue the alternative resources of self that they have available. Before long, these possibilities begin to "atrophy," to use Vaughan's word. Withdrawal from interaction, in general, limits your relationship possibilities, not to mention that a discussion of your failed relationship hardly gets a new one off on the right foot. In addition, friends and family tire of the endless negativity and introspection. Long stretches of unemployment complicate getting back to work. Victimization thus intensifies the shortage of Institutional resources by devaluing them as potential sources of the narrative of the self. Before long, a shortage of resources becomes an absence of them. Meanwhile, victims rationalize the absence of resources by dismissing the importance of social structure altogether. After all, who wants to work when you have to cultivate the "needs" of the inherently worthy inner self?

But the "needs" of the self will remain elusive, perhaps because they fasten so tightly to interests, and because interests and self interact dialectically. As I define what I want, the stories I tell about myself change. At the same time, my new stories shape my emerging interests. People may also—intentionally or not—resist clarifying outright what they want. As Goldstein and Rayner (1994) put it, "No matter what I get (what interests are satisfied), I may continue to wonder if what I get really recognizes who I am" (367). Given adequate resources, the search for interests can expand exponentially, since the simultaneous effort to tell the story of the self changes the course of that search even as it occurs.

The conflation of interests with identity explains much of Richard's apparent self-indulgence. As of our last interview, he had enough money to buy the time to pursue his interests. By living off the money from the sale of his house, he could forestall gainful employment and devote his days to meetings. But, gradually, he began to see that he "needed" more than just CoDA. His emerging definition of self now "needed" Overeaters Anonymous, Parents Anonymous, and a gym membership, as well. The "new" Richard could not tolerate the clothes and shoes he used to wear; he would no longer "walk around with holes." Eventually, he could not even drive around in the same old van; he found that a sport utility vehicle better suited his present definition of self. A man who once devoted himself to his family and his business now describes that past as having been "so codependent that I didn't have a life." He has only contempt for having once "let others tell [him] who to be and what to feel." Now, only the freedom to do whatever he wants to do will suffice for expressing who he has become. He seems engaged in the continual pursuit of interests that eventually lose their power to define who he believes he is.

The victim narrative has its merits. It can provide a way to seek temporary comfort during a painful and confusing experience. While this can be valuable to partners, it cannot be equated with establishing anchors for an identity separate from the relationship. Indeed, by using the "abuse" of the relationship to justify all manner of self-indulgence, victimization can actually prolong a partner's attachment to an initiator. Victims will not gain what Alex gains from service, for example, or what Liz gains from refusing to wait for someone to invite her to start having a good time. The things a victim does or buys to fulfill his or her "needs" will pale in comparison with the power these other strategies have for allowing you to move on. For by continually attributing your current thoughts, desires, and interests to your past relationship, you can surely never move beyond it.

Conclusion

Just as the discourse of codependency can generate varying life narratives, so the attempts to explain the appeal of codependency can generate varying narratives of the state of American culture and selfhood. Moreover, just as the narratives that I presented here manifest particular concerns of their narrators, so the narratives of what codependency means for this culture manifest narrators' concerns. It seems that Americans are always thought to be taking one thing or another to extremes, and this proclivity offers ample basis for stories about codependency's widespread popularity—depending, of course, on what it is that one sees as being taken to extremes.

It could be said, for example, that codependency's appeal indicates an extreme form of individualism. One could tell a story in which CoDA members epitomize or exaggerate the individualistic tendencies that Americans have shown throughout their history. It would be easy to argue that CoDA encouraged Paul to selfishly "detach" from his children, and even easier to make an example of Richard. In this sense, CoDA members are the contemporary representatives of a preoccupation that dates back to Tocqueville ([1832] 1969) and Crèvecoeur ([1782] 1981). The combination of Puritanism, democracy, capitalism, migration, and mobility has allegedly made Americans independent to the extreme. They "form the habit of thinking of themselves in isolation," Tocqueville wrote, in a depiction that could apply as easily to Richard, Susan, Paul, or Liz as it could to the Americans he visited over a century and a half ago. This theme of radical individualism—its negative and excessive aspects, in particular—has been a focal point for observers of the American social character ever since. The list of leading tellers of this type of tale includes Slater, Lasch, Yankelovich, and Bellah et al.

At the same time, CoDA could just as easily be portrayed as an antidote for the alienation that is the downside of excessive individualism. A story could be told, for example, in which the group fulfills unmet needs for connection. Kaminer spins such a tale in claiming that the numbers of people flocking to meetings suggest a "hunger to belong." This, too, has a long history. The same people that Tocqueville described as "thinking of themselves in isolation" were banding together in impressive numbers of voluntary associations. CoDA could be seen as a contemporary version of this characteristically American trait.

But it is *also* characteristically American to take affiliation to extremes. In this formulation, CoDA would be indicative of the conformist tendencies that appear throughout our history. As Whyte, Riesman et al. and Bellah et al. have argued, in varying terms, the slope between voluntary association and people-pleasing is slippery indeed. Those who lack external standards by which to measure their views will eventually rely on others for verification, making morality but a hollow shell. If one finds this view convincing, there is sufficient evidence to portray CoDA members as other-directed conformists who cannot "be" who they are without the group. They surround themselves with people who will share about what they want to hear, and they will exclude those who, like the developmentally disabled Beth, make them uncomfortable. Moreover, they lack the originality to reinvent themselves, preferring instead to craft their life narratives along a preestablished narrative formula.

There are numerous other stories that one could tell about what CoDA and codependency say about American culture and the state of the self. I would gain nothing by enumerating them all. Rather, I want to call attention to their variety in order to make two related points. First, each story represents a particular view of the issues at stake. This is the case not only for accounts of the cultural meaning of codependency, but for the expansive literature on the American character. Just as the terms "dysfunction" and "abuse" indicate specific ways of understanding the world and one's relationship to it, terms such as "individualism" and "conformity" also indicate specific views. And, just as the teller of a codependency narrative must omit things that do not fit the formula, so the teller of a story of American individualism must, inadvertently or not, leave out what does not fit. This is not to say that either type of story is somehow untrue, for both are true for the tellers. In both cases, however, the formulas shape the stories. As a cultural phenomenon, codependency could potentially mean many different things. The formula one uses to tell one's story will use evidence selectively. My goal in this book has been to create a story that includes as much evidence as possible.

The second point that I want to make is that CoDA is not simply today's answer to age-old concerns. Herein lies the difficulty: codependency's appeal undoubtedly centers on the relationship between the individual and society, but not necessarily in the formulaic terms that have typically described this relationship. Today's Americans do not move in Tocqueville's world. Their world contains uncoupling, single parenthood, serial monogamy, job uncertainty, and a host of other forms of disruption and complication previously unknown. CoDA is not out to stem this tide; it is helping people adapt to it. It may even *encourage* disruption by making it easier for people to dissolve relationships and lead more flexible lives. For example, while some might look at Paul's "personal growth" and see someone trying to assert his individualism, there is more evidence to see him as someone trying to adapt to the kind of life he must face, which is a life as a divorced father about to begin a second marriage. Should the second marriage end, too (as it is likely to do), Paul will be better prepared for what happens. It would be a mistake to understand this kind of preparation for disruption as something that has long existed in the American character. Moreover, it would be a mistake to blame the group for Paul's divorce. I saw no evidence that CoDA fosters disruption in lives that are unruffled, for those who lead such lives would not be attracted to what the group offers. Rather, CoDA appeals to people who, like Paul, Liz, Richard, and Susan, must live with disruption. Granted, the adjustment can sometimes go to extremes, as it did with Richard. More typically, however, CoDA helps people come to sensible terms with disruption once it has already occurred. In short, CoDA is not equipping people to buck the system, but to live peaceably with the system's bucking.

CoDA is also helping people live with the system's failures. The group is not fostering individualism as much as it is helping people adjust when its promises fail them. Recall that, in Alex's case, the economic, professional, and romantic accomplishments that have long been taken-for-granted aspects of American adulthood had eluded him. In CoDA, Alex found a way to live with that disappointment. Susan, as well, found in CoDA a way to accept the reality of her circumstances, instead of feeling overwhelmed by the lack of a successful career and lasting marriage. Both Alex and Susan adjusted to significant disappointment through belonging to the group. This does not imply that they can be summarily dismissed as conformists, however. They simply learned from other members of the group who had already weathered similar transitions.

To describe the group in which this learning takes place as a current manifestation of a characteristic American need for association is to describe it inaccurately. The Institution "lite" is not another way of satisfying a gnawing "hunger to belong." It is indicative of new appetites altogether, which were unknown in Tocqueville's era. Belonging to CoDA means something very different from belonging to the PTA, the Jaycees, or the Garden Club. While the clubs that Tocqueville observed as characteristically American eventually led people into broader civic involvement, CoDA does nothing of the sort. Most of the members of CoDA have relocated often enough to find civic involvement impractical. Others may view such involvement with suspicion. In any case, CoDA's distance from a civic tradition does not justify jumping to the conclusion that the group encourages the detached behavior that Putnam calls "Bowling Alone" (1995).[1] Some of its members may indeed bowl alone, but not because CoDA has prompted them to do so. As an Institution "lite," CoDA has other purposes altogether. Chief among these is offering a portable form of association that dovetails with failures of social-structural support that were unknown to previous generations of Americans.

The evidence that I saw and heard in CoDA dissuaded me from spinning yet another chapter in the continuing saga of American individualism. It suggested, instead, that there are many ways of "being" an individual, and that individualism exists in dynamic tension with numerous other ideas. No single idea—practiced in excess or deficiency—is responsible for producing either the codependency discourse or the problems to which it responds. Most CoDA members would disagree with this. They would describe the group as an antidote to a "dysfunctional" society. Indeed, for many, this is what CoDA seems to accomplish. But it is doing something more and something different. Codependency, as a phenomenon, should not be understood as an antidote for what is wrong or an alternative to what is missing, but as a way of giving meaning to what is here. Codependency's appeal lies in its capacity for helping people create meaningful lives, especially when their sources of meaning have become unreliable. As the previous chapters have shown, the *meaning* of that meaning can vary. The process of creating it does not vary, however; human beings create meaning narratively. Meaningful lives are the premise and the result of the stories you tell about yourself, to yourself as well as to others. On the weight of evidence, this story of the appeal of codependency, as a cultural phenomenon, is *particularly* convincing.

If Americans grow up assuming that they are individuals, possessed of autonomous selves, if selfhood does not need to be put to the test, why even *talk* of the self, much less worry about its meaning? To some readers, these questions will seem hopelessly dated. "Mutability" has allegedly been taken to such extremes that it no longer makes sense to speak of the self as an entity that you can "have." In its place, postmodern men and women have become tricksters or shape-shifters, becoming what they need to be, according to their own standards. They simply pick up and dispose of identities more or less at whim, drawing from sources so diverse that selfhood can no longer be thought of as something that you possess.

Among the people I met in CoDA, the self is alive and well. They wanted no part of ad hoc identities, but longed for a coherent sense of who they are, instead. Although I readily characterize selfhood as a series of stories, this is not how the members of CoDA would see it. They cling to the idea of a "true" self, deep within them—a very modern image of selfhood, characterized by a search for a continuous, authentic character. They struggle with questions of "Who am I?" in an enduring sense, not just "Who am I today?" or "Who am I with this person?" They make subjective statements such as "I am a good person," not viewing those qualities as fleeting, useful only in passing situations, but as lasting ones. Their stories suggest a belief in an essential self, not fragmentation. Indeed, they had come face to face with fragmentation, and were not one bit pleased about it. In response, they devote themselves to cultivating a sense that they are now somehow what they always were and will be. CoDA offered them a chance at authenticity, and they took it. Through the discourse's emotional basis for morality, they have access to what is perhaps the last remaining way to justify your decisions and preferences as thoroughly and unquestionably your own.

Circumstances will surely change, as the members of CoDA know well, but they will *somehow* remain the same, in James's "peculiarly subtle" sense. Perhaps they will even improve with experience. In either case, the sense of what we "are" can only be brought to bear through stories, especially those we tell in "internal conversations." Throughout this work, I have held to the claim that selfhood is accomplished in the stories that people tell others and themselves. People can somehow remain the same because they preserve what they "are" in stories. They improve in the same way, through incorporating what they have endured and overcome, and how they have changed, into their stories. This is not to diminish the role of experience, for without it, your stories would be merely fantasies. But experience is given weight through narrative— especially, but not solely, through those that you convincingly tell your- self. This is what makes for a meaningful life. For understanding the process of making it, stories are indispensable sources of data.

I came to this understanding when the existing terms used to discuss selfhood failed to capture what people described. Because researchers lack direct access to any such entity called the self, depictions of its supposed location or "behavior" will always miss a step. Those who as- sume the existence of the self mistake the topic for the resource (Zim- merman and Pollner 1970). Instead of presupposing that the self exists and asking, for example, where it is located, more productive questions would ask what makes the experience of selfhood possible. As Maines (1993) puts it, the process of self-abstraction—of *having* a self—can best be understood in terms of narrative. "The self-abstracted person . . . is one who has acquired a biography and thereby can tell his or her life story. A person thus is defined as a self-narrating organism" (23; see also Gergen and Gergen 1988; Polkinghorne 1991). If selfhood is a narrative achievement, stories offer the first empirical access to it. The self is not dead. It lives in the stories people tell.

As a field of study, narrative has long been the domain of fields other than sociology. For the most part, stories were studied by the humani- ties, while the social sciences sought more "objective" data.[2] Perhaps stories were considered too subjective for the kind of knowledge sought by social science. Or they were assumed to convey unreliable informa- tion, and the narrators were not representative of a particular "universe" (see Plummer 1990). Moreover, stories do not often lend themselves to the causal and nomothetic explanations favored by social science (see Somers 1994, 614; see also Maines 1993). Admittedly, stories are not suited to all types of social scientific research. But for understanding the social origins of subjective experience, they are ideal. For this rea- son, there has recently been a surge of interest in the study of narratives among qualitative researchers. This raises the question of what sociology can bring to the task. It makes sense to suggest that it should bring what it does best, which is the analysis of culture, social structure, and Institutions.

One of the weaknesses of narrative study as it has been done in the humanities is that it usually focuses on representational aspects applied to epistemological purposes. A given narrative is broken down into its constituent elements, and the reader or listener is presumed to appropriate the tale as a means of knowing what to do. He or she substitutes him or herself for the character in the story, and learns to behave as the character might. But knowing what to do depends largely on knowing who you are, and this knowledge is always situated in networks of Institutions and structure. Moreover, what you do with that knowledge depends on your "repertoire" of capacities, desires, needs, skills, and habits—or the "tool kit" known as culture. You do not simply pick a story, any story. To be sure, each person has a range of narratives available for accounting for his or her life. Ultimately, however, your alternatives are limited by individual structural circumstances, which determine the narrative formulas that you may need, and by culture, which determines what you will do with a given narrative formula. For example, consider a formula such as the one CoDA offers. The person who, like Paul, has a new relationship to move into will develop a story that justifies that action. The person who, like Richard, has experienced a failure of social structure will develop a story that justifies that failure. Paul would not tell a story like Richard's because doing so would mean the end of his relationship. His range of possible stories is limited by the structures within which he moves. Likewise, Richard could not tell a story like Paul's; he is not "learning to love, for real." The absence of social structure in his life has led Richard to create a story with a very different meaning. Neither man created a narrative by simply substituting himself for an existing character in an existing plot or inventing a fanciful story out of thin air. Rather, both men adapted an Institutionalized formula to the structure they faced, using the tools at hand. In short, we "come to be who we are (however ephemeral, multiple, and changing) by being located or locating ourselves (usually unconsciously) in social narratives rarely of our own making" (Somers 1994, 606). Our narratives cannot transcend our resources, but they can allow us to make the best of them.

Ironically, what sociology can contribute to the study of self-narrative is what has supposedly declined in importance for selfhood. But the argument that Institutions have lost their ability to define the self reflects the leanings of those who tell that particular story. It is also an argument that cannot be sustained. If you believe that people now take on and discard fragments of what the world has to offer, then, as I see it, you are left with two ways of thinking about the experience of "personhood." One possibility is that the person is nothing more than a container for a stimulus and response process, which leads people to enact "appropriate" identities. This hollow view of the person leaves no way to account for change and conflict. This objection aside, if there *were* such a process at work, it would have to allow people to accomplish certain tasks. It would have to respond to—or create—Institutions.

Another possibility is that something or someone orchestrates the action, some presocial homunculus, spirit, or force within each person. Whatever this is—and I picture the Wizard of Oz when Toto pulls back the curtain—it must have some basis for choosing among alternative courses of action. If this were truly a wise and powerful something or someone, then it, too, would allow people to accomplish certain tasks. And it, too, would lead back to Institutions.

If it were the case that Institutions had indeed lost their ability to define the self, I would not have found people who, when faced with the loss of Institutional anchors in their lives, hurried to restore structure and regain affiliation. If contemporary selfhood were truly "mutable" and fragmented, I would not have found a group of people dedicated to crafting stories that they themselves found convincing. I would also not have found people who strove to create seamless narratives that made the present seem like the logical outcome of the past, no matter how traumatic. What sociology can contribute to the study of narratives is an understanding of how they are shaped by Institutions. Sociology can also show how Institutions have changed, and reckon with new forms such as the Institution "lite."

The appearance of the Institution "lite," as well as the discourse that supports it, does suggest something about Americans that is entirely consistent with claims that have long been made about them. If codependency, as a cultural phenomenon, says anything about Americans, it says that they are remarkably durable and optimistic. They believe that they deserve to live lives that are better than the ones they have. They also believe that they have the ability to figure out how to do so. This is the promise of modernity. Americans may live in a postmodern world, but a good number of them seem to understand their relationship to it in very modern terms. They invent ways of accounting for even the most chaotic events of their lives.

One striking thing I have learned about the experience of selfhood—through this research, but also through conversations—is that the idea of an inner self seems inviolable. A few dedicated postmodernists notwithstanding, most people continue to cherish an image of a "true" self that directs their actions, not in a mechanical sense, but in ways that are consistent with an overall meaning and purpose of an individual life. This image holds tremendous power, perhaps because of its connection to the idea of a soul. More likely, the idea of a "true," inner self persists because the possibility that the self is nothing more than its description of itself is so perplexing. It can also be frightening. Most people have no difficulty accepting a narrative concept of the self, in theory, but they have great difficulty putting that idea to the test in their own subjective experience of themselves. Without the comforting delusion that there is a permanent basis for their narratives, people must either collapse in panic or shoulder the burden for creating their own meaning. There may be a handful of postmodern theorists who feel comfortable proclaiming the death of the self, but there are far more people who have heard that story and do not want to believe it. For this majority, the more convincing—and meaningful—stories will continue to be those of the "true" self.

INFORMED CONSENT AND FIELDWORK
IN TWELVE STEP GROUPS

Codependent Forevermore reports the results of ethnographic research. The project required this type of study. I could not have surveyed a representative population of people who identify with codependency. I also could not have learned what codependency says about selfhood from reading a sample of the popular advice books. In order to learn what takes place among codependents, I had to go to CoDA. Once there, I had to become a participant—or, at least, look like one. This is an account of my experience. I think it is worth reporting not only because it was so different from the experience that I intended to have, but because of what that difference reveals about the assumptions underlying "ethical" sociological research.

> *Friday March 24, 1995.* Just got kicked out of a meeting. Well, I didn't get kicked out exactly, but it became very obvious to me that I should leave. I **had** to leave. Forced out, kicked out, same thing. I wanted to get in with this group because they hang out a lot afterwards at the diner, in a huge group. A very big, very social group. It took me almost a year to get comfortable there. Now I have enemies. *(excerpt from fieldnotes)*

On this particular March night, we had arrived at the moment in the meeting when the leader asks the group if anyone has any announcements to make. Several times before, I had planned to announce that I wanted to interview people and had lost my courage each time. Tonight, however, I felt more sure of myself, probably because Laura led the meeting that night. I liked her. I saw her as a kindred spirit of sorts, since she looked about my age and she had just gone back to college. I took her leading the meeting as a good sign. Looking back, I see why I don't usually put any stock in signs.

"There's a new Step Study starting, and you have two more weeks to sign up," said a guy named Jim. "It involves a big commitment, because they ask that you stick with it through all Twelve Steps. You have to buy a workbook and you really should do all the assignments. I left some flyers on the table for anyone who wants to check it out."

Jim took his recovery very seriously. He served as the treasurer of this particular group, and he went to several other CoDA meetings each week, as well. He got involved with planning all the social events. Because he had contact with so many groups, he always had announcements to make. Tall and burly, I thought of him as "*Big* Jim," not just "Jim." He hung around with a short, chubby, balding guy named Glen, and together, they made something of a Stan-and-Ollie pair.

Laura thanked him and, while looking around the circle, asked if anyone else wanted to announce anything. I felt my heart speed up a bit. I had given up a lot of Friday evenings to fieldwork, and the payoff hinged on what I was about to do. If I kept quiet, I could continue to approach individual members for interviews. It would take a considerable amount of time, since each approach required an icebreaking conversation in which I tried to get a sense of whether the person might be willing to be interviewed. If I announced that I wanted to do interviews, I could conceivably "recruit" a number of people in one night, but I would run the risk of inciting those members who thought researchers had no business being in the group. I mustered the courage and raised my hand.

"I have an announcement," I said out loud. Thirty-nine pairs of eyes looked in my direction. "A few of you know that I'm writing a dissertation on codependency. I've interviewed about a dozen people, and I need to talk to more. I'd like to pass around this notebook, and if you want to do an interview with me, write down your name and phone number, and I'll call you and make an appointment." As I finished my sentence, a rush of chatter erupted to my right.

"I'm not comfortable with this."

"I feel violated."

"Yeah, me too," said Big Jim. "How did you get in here?"

"Are you impersonating a Ph.D.?" Glen asked, not realizing how close to home his remark could strike.

"I'm a graduate student in sociology," I said. "I'm doing research for my Ph.D. I want to interview people about how codependency and recovery work in their lives. I've talked to a few people here already. Because this is a big group, I thought I could make one announcement, rather than approaching people one at a time."

"But did you come here as a doctorate or a codependent?" Glen asked.

"Now wait a minute," Richard cut in, much to my relief. I had always liked him. He was the closest I had come to having a "Doc" or a "Tally," the exemplary gatekeepers of classic sociological field studies. His easygoing manner made him the first person I had approached for an interview. He gave Glen an answer that I would not have thought to give: "If you heard her talk in small group," he said, "you'd know she's codependent. I did an interview with her, and it really helped me."

"Richard, I don't care if it helped you," Big Jim responded. "She should have brought this up in a business meeting first." If anyone would want to follow a set of procedures, Jim would.

"Oh, come on," Richard said. "You know what would happen. Nobody comes to the business meetings. If it bothers you, just don't sign up for an interview." Later, Richard would tell me that he and Jim had locked horns on a few matters before. "He can really push my buttons," he said, with a look that betrayed a history of disagreement.

While the discussion continued, a woman on my left leaned towards me, took my notebook and pen from my hand, and quietly said, "Let's start passing this around." She signed up for an interview, and the book began to make its way around the circle.

By this time, the group had split into three factions. Some members, like Richard, supported me. They understood that the interviews were voluntary, and those who objected should simply not sign up. Others felt violated by my mere presence in the meeting. They felt betrayed by the fact that I had "come out," in a manner of speaking, as a person they might not want in their midst. They felt threatened by the fact that I wanted to study them. I explained that I wanted to respect the anonymity that Twelve Step groups provide their members, but in order to learn about the group, I wanted people to tell me their stories for the record, on audiotape. I explained that the university's Committee on Research Involving Human Subjects had approved the project. I explained the consent procedure. I told them that I removed all names and identifying references when I transcribed the tapes. I said that each person would receive a transcript of the interview, and if anyone thought I had misquoted or misinterpreted him or her, I would listen to the tape again. If necessary, we would listen to it together. I would do what I could to put things right.

"I trust her," said a woman sitting next to Richard.

"I don't know who she is," Big Jim replied.

"She's been coming to this meeting for months," someone said in my defense.

A third faction—about a half dozen or so people—voiced their objections to the way I had made the announcement. Big Jim's sidekick Glen raised the issue of the business meeting again. Once more, Richard came to my defense. "But no one ever stays for the business meetings, Glen. You know that. It wouldn't do her any good."

Richard's point was something I had already realized. In CoDA, the "business" meeting does not have the power that its title might suggest outside of Twelve Step circles. Those who volunteer to attend these meetings do not speak for or have authority over their groups. Any proposal brought before a business meeting has to be approved at individual meetings, anyway. The experience of another sociologist shows where this can lead. Rice (1996) identified himself as a researcher at one of the many CoDA meetings he visited. The members asked him to leave the room while they voted on whether to let him stay. They decided in his favor, but they had to repeat the vote each time a member arrived late, and they would have to repeat the entire procedure each time he attended. Rice and the members agreed that this interfered with the meeting, and he stopped attending. From then on, he simply observed the meetings of other groups. The business meeting, I knew, was a replication of this process.

"What if I *had* done that?" I said, looking towards Jim and Glen. "What if I *had* gone to the business meeting, and they gave me permission to make the announcement, but you hadn't been there to get in on the decision. I'd have done things your way but still come out wrong. I talked to someone from Intergroup," I said, explaining that I had sent a packet of materials—sample interview questions, a consent form, a copy of my approval from the university—to the CoDA committee that makes decisions that affect local groups. I had done this out of ignorance of how Twelve Step groups work. The representative who had spoken to me had said that Intergroup could not make decisions for individual groups. While he personally did not think I should use meetings for my research, only the individual groups could decide for themselves. "This seemed like the only way to do it," I said, somewhat apologetically. "A group announcement made sense to me. I didn't mean to offend anyone. You don't have to sign up for an interview if you don't want to."

By now, the meeting had dissolved into near chaos, with everyone talking at once. I began to regret my decision to speak up.

"How else could I have done it?" I asked. "I tried it at the Wednesday meeting, and they had no trouble with it."

"Well, we're not Wednesday," said Big Jim.

"Jim, you're not listening to her," said Richard. "She knows we're not Wednesday. How was she supposed to know what would happen unless she tried?"

I told them that, since I did not want to make anyone uncomfortable, when I got my notebook back, I would leave. That brought on another wave of discussion. A number of members felt uncomfortable about making me so uncomfortable that I felt I had to leave. Big Jim also took the lead in this. "We don't want you to leave," he said. "We didn't mean to make you feel like you had to leave." By then, I had run out of patience. I said, "Maybe you should have thought about that earlier." I walked across the room to collect my notebook.

As I recrossed the room for my coat, a man I had never seen before stood up and spoke. He said that he had come to that particular meeting for the first time that night, and would never come back again. "How is anybody going to learn anything about CoDA if you get so worried about having somebody study you?" he said to the group. The whole thing made him sick, he said, so he wanted to leave, too. He and I left the room together. As we did, three more members followed me, wanting to sign up for interviews. Like autograph seekers in reverse, they grabbed my notebook out of my hands as I headed down the narrow hallway that led out.

The man who left with me—call him Don—suggested that we sit in the lobby for a while so that I could calm down before driving home. I felt absolutely drained, and yet agitated at the same time. I have driven in that adrenaline high before and I know what it does to my ability to pay attention, so I took his advice. He made an obvious effort to distance himself from what had happened. He told me that he usually goes to another Twelve Step group, Families Anonymous, and he thought that they would welcome me there. He described them as "much nicer people." He called this group "a bunch of Lilliputians, looking to see which side of the egg they should crack." He clearly disliked Big Jim and Glen, and he spat out something about how "those two, the ringleaders, run the whole show."

Don and I sat in the dim lobby for a few minutes. I sprawled on a secondhand brocade sofa. Don sat in an armchair to my left. I found it hard to hold my head up. I tried to rest it on the back of the sofa, but I could not focus on Don when I did. He talked about his family and his job as a salesman. I listened with only one ear for the first few minutes while my mind raced on its own. What would this mean for my research? What would I do now that I had blown it with this group? What would happen with the people who also go to other meetings? Would they still talk to me?

After a few minutes, the sound of laughter came from the meeting room. I did not know if it meant anything for me, and if so, what, but it came as a great relief. At the very least, I thought, the group had moved on. Meanwhile, Don continued to talk about his family and his job. His son abused drugs, he told me, in a very candid and direct, but practiced, delivery. "My son is a drug addict." Later, after I had written up my notes, I realized what I had seen there. I had not tried to steer Don with what few interview skills I could have mustered in that state. I had not needed to. He had gone to the meeting to talk about his troubles with people who would not flinch at the messy side of life. The meeting had not gone the way he expected, but he would still talk. He had a listener, and he used the opportunity. He had to practice his line—"My son is a drug addict"—until he could say it without shame. I would hear that same delivery from other people in CoDA: "My son is a drug addict"; "My mother was in and out of mental hospitals"; "I never knew my father"; "I had a nervous breakdown"; "I attempted suicide." I heard them interpret these parts of their lives through "dysfunction," "abuse," "codependency," and "recovery," rehearsing the script until they could successfully deliver their lines. It takes a lot of practice, which usually comes through sharing. Having missed his opportunity to share, Don practiced there, on me.

We sat for a while, with him talking and me listening, and eventually, I felt calm enough to drive home. As I collected my things, a man named Allen walked out of the meeting room and joined us. He said that it had taken him a while, but he had decided to leave, too, and the incident had upset him so that he would not come back to that particular group. I had seen Allen several times before. Our paths had crossed at this meeting and at other locations, as well. I always felt a little uncomfortable around him because I sensed his attraction to me, and I did not feel the same in return. His liking me put me in a very awkward position. While I did not want to encourage him, I could not avoid him, either.

I knew that he, like the other members of the group, had things to teach me. When he signed up for an interview, I had my suspicions. A few days later, when I called him to set up an appointment, he responded far too enthusiastically. He suggested that I come to his apartment for the interview. I said that I preferred to meet over coffee at a diner in his neighborhood. I wanted the neutrality and safety of a public place. He explained that his car insurance had just lapsed and he did not want to risk driving, and besides, he could make me a cup of coffee. Feeling boxed in, I agreed to interview him at home. When I pulled up at his address, I saw him waiting proudly for me out front, dressed in the only outfit I had ever seen him wear. As we sat at his cluttered kitchen table, my tape recorder between us, he told me about the "violent impulse" he felt towards me. My mind went numb. I stared at my notes and tried to buy some time by asking him to explain what he meant. He said that he wanted to punch me in the nose, but laughed it off as "misplaced affection." Later in the interview, he would show me a two-month-old scar on his neck, inflicted by the knife-wielding young woman he wanted to call his girlfriend. Later still, after he asked me if I had a man in my life, I placed a fake phone call to a mythical "boyfriend," who ostensibly waited for my safe and immediate return.

I called all the people who signed up for interviews on that chaotic Friday night within two days. I knew better than to let too much time elapse, or their enthusiasm and interest would disappear. I had seen most of those who signed up at meetings before, but a few I had not. I knew these others only as first names and voices over the phone. As I drove to the home of one man in this category, the reality of what my lack of knowledge involved hit me squarely in the gut. He lived some distance away, in an area where the suburban landscape quickly becomes rural. I drove an unfamiliar, two-lane road that, according to my map, did not intersect another main road for several miles. The distance between houses gradually grew wider and wider, some of it peppered with horses and old American cars up on blocks. After a while, I passed no convenience stores, no gas stations, no telephones. I repeatedly checked the directions he had given me against my map; yes, I should keep going. Finally, I saw his house number on a mailbox and turned in the dirt driveway. All manner of objects littered the property: rusted barrels, bicycles, broken furniture, a swing set minus the swings, several defunct barbecue grills, and, against one corner of the sagging porch stood my personal favorite, a naked, armless, female mannequin with a chip in her forehead. Three mangy dogs headed for my truck as I inched it toward the house. I stopped trusting dogs two years ago after a "friendly" German shepherd attacked me. I sat paralyzed, with the windows rolled up. I tapped the horn and saw the screen door at the front of the house swing open. A man stepped on to the porch, clapped his hands, and called the dogs off. I thanked him as I got out of the truck. "They won't hurt you," he said. "They just want to check you out." He wore faded jeans that came up to a sizeable stomach, over which strained a plaid flannel shirt and down vest. The requisite baseball cap— worn even in the house—shaded his puffy eyes and completed what makes for something of a uniform in areas such as this. He had not shaved that morning, nor, it seemed, for several mornings before. He had lived alone in the house since his wife had taken their four children and moved in with her mother. Within the first few seconds of the interview, he told me that he had not had a drink in a week, and he would soon enter a counseling program for husbands who batter. I drank countless cups of his strong coffee to keep my mouth from going bone-dry.

The interview went very smoothly; I had nothing whatsoever to fear from him. But the experience shook me, and afterwards, on the advice of friends, I left the addresses and phone numbers on my refrigerator when I left for an interview, just in case.

IT'S NOT JUST A JOB, IT'S AN ADVENTURE

When I thought about studying CoDA, I had not imagined that I would be forced to leave meetings or that I would interview strange men who were potentially violent. I did not—and still do not—think of CoDA as a risky research setting, and I am not trying to win any kudos for the unexpected dangers that I faced. Rather, I recount these instances to make a point about the unbridgeable chasm between the assumptions that sociologists often hold about how the world works, which are reinforced by the process of seeking permission to carry out our research, and how it actually does work. I went into the field intending to identify myself as a sociologist. I thought I would get permission from group leaders and openly recruit subjects for interviews. I found myself in a group in which outside identities count for nothing, in which there are no leaders who have authority to grant permission, and in which the open recruiting of subjects constitutes a violation of the group's norms.

Although I knew of CoDA's anonymous tradition before I began my research, I had not foreseen what it would mean for me as a researcher. Because little empirical work on CoDA existed, the literature offered no guidance, and I did not want to assume that the findings from studies of AA would necessarily apply to CoDA. To learn about the group, I would have to attend meetings. I could not do so, however—at least not as a researcher—without first having permission from my university's Committee on Research Involving Human Subjects. Even though CoDA meetings are open to the public, I did not want to appear to be "just checking it out," only to turn up later as a researcher. I sought the required approval to do the research, and in doing so began to presuppose a formality that did not exist in the setting I proposed to study.

As most readers will know, since the 1970s, the Department of Health, Education, and Welfare has regulated social research in the United States in keeping with the National Research Act (DHEW 1974, 1978). These regulations emerged in response to decades of research that put participants at considerable risk without their knowledge. The better-known instances of research prior to regulation include the Nazi abuses, the Tuskegee Syphilis Study, the Jewish Chronic Disease Hospital Case, and the Willowbrook State School controversy (see Faden and Beauchamp 1986, chapter 5). In psychology, Milgram's research on obedience stands out. In sociology, the best-known studies are Vidich and Bensman's *Small Town in Mass Society* ([1958] 1968) and Humphreys's work entitled *Tearoom Trade* (1970). Out of these and other cases, the U.S. developed a set of policies requiring the consent of those participating in research. In addition, individual disciplines developed professional codes of ethics. To enforce the new consent requirements, universities established Institutional Review Boards (IRBs) that review proposed research. IRB applications typically require a discussion of the scientific significance and goals of the study, an estimate of the number of "subjects" involved, an explanation of how the researcher intends to recruit them, a discussion of potential risks and benefits they may face, and a description of how the researcher intends to obtain their consent. All institutions and projects that receive federal funding must comply with these regulations, which also apply to research carried out by students.

Qualitative researchers have questioned the feasibility of answering these sorts of questions about the research before it is carried out (see Cassell 1978, 1980; Emerson 1983; Thorne 1980; Wax 1980, 1983). As Wax puts it, "To know the exact questions to study and the precise procedures for studying is in fact to know most of the answers" (1983, 294–

95). Fine adds, drawing on Glaser and Strauss's *Discovery of Grounded Theory* (1967), "that good ethnographers do not know what they are looking for until they have found it" (1993, 274). The ability to obtain the consent of those being studied has also been a source of continuing debate among sociologists (see Erikson 1967, 1995, 1996; Fine 1993; Leo 1995, 1996; Punch 1983; Thorne 1980; Roth 1962; Wax 1980, 1983). Indeed, recent controversy over deception in field studies has been portrayed as something of an academic scandal (see Allen 1997).

Human-subject regulations protect innocent people from undue harm at the hands of unprincipled or overzealous researchers. In my experience, however, they can constitute a force that shapes research according to a formality that does not exist in many groups. In settings such as experiments, focus groups, and surveys, that formality does exist. The researcher can assume an "official" identity and "subjects" can be openly recruited. In other settings, however, a researcher cannot interrupt routinely occurring social interaction to explain what he or she is doing and ask for consent. Presupposing the right to do so shows little sensitivity to the dynamics of the group one hopes to understand. Sometimes, identifying oneself as a researcher can be more problematic than engaging in covert observation—something I had not anticipated when I began my research.

I started out by trying to get blanket permission to do the research from an official gatekeeper in CoDA. Organizations are hierarchical, I thought, so I will go to the top. I had already spoken with someone at CoDA's headquarters in Arizona often enough to know that they had no authority over individual groups, so I found "Codependents Anonymous" in the local phone book and called the number. I left a message after the recording of area meeting times and locations. A few days later, I received a call from a man who identified himself as the chair of Intergroup, the committee that orchestrates joint functions among CoDA groups in the area I was studying. I told him I wanted permission to do my research. He said that he could not help me because Intergroup had no power over individual groups. Indeed, it was becoming clear to me that no organizational body or individual in CoDA has authority over individual groups. He said that researchers—mostly therapists—had studied CoDA before and it "had not gone well." Some people feel like guinea pigs, he said, and others "grandstand," hoping to appear in somebody's book or article. Both behaviors violate the principles of the group. I pressed him to help me find a way to do the research. Perhaps I pressed too much, however, because he encouraged me to start going to the meetings, but to go for what he saw as my obvious "codependent tendencies." He asked if I agreed that I was codependent. I knew better than to say that I did not; any "denial" would only indicate to him the depth of my codependency. I said that I probably had my share of "issues" to work through, but my real interest was in studying CoDA. As our conversation ended, I was convinced that I could seek permission from the "leaders" of individual groups.

I went to my first meeting expecting to do just this. Groups have leaders, I thought; I would find someone in charge. I believed that the credibility attributed to the word "research" would open doors for me. I planned to sit and watch the meeting without disturbing the interaction. I had with me a stack of IRB-approved flyers asking for volunteers for interviews. I hoped that, after I announced who I was and what I was doing, I could hand the flyers out to the members, who would welcome a curious scholar into their midst. Instead, I found no one in charge. "Leading" a CoDA meeting consists of reading a standard, printed text. The "position," such as it is, is voluntary. It lasts only for one meeting and has no power attached to it. As the meeting began, I waited for the moment at which I could make my introduction. I soon discovered that CoDA meetings purposely have no such moment. Those in attendance introduce themselves using first names only. I quickly realized that it would have been a gross violation of the group's norms to have given my full name and mentioned my occupation. It took only seconds for me to understand that I would have disrupted the meeting if I did what I planned to do.

Even if I *had* been able to make an introduction, I would have had no idea who my audience was. Not only had I not found anyone in charge, I had not found anything that I could readily call "The Group." There are no means through which to identify official "members" of CoDA. I could not tell those who had made a commitment to the group from those who were only marginally involved or just "checking it out." For all I knew, most of the others were there doing research, too. I sat through that first meeting in stunned silence, seeing my best-laid plans fail at every turn. Without a gatekeeper at the organizational level or at the meeting itself, and with an introduction out of the question, I would have to find another way. I would also have to keep coming to meetings in order to find it.

Initially, I thought that the time set aside for announcements might be the place in which to announce my research, say that I wanted to do interviews, and pass out my flyers. I waited for a few weeks until I had a better sense of the scene. I gradually discovered problems with this strategy, too. CoDA, like other Twelve Step groups, does not promote or endorse any outside concerns. This is explicitly stated in the Twelve Traditions, which are read at every meeting. All the announcements made at meetings have to do with Twelve Step activities. As I became familiar with the group, I realized that my research would count as an "outside" concern. This also ruled out distributing my flyers or even leaving them in the meeting room. The only literature available at meetings has to do with the Twelve Steps and Traditions. CoDA does not promote any causes or accept any outside sponsorship. A person cannot simply leave brochures on a table at a meeting. In short, although the announcement and the flyers had seemed like perfectly neutral tactics to me—and to the IRB—they became controversial in that particular setting.

During the first few meetings that I attended, I tried to absorb as much as possible about the group's interaction. Soon, however, I realized that would have to change, too. CoDA's meeting format encourages everyone to "share." The codependency discourse claims that codependents put everyone else's wants and needs before their own (see Beattie 1987, 1989). On occasion, someone will pass up the chance to share, but doing so is thought to foster the codependent behavior that one goes to CoDA to overcome. Sharing is the means for the "identification and hope" seen as essential for recovery (CoDA 1989). Consistently not sharing would be so unusual as to arouse the suspicions of those at the meeting (*"Why can't we hear about **her** experiences?"*). Moreover, silent observation would have defeated my research goals. The kind of knowledge I sought about group interaction required sustained attendance, which in turn required participation. I could not have said that I only wanted to learn more about CoDA over the entire course of my research. Rapping (1996) used this strategy to study several Twelve Step groups. It made her feel less "sleazy" than outright deception, which she initially tried, but she found maintaining silence over time both "awkward" and "anxiety provoking" (1996, 95).

In sharing, I did not have to lie, as I would have if I had tried to "pass" in Alcoholics Anonymous or other Twelve Step programs. Given the ambiguity of the concept of codependency, I had absolutely no trouble finding things to talk about. I suspect most other adults would find this the case, as well. Concurrent with my research, my five-year, live-in relationship ended. Before that, I had experienced a divorce. I came to CoDA fully qualified to talk about failed relationships. I met other requirements, too. As the elder daughter of two hardworking professionals, responsibility and competence were expected of me from an early age. My sister and I were latchkey kids before the term was in use. My parents divorced when I was a teenager. In CoDA, that combination indicates a wounded "inner child." I do not like to disappoint people and will often do things for the sake of being a good sport, which makes me a "people-pleaser." In many areas, I would describe myself as an overachiever. When I know how to do something, I tend to take over. In the language of CoDA, that translates into "control issues." In short, I did not have to embellish any of the events in my life. As I have argued in preceding chapters, the concept of codependency has sufficient leeway to accommodate almost anyone's life history; therein lies much of its appeal. This also makes it difficult to claim that you are not codependent. In CoDA, you are either codependent or in denial. As Ramona Asher explains, codependency's "generality and vagueness make individual resistance to or rejection of the label difficult" (1992, 191). Although my sharing inevitably led the members to think that I identified with codependency in the same way that they did, I saw no way around this situation. For my part, I simply hoped that the words of Herbert Gans would ring true for me: "Most people are too busy living to take much notice of a participant-observer once he [or she] has proven to them that he [or she] means no harm" (1982, 405).

While I did not find it hard to think of things to say at meetings, I did find it difficult to actually speak. I did not like confiding in strangers. As one woman in the group once put it, the talk in CoDA comes "from the gut." Typically, I spill my guts only to my closest of friends. The one-dimensionality of the interaction grated on me. I knew the people in CoDA—and they knew me—mostly as a set of problems. Other researchers have found attending CoDA equally unsettling for similar reasons. Carol Warren, for example, "attended one meeting and found the experience too intense to return" (Mitchell-Norberg, Warren, and Zale 1995, 129).

Even though I found it relatively easy to talk the CoDA talk, I did not find it easy to interact with the members knowing that I was not walking the walk. I cringed when others thanked me for something I had shared in a meeting, or when a member told me that I had said something that she "really needed to hear." I could not have foreseen that I would contribute to anyone's recovery program. I wanted to say,

"Don't pay any attention to me. I'm just a sociologist." I wanted to tell them that I did not really believe I had a problem, but my resistance would only have signaled to them the depth of my need to be there.

FALLACIES OF INFORMED CONSENT

Initially, of course, I had not anticipated ending up in this predicament. I assumed that I could rely on the safety of detached observation. In the field, however, I could not act on that assumption. My transformation from open observer to participant and covert observer raised some important sociological issues.

There are strong reasons why it is usually preferable to give people the information they need to consent to participate in a study. While insisting on informed consent makes good sense in principle, however, it often makes little sense in practice. It reveals a striking lack of reflection on the realities of lived experience. Most everyday social settings lack clear points at which consent becomes an issue. These points do not suddenly become clearer when researchers arrive on the scene. Obtaining informed consent becomes a sociological impossibility, as does the open recruitment of "human subjects."

Regulations for the protection of "human subjects" are based on a model of experimentation. They assume a formal setting in which a researcher can openly disclose his or her identity to less powerful "subjects," who, on an individual basis, consent or refuse to participate in the research. Informed consent, in principle, not only assumes that a researcher knows what he or she is looking for, it assumes that he or she is looking for the same information from each person. In the context of qualitative research, this kind of prescience seems absurd. But even in the arena in which it originated, informed consent has obvious shortcomings.

As a legal doctrine, informed consent came out of a 1957 California court decision (*Salgo*) that held physicians liable for withholding information necessary for consent to proposed treatment (see Faden and Beauchamp 1986; Lidz et al. 1982; Lidz et al. 1984). With *Salgo*, " 'informed' was tacked onto 'consent,' creating the expression "informed consent" (Faden and Beauchamp 1986, 125). Informed consent is "intended to enable patients to make decisions about their own medical care by requiring physicians to provide them with sufficient information about the risks and benefits of treatments and procedures as well as about alternatives to any proposed treatment or procedure" (Zussman 1992, 82). Even in medicine, however, the assumptions underlying consent seldom correspond with actual practice. Consent assumes "that medical practice is discrete—that is, broken into distinct parts, or decision units—and that there can be consent by the patient to each of these individual parts" (Lidz et al. 1982, 401). In practice, medical treatment takes place on a continuous, not a discrete, basis. Prior treatments change the degree and kind of risk incurred by subsequent treatments, making the possibility of providing truly accurate information about each unlikely. In addition, many patients have no desire to become as involved in the process of consent as the doctrine allows. Others, due to the severity of their illness, simply cannot participate in the decisions that affect them (see Zussman 1992). In short, the concept of informed consent, though intended for use within the practice of medicine, does not articulate with the realities of medicine as practiced.

If consent presupposes a formality that does not exist even in the setting for which it was designed, its pitfalls become even more glaring in informal group settings. Consent assumes that the researcher "confronts a series of individual subjects" (Emerson 1983, 264) over whom he or she has power. In groups, however, researchers confront complex and continuous interaction. As Thorne has explained, "The contours of the natural groups and settings of field research run against the individual model of informed consent" (1980, 264). This continuous quality became clear to me when I started visiting CoDA meetings and saw no way to intervene in the course of events and explain my presence.

Even if I *had* had the opportunity to disclose my identity, I would have had no control over what the members of CoDA made of the information I gave them about myself. In that setting, the power of "Codependent" as something approximating a "master status" would have overridden any other information I could have given. For example, those who knew about my research from my sharing fit their ideas about the research into their understanding of me as a fellow codependent. They assumed that I had an urge to "help" people (a "symptom" of codependency) that had led me both to the group and to my chosen profession. They confused "sociologist" with "social worker" or "therapist," and assumed that my research would help people who "had" codependency. When I explained that I planned to become a university professor, they often responded by saying, "Well, that's helping people, too." I had little power to shape their understanding of my interests. They saw what they were prepared to see, as we all do. They filtered new information through their existing presuppositions.

Similar ambiguities enter into the process of obtaining consent. As Roth (1962) put it, "Even if the subjects of a study are given as precise and detailed an explanation of the purpose and procedure of the study as the investigator is able to give them, the subjects will not understand all the terms of the research in the same way that the investigator does" (284). My stock explanation—and the one that appeared on the consent forms I used in my interviews—was that I was studying "codependency and emotion management." Most of the time, however, even *I* would have been hard-pressed to explain exactly what that meant. Moreover, sometimes I became interested in things far removed from emotion management. In those instances, what was the purpose of the research in which my "subjects" would consent to participate? The "truth" is always far more complicated and difficult to communicate than the concept of informed consent allows.

There will be readers who believe that covert research should not take place. Some will want to argue that ethical regulations should be upheld at all costs. To be sure, informed consent requirements have prevented untold abuses. But, as Bronfenbrenner asserts, "the only safe way to avoid violating principles of professional ethics is to refrain from doing social research altogether" (1952, 453). Thus, the question is not whether to uphold ethical principles, but which principles to uphold. In field studies, this decision cannot be made outside the research setting. Doing so manifests a methodological arrogance that defeats the goals of field research. As my experience shows, the weight of the IRB's regulations, light though it was, gave me an inflated sense of my status as researcher, created through the assumption that I should—and could—seek and obtain the consent of those I wanted to study.

Assuming that one can obtain consent entails additional assumptions about the way interaction occurs and the role that one can have within the group. If one's ideal is detached objectivity, then methods other than field study lead to it more directly. But if one wants to understand what takes place within group settings, it is essential to understand—and respect—the ethical standards of the group. Anything else contradicts the reflexive involvement that ostensibly drew the researcher to the study of natural groups.

The issues of disclosure and consent, along with the companion issue of disguised observation, have often been framed in ethical terms (for the classic example, see Erikson 1967). But framing the issue in ethical terms neglects what I see as the larger issue. While insisting on full disclosure and informed consent makes good *ethical* sense, it makes little *sociological* sense. It reveals an unsociological approach to the world of everyday experience. A person who gets a job in a restaurant, a mental hospital, a porn shop, or an organization and *also* does a sociological study might not discuss the study with his or her employers and coworkers. He or she might not have had access to one of these domains without becoming an employee. But, as Roth argues, most social settings lack a clear point at which consent becomes an issue. He asks, "Is it moral if one gets a job in a factory to earn tuition and then takes advantage of the opportunity to carry out a sociological study, but immoral to deliberately plant oneself in the factory for the express purpose of observing one's fellow workers?" (1962, 284). If we push the idea of disclosure to its logical conclusions, sociologists could produce few ethnographic studies at all.

During one interview, I discussed my predicament with a long-time member of CoDA. She did not see me as having an ulterior motive, for the simple reason that the meetings can accommodate a range of needs that people bring to them.

> People come to CoDA for all sorts of reasons. Not everybody in these rooms is working a program. Some people just need contact. They're lonely. Some people have nothing to do on a Friday or a Monday night. Some people come here looking for a date, or a mate. Some people are just checking it out, and it might take some time for them to figure out if they belong here or not. But CoDA welcomes anyone. We don't ask what your reasons are for coming.

By the IRB's standards, I deceived the people in CoDA by not getting their permission to study them. By the standards of the group, I did not do anything that does not take place in CoDA already, when someone goes to a meeting but does not "work a program." Moreover, seeking their permission would have disrupted the group. The woman quoted above shows a more sociological understanding of the range of interaction that could take place within the group than do most of the guidelines for research.

My decision to misrepresent my purposes to the people I studied evolved in the field. Most sociologists know that decisions about research strategies often take place there, in the thick of things, and not in the office, where the proposals are written. And yet, seldom does the literature on research methods take this discrepancy seriously. The texts that introduce most of us to methods describe versions of the "research wheel," with a chapter on ethics somewhere in the back of the book. Our journals offer sanitized reports of projects smoothly carried out, with discussions of ethical dilemmas reserved for specially dedicated volumes. Our code of ethics suggests discussing potentially problematic situations in our research with knowledgeable colleagues; a sound idea, provided that one anticipates one's problems and does not have to make decisions while in the field. Sociology would benefit from acknowledging the necessity of making ethical decisions in the midst of interaction that is fluid and continuous. In other words, the discipline would benefit from applying what it already knows.

INTRODUCTION

1. Additional works that have influenced my approach to the self include Bruner 1987, 1994; Giddens 1991; McAdams 1993; Mitchell 1981; Neisser and Fivush 1994; Polkinghorne 1988, 1991; and Taylor 1989.

Sociology has recently enjoyed a burgeoning of studies that take narrative seriously, as a topic and a method. Examples include Plummer 1983, 1995; Chase 1995; Karp 1996; Kleinman 1988; and Riessman 1990. For examples in the social sciences, more broadly, see the volumes edited by Mitchell (1981); Rosenwald and Ochberg (1992); and Sarbin (1986); and the Sage Series *The Narrative Study of Lives* (Josselson and Lieblich 1993; Lieblich and Josselson 1994; Josselson and Lieblich 1995; and Josselson 1996).

2. The Serenity Prayer originated in AA. Although used in all Twelve Step groups, it has also become part of mainstream culture, appearing on inspirational decorations of all kinds and all levels of quality.

3. At each meeting, the leader announces that "the Seventh Tradition reminds us that we are self-supporting through our own contributions. We ask that you donate only as you can. Donations are used for meeting expenses, literature, and general CoDA expenses." During the course of my research, I saw no one donate more than $1.00. Should anyone aspire to greater generosity, CoDA's Service Office sets a limit of $1,000 annually per person. In order to avoid alliances with or obligations to outsiders, CoDA, like other Twelve Step groups, accepts no outside contributions. The Service Office recognizes "that nothing can so surely destroy our spiritual heritage as futile disputes over property, money, and authority" (CoDA 1992, 4). Individual groups are instructed not to maintain more than "*a prudent reserve,* usually one or two months expenses" (emphasis original). If any balance remains, each group should send 60 percent to Intergroup, 30 percent to the Service Office, and 10 percent to the State committee. Quarterly financial reports appear in each issue of CoDA's magazine, *Co-NNECTIONS,* along with a "Financial Bill of Rights" that grants members the right to know how the group spends its money—and to take part in the decisions about spending, as well. In speaking with the treasurers of several groups, however, I learned that even very

large groups seldom have much left to pass along. CoDA simply does not have vast reserves of wealth. Twice during the course of my research, the Service Office reduced its already small paid staff due to budget shortages.

4. I also interviewed three therapists about their practices and about the diagnosis and treatment of codependency. At the outset, I planned to interview more, but since they gave virtually identical responses to my questions, and since their viewpoints lost relevance as the central focus of the research emerged, I did not continue with those interviews.

5. I thank Lynn Appleton for this metaphor.

PART ONE

1. This aspect of the discussion builds on Rice's work (1996), although what I offer takes a far more schematic form.

CHAPTER ONE

1. See Rice 1996 for an especially thorough treatment of this.

2. Sales of therapeutic books also evince this trend. Between 1963 and 1973, fourteen self-help books reached the bestseller list; during the next decade, that number nearly quadrupled.

3. Much of popular culture, especially television and novels, has this same open quality. For example, John Fiske (1986) explains that, in order to maintain popularity, a single TV show can, and indeed must, respond to the interests of different audiences. When a female television character assumes a southern accent and says "'Oh, that's the cutest thing you've ever said to me, sugar,'" some audiences will understand this as a "traditional chauvinist discourse of gender," while others will see it "as a more modern, liberated one" (Fiske 1986, 394). In other words, one program can serve the interests of two groups at the same time. This quality is part of what makes television "work." In a similar fashion, Janice Radway (1984) has argued that the heroine of a romantic novel can express contradicting qualities simultaneously. Some readers might identify with her through a stereotypically feminine quality such as nurturance. At the same time, others can admire her for her rebellious independence. Readers' own backgrounds provide different bases—or social contexts—for their interpretations of the "meaning" of the story.

4. Evidence for the lack of fit between codependency and the existing groups comes from other sources, as well. For example, journalist Melinda Blau writes of AA: "Whenever somebody who's been called on to 'share' (respond to the speakers' story of his recovery or to the chosen topic) launches into the dread phrase 'I've been going through some changes' or 'I'm in a lot of pain today,' AA veterans get that sinking feeling. They know they're probably in for a fuzzy monologue about the pills the speaker has popped, the cocaine he's snorted, the food she's binged on, arguments he's had with his lover, the Prozac she's been taking for depression, her co-dependency—everything but alcohol" (1991, 32).

CHAPTER TWO

1. "Middlebrow" critics are numerous. They include Jimenez and Rice (1990); Kaplan (1990); Faludi (1991); Rieff (1991); Scott (1991); Mitchell-Norberg, Warren, and Zale (1995); Rapping (1996); and Simonds (1992). They also include the following, whose work has been collected in Babcock and McKay's (1995) edited volume of feminist critiques: Babcock (1995); Hagan (1995); Kaminer (1990, 1991); Krestan and Bepko (1990); Lodl (1995); McKay (1995); Tavris (1989, 1990); Tallen (1990); Van Wormer (1989); and Walters (1990).

2. Further evidence of publishers' interest in trends, not specifically in codependency, is available in the recent shift of interests. For example, codependency began to fade from media attention during the early 1990s. The experts no longer made appearances on *Oprah* and *Donahue.* Publishers, seeing that the market had reached saturation, began to redirect their efforts. The subtitles of one of the magazines published by HCI indicate a series of transitions throughout the 1990s. What originated as *Changes: For and About Adult Children,* became *Changes: The Magazine for People in Recovery,* then *Changes: The Magazine for Personal Growth,* and finally, *Changes: The Recovery Lifestyle Magazine.* "That's our latest incarnation," said Jeff Laign, the magazine's managing editor. *Changes* began to focus less narrowly on recovery as popular interests shifted. This "latest incarnation" avoids alienating those readers who have become saturated with recovery by including what Laign calls "a good mix of interests." On the same note, Gary Seidler said that, in terms of books, the firm now focuses less on addiction and recovery and more on the next trend, spirituality. Their professional conferences have gone in that direction, too, Seidler claims. They now may have only one workshop on codependency, since both professionals and readers "have been saturated with material regarding codependency. . . . It started with addictions, then it went to ACoA [Adult Children of Alcoholics], then it went to codependency and dysfunctional families, and now to spirituality." In sum, publishing, even with its linkages to substance abuse treatment, did not create the market for codependency, but followed existing market trends.

3. For the initial framework on exiting one career by carrying features of it into a new one, see Ebaugh 1988.

4. For a thorough treatment of this phenomenon, see Gray 1991, especially chapter 3.

5. Mitchell-Norberg, Warren, and Zale cite Secunda's (1990) article in *New Woman* magazine as the source of this figure. Secunda herself cites no source for it.

CHAPTER THREE

1. The extent to which an observer sees this as remarkable seems to come with age. During the course of my research, I took a friend, then in her mid-twenties, to a meeting with me. Having had only two significant relationships herself, she saw the members of CoDA as "losers." I took another friend who was closer to 40. Although the discourse of codependency did not appeal to him, he saw that the members had had experiences very similar to his own.

2. For several years, the figure most commonly used to document this loss came from Weitzman (1985). She reported a 73 percent decline in women's status of living after divorce, and a 42 percent improvement in the status of living enjoyed by men. Re-analysis of her data proves these figures erroneous (see Duncan and Hoffman 1985; Hoffman and Duncan 1988). The most recent correction suggests a 27 percent decline for women, and a 10 percent improvement for men (Peterson 1996).

3. For a discussion of the variables that contribute to one's response to separation, see Spanier and Thompson 1983.

4. The term comes from Dworkin (1993), who describes the experience of immobilizing illness as leaving one's life a "narrative wreck, with no structure or sense."

5. Gerstel (1987) found that stigmatization is contingent on the specific conditions of the divorce and on gender. Among men, those who had affairs while married and continued them during separation reported experiencing the most disapproval. Among women, those with children did so, especially if the children were young.

6. Several studies have examined more generally the importance of talking about uncoupling. For example, Vaughan (1986) points out the importance of talking to confidants and "transitional people" (chapter 2). Riessman (1990), who works in the narrative analysis tradition, documents a prevailing theme of the failure of the marriage to measure up to a companionate ideal (chapter 2). Weiss (1975, chapter 2) and Davis (1973, chapter 8) both note a consistent effort to allocate blame.

7. Similar strategies have been addressed by Mills (1940), Hewitt and Stokes (1975), and Stokes and Hewitt (1976).

8. This group includes Turner (1976); Zurcher (1977); Lifton (1968); and Hewitt (1994) (although Hewitt disputes and reconceptualizes the shift from an institutionally grounded self to an impulsively grounded one).

9. Turner himself makes no claims about the existence of a "real self." He writes that "there is no objectively, but only a subjectively, true self" (1012); his essay examines the *experience* of self, not the existence of it. He points out that "each person develops at least a vague conception by which he recognizes some of his feelings and actions as more truly indicative of his real self than other feelings and actions" (1011).

10. The trend towards impulsively anchored images of self has the support of two national studies. *The Inner American,* by Veroff, Douvan, and Kulka (1981a) reports that between 1957 and 1976, Americans had moved from a "social" to a "personal" paradigm for structuring well-being. According to data from a 1957 survey, people of that era took "comfort in culture," as did Turner's institutionals. The 1976 population had become more impulsive, "gathering much more strength in its own personal adaptations to the world" (529). The research team noted three types of changes consistent with Turner's trend towards impulsivity: (1) the diminution of role standards as the basis for defining adjustment; (2) increased focus on self-expressiveness and self-direction in social life; and (3) a shift in concern from social-organizational integration to interpersonal intimacy (529). In the seventies, people thought more in psychological terms, instead of the moral or material terms of the fifties. In 1957, people would have asked them-

selves "Should I do this?" or "What will this get me?" when weighing alternatives. In 1976, they asked "How does this make me feel?" (see Wilkinson 1988, 44).

The same year that *The Inner American* appeared, opinion pollster Daniel Yankelovich's *New Rules: Searching for Self-Fulfillment in a World Turned Upside Down* noted many of the same trends. Using data from surveys and interviews, he documented varying degrees of preoccupation with self-fulfillment, with a trend suggesting an overall increase in such concerns. He claimed that post–World War II generations had rejected the "giving/getting covenant" that had motivated earlier generations to work, as well as to enjoy the fruits of their labors. Instead, the Baby Boomers wanted fulfillment without much sacrifice, and psychological fulfillment, in particular, had moved to center stage.

In many ways, the argument in *New Rules* takes up where *The Lonely Crowd* had left off (Riesman, Glazer, and Denney 1950). Yankelovich attributed this "psycho-culture" largely to the growth of the consumer economy. He speculated that the emphasis on fulfillment, especially in its extreme version expressed by what he called the "strong formers," would eventually have devastating economic consequences. He also saw a positive side to the changes, in the form of a new tolerance that could prove productive in times of austerity. He also documented that the mid-to-late 1970s saw an upsurge in membership in voluntary associations, belief in the value of commitment to others, and civic involvement, all trends remarked upon by Riesman (1980) in his reappraisal of the American social character.

Over the same period of time, in social-psychological research involving instruments such as the Twenty Statements Test, which asks for twenty answers to the question "Who am I?" fewer people defined themselves by their roles, and more used individualistic, attitudinal traits. In the language of the Test, the answers began to shift from B mode roles ("I am a father," or "I am a teacher") to C mode attitudes ("I am a happy person," or "I like music") (see especially Zurcher 1977).

11. For a discussion of how the culture of Romanticism rested on the innovative belief in the self, see Gagnon 1984 (see also Gagnon 1992).

12. Sharing, or, more generally, storytelling, is commonplace in small groups of all kinds. For more on this, see Wuthnow 1994, especially chapter 10. There are many other "narrative auspices," or "people processing institutions that increasingly elicit, screen, fashion, and variously highlight personal narratives" (Gubrium and Holstein 1998, 164). These include schools, clinics, hospitals, jails, and counseling centers, just to name a few.

13. Gubrium and Holstein (1998) use the phrase "formal narrative control" to address the ways that stories are "geared to institutional agendas, with preferred plot structures, 'points,' or morals" (173). Rice also makes note of "how thoroughly faithful [CoDA] speakers are to the norms governing their role" (1996, 149).

14. Arthur Frank refers to people in this position as belonging to "the remission society" (1995, 8). He puts in this group people who have had cancer or heart conditions, diabetes, allergies, people with prostheses of various sorts, and former drug addicts and alcoholics.

15. This reliance on the group has often been misunderstood as replacing one "addiction" with another (see Katz and Liu 1991).

CHAPTER FOUR

1. This is consistent with what Americans, on the whole, consistently report to believe. Roughly 80 percent of the public agreed with statements such as "a person can be a good Christian or Jew if he or she doesn't attend church or synagogue," and "an individual should arrive at his or her own religious beliefs independent of any churches or synagogues" (Gallup 1988).

2. This is not the case in the older Twelve Step groups, such as AA, which are not "lite," or at least not as "lite" as CoDA. AA, for example, verges on the "greedy" with its sponsorship and the "90/90" challenge (encouraging new members to attend ninety meetings in ninety days). AA does not expect new members to forsake competing claims to time and identity, but it uses other means of surrounding them with the AA perspective. Moreover, AA seems to recognize the tension and resentment this level of involvement can create in marriages and relationships. It minimizes and, in the best of cases, resolves this by offering to bring spouses and partners into the AA worldview through "auxiliary" organizations like Al-Anon (see Greil and Rudy 1984). Single AA members are encouraged not to date or develop relationships for the first year of recovery.

In CoDA, members may attend as many meetings as they wish, and their significant others are free to attend CoDA or any other group. But neither suggestion would be made, however, because the idea that anyone else could or should guide another's recovery is heresy. For this same reason, CoDA does not encourage an active program of sponsorship.

3. See Wuthnow's *Sharing the Journey* for a general discussion of spirituality in small groups.

CHAPTER FIVE

1. This is also known by other terms. McCall and Simmons (1978), for example, refer to "hierarchies of prominence."

CHAPTER SIX

1. This is a version of what is known as the "innate" or "organismic" model of how emotions work. Inherited from Charles Darwin, William James, and Sigmund Freud, the organismic model grants the emotions "a prior existence apart from introspection" (Hochschild 1983, 205). It portrays emotions as entities independent of those who feel them, and grants them the ability to convey accurate and reliable information about character. The "organismic" model contrasts with an "interactional" model (see Hochschild 1983), in which emotion is understood to be produced and managed according to "feeling rules" and "expression rules." For more on this, and for other perspectives, as well, see Kemper 1978.

2. The term "emotional culture" refers to norms that indicate the appropriate and desirable emotions for given situations. For more on this, see Stearns 1989a, 1989b, 1994; Hochschild 1975, 1983; and Goffman 1959.

3. The question of why this happened, while not essential for the present discussion, can be answered in brief. In part, the fading of intensity accompanied

the demands of an advanced industrial society, combined with new family patterns and increasing consumerism. To these, Stearns (1994) adds the importance of a twentieth-century shift away from excessive religious spirituality and a new emphasis on health.

4. Americans have a far greater tendency than members of many other cultures to define emotions they find unpleasant as negative (see Sommers 1984). The Chinese, for example, find certain emotions difficult or even unpleasant, but they simultaneously recognize that those emotions could have important functions. Americans, in contrast, largely disapprove of unpleasant emotions and see them as dangerous, not potentially useful. They also tend to deny or conceal their experience of unpleasant emotions. As a result, the American emotional vocabulary manifests a relatively simplistic pleasure/pain dichotomy. Americans differ strikingly from several other cultures, not only in their disapproval of emotions such as jealousy and guilt, but also in their desire to conceal those emotions and their pride in the ability to do so.

5. A classic statement on this can be found in Sartre 1948.

6. This discussion touches on issues that are included in the debate about postmodernism. I have not taken my argument in that direction because I doubt that it would add to it significantly. I can, however, refer readers interested in such issues to an indispensable, marvelously written book. This is Charles Lemert's *Postmodernism Is Not What You Think* (Malden, MA: Blackwell, 1997).

7. I am of a mixed mind about whether to call serenity an emotion. It indicates a freedom *from* emotions rather than an emotional state. More precisely, it refers to the successful management of all intensity.

CHAPTER SEVEN

1. This is one of many instances in which a literal reading of the texts—the favored method of codependency's critics—fails to show how the discourse is used.

2. My discussion of the historical linkages among gender, intimate relationships, the family, and the economy is necessarily limited. For more thorough treatments of various aspects of this history, see Cancian 1987; Cott 1977; Cott and Pleck 1979; Cowan 1976, 1983; D'Emilio and Freedman 1988; Kimmel 1996; Ryan 1979, 1981; Seidman 1990; Swidler 1980; and Zaretsky 1976.

3. Gerson and Peiss (1985) suggest that the dichotomy of the separate spheres fails to capture the changing patterns of social relations between the sexes. They propose replacing the term "separate spheres" with the term "boundaries." This opens up the possibility of analyzing the change and crossover through the processes of negotiation and domination.

4. In CoDA, there is a belief that new members who are not in a relationship should remain unattached for the first year, while they focus on recovery. Although I did not find a statement to this effect in any of the CoDA literature, I often heard it repeated by members. A long-time member of AA told me that it had started there.

5. Vaughan (1986) talks about the importance of confidants during uncoupling.

6. For similar critiques, see Babcock and McKay's volume (1995); Rapping 1996; and Kaminer 1991.

7. For an opposing view, see Rapping 1996. She argues that the recovery movement "borrowed" what was good about feminism, namely the consciousness-raising technique, and then negated its political content and purpose.

8. For other examples of how women create alternative, resisting meanings, often while appearing to acquiesce to the status quo, see Fisher and Davis 1993; Kaufman 1991; Lewis 1990; Paules 1991; and Radway 1984.

9. A male friend suggested that maybe men go to CoDA to meet women. Although he meant it in jest, the comment does merit addressing. No doubt some men do go to CoDA looking for a date—but surely women do this as well. Within Twelve Step culture, this is known as "Thirteenth Stepping," and it is discouraged. I asked several longtime members about dating in the group, and they said that some does take place, although not a lot. The consensus was that, when you are serious about "working a program," you respect the norms of the group. Among these norms are the expectation that you will avoid starting a new relationship during the first year of recovery, and that you will not date anyone in the same group. Of the thirty-six people I interviewed, only two claimed to have dated other members (and I found out later that they had dated each other).

10. I recorded the topics raised at meetings and the gender of the person who raised them, and I could not draw any conclusions about the relationship between the two.

CHAPTER EIGHT

1. Although in the actual process of uncoupling the two people may alternate roles several times, one person typically expresses discontent first. Vaughan distinguishes between the "initiator" and the "partner"; Weiss calls them the "leaver" and the "left."

2. Vaughan found no initiators who turned to religion, though it was common among partners. Because religion emphasizes commitment to relationships, initiators would be less likely to adhere to it. Partners, in contrast, typically do, "at least in the early stages of separation" (1986, 162).

CONCLUSION

1. I thank Michael Layton for pointing this out.

2. Exceptions to this come mainly from the life history approach, the classics of which in sociology include Thomas and Znaniecki's *Polish Peasant* ([1918–1920]1958; but see Maines 1993 for a convincing argument that Thomas and Znaniecki used the narrative approach to strive for a nomothetic sociology), and three studies by Shaw: *The Jack Roller* (1930), *The Natural History of a Delinquent Career* (1931), and *Brothers in Crime* (1936). More recent uses of life history include Harper 1987 and Plummer 1983. For examples of recent work using an explicitly narrative approach, see the notes for chapter 1.

Alcoholics Anonymous (AA). 1957. *Alcoholics Anonymous Comes of Age: A Brief History of AA.* New York: Alcoholics Anonymous Publishing.

Allen, Charlotte. 1997. "Spies Like Us: When Sociologists Deceive Their Subjects." *Lingua Franca,* November.

Anderson, Charles, Deborah J. Carter, and Andrew G. Malizio. 1990. *Fact Book on Higher Education.* New York: Macmillan.

Anderson, Walter Truett. 1997. *Future of the Self: Inventing the Postmodern Person.* New York: Penguin Putnam.

Asher, Ramona. 1992. *Women with Alcoholic Husbands: Ambivalence and the Trap of Codependency.* Chapel Hill: University of North Carolina Press.

Asher, Ramona, and Dennis Brissett. 1988. "Codependency: A View from Women Married to Alcoholics." *The International Journal of the Addictions* 23:331–350. [Reprinted in Babcock and McKay 1995.]

Babcock, Marguerite. 1995. "Critiques of Codependency: History and Background Issues." Pp. 3–27 in *Challenging Codependency: Feminist Critiques,* edited by Marguerite Babcock and Christine McKay. Toronto: University of Toronto Press.

Babcock, Marguerite, and Christine McKay. 1995. *Challenging Codependency: Feminist Critiques.* Toronto: University of Toronto Press.

Baudrillard, Jean. 1983. *Simulations.* New York: Semiotext[e].

Beattie, Melody. 1987. *Codependent No More: How to Stop Controlling Others and Start Caring for Yourself.* New York: Harper/Hazelden.

———. 1989. *Beyond Codependency: And Getting Better All the Time.* New York: Harper/Hazelden.

———. 1990. *Codependents' Guide to the Twelve Steps.* New York: Prentice Hall/Parkside.

Bell, Daniel. 1976. *The Cultural Contradictions of Capitalism.* New York: Basic Books.

————. 1980. *The Winding Passage: Essays and Sociological Journeys 1960–1980.* Cambridge, MA: Abt Books.

Bellah, Robert N., Richard Madsen, William M. Sullivan, Ann Swidler, and Steven M. Tipton. 1985. *Habits of the Heart.* New York: Harper and Row.

Berger, Peter. 1963. *Invitation to Sociology.* New York: Anchor Books.

Bethune, John. 1990. "Pens and Needles." *Publishers Weekly* 20 (July): 23.

Blau, Melinda. 1991. "Recovery Fever." *New York,* 9 September, 31–37.

Blumstein, Philip, and Pepper Schwartz. 1983. *American Couples.* New York: William Morrow.

Bourdieu, Pierre. 1977. *Outline of a Theory of Practice.* Cambridge, UK: Cambridge University Press.

Bronfenbrenner, Urie. 1952. "Principles of Professional Ethics: Cornell Studies in Social Growth." *American Psychologist* 7:452–55.

Brown, J. David. 1991. "The Professional Ex-: An Alternative for Exiting the Deviant Career." *Sociological Quarterly* 32:219–30.

Bruner, Jerome. 1987. "Life as Narrative." *Social Research* 54:11–32.

————. 1994. "The 'Remembered' Self." Pp. 41–54 in *The Remembering Self: Construction and Accuracy in the Self-Narrative,* edited by Ulric Neisser and Robyn Fivush. Cambridge, UK: Cambridge University Press.

Cancian, Francesca M. 1987. *Love in America: Gender and Self-Development.* New York: Cambridge University Press.

Carroll, John. 1985. *Guilt: The Grey Eminence Behind Character, History, and Culture.* London: Routledge and Kegan Paul.

Cassell, Joan. 1978. "Risk and Benefit to Subjects of Fieldwork." *American Sociologist* 13:134–43.

————. 1980. "Ethical Principles for Conducting Fieldwork." *American Anthropologist* 82:28–41.

Charmaz, Kathy. 1983. "The Grounded Theory Method: An Explication and Interpretation." Pp. 109–26 in *Contemporary Field Research: A Collection of Readings,* edited by Robert M Emerson. Boston: Little, Brown and Co.

Chase, Susan E. 1995. *Ambiguous Empowerment: The Work Narratives of Women School Superintendents.* Amherst, MA: University of Massachusetts Press.

————. 1996. "Vulnerability and Interpretive Authority." Pp. 45–59 in *The Narrative Study of Lives,* vol. 4, *Ethics and Process,* edited by Ruthellen Josselson. Thousand Oaks, CA: Sage.

Cherlin, Andrew J. 1978. "Remarriage as an Incomplete Institution." *American Journal of Sociology* 84: 634–50.

————. 1992. *Marriage, Divorce, Remarriage.* Revised and enlarged edition. Cambridge, MA: Harvard University Press.

Clecak, Peter. 1983. *America's Quest for the Ideal Self: Dissent and Fulfillment in the 60s and 70s.* New York: Oxford University Press.

Co-Dependents Anonymous (CoDA). 1987. "The Bear Facts of Co-Dependents Anonymous, Inc." Vol. 1, no. 1, October.

———. 1988. *Preamble and Welcome.* Phoenix: CoDA Service Office.

———. 1995. *Co-Dependents Anonymous* [also known as *The CoDA Book*]. Phoenix: CoDA Service Office.

Collins, Randall. 1982. *Sociological Insight: An Introduction to Non-Obvious Sociology.* New York and Oxford: Oxford University Press.

Conrad, Peter, and Joseph W. Schneider. 1992. *Deviance and Medicalization: From Badness to Sickness.* Expanded edition. Philadelphia: Temple University Press.

Coser, Lewis. 1974. *Greedy Institutions.* New York: Free Press.

Cott, Nancy F. 1977. *The Bonds of Womanhood.* New Haven: Yale University Press.

Cott, Nancy R., and Elizabeth H. Pleck. 1979. *A Heritage of Her Own.* New York: Simon and Schuster/Touchstone.

Cowan, Ruth Schwartz. 1976. "Two Washes in the Morning and a Bridge Party at Night: The American Housewife between the Wars." *Women's Studies* 3:147–72.

———. 1983. *More Work for Mother: The Ironies of Household Technology from the Open Hearth to the Microwave.* New York: Basic Books.

Crèvecoeur, J. Hector S. John. [1782] 1981. *Letters from an American Farmer.* New York: Penguin.

Davis, Murray. 1973. *Intimate Relations.* New York: Free Press.

D'Emilio, John, and Estelle B. Freedman. 1988. *Intimate Matters: A History of Sexuality in America.* New York: Harper and Row.

Department of Health, Education, and Welfare (DHEW). 1974. "Protection of Human Subjects." Washington, DC: *Federal Register,* 30 May (39 FR 18914).

———. (1978). "Protection of Human Subjects: Institutional Review Boards." Washington, DC: *Federal Register,* 30 November (43 FR 56174).

de Swaan, Abram. 1981. "The Politics of Agoraphobia: On Changes in Emotional and Relational Management." *Theory and Society* 10:359–85.

Duggar, Benjamin J. 1991. "Community-Based Drug Treatment Reimbursement: Progress and Barriers." Pp. 148–64 in *Economic Costs, Cost-Effectiveness, Financing, and Community-Based Drug Treatment,* edited by William S. Cartwright and James M. Kaple. NIDA Research Monograph 113. Rockville, MD: NIDA.

Duncan, Greg, and Saul Hoffman. 1985. "A Re-consideration of the Economic Consequences of Divorce." *Demography* 22:485–97.

Durkheim, Emile. [1915] 1961. *Elementary Forms of the Religious Life.* New York: Collier-Macmillan.

Dworkin, Ronald. 1993. *Life's Dominion: An Argument about Abortion, Euthanasia, and Individual Freedom.* New York: Knopf.

Ebaugh, Helen Rose Fuchs. 1988. *Becoming an Ex: The Process of Role Exit.* Chicago: University of Chicago Press.

Eco, Umberto. 1979. *The Role of the Reader: Explorations in the Semiotics of Texts.* Bloomington: University of Indiana Press.

Emerson, Robert M. 1983. *Contemporary Field Research: A Collection of Readings.* Boston: Little, Brown and Co.

Erikson, Kai. 1967. "A Comment on Disguised Observation in Sociology." *Social Problems* 14:366–73.

———. 1995. "Commentary." *American Sociologist* 26:4–11.

———. 1996. "A Response to Richard Leo." *American Sociologist* 27:129–30.

Faden, Ruth R., and Tom L. Beauchamp. 1986. *A History and Theory of Informed Consent.* New York: Oxford University Press.

Faludi, Susan. 1991. *Backlash: The Undeclared War against American Women.* New York: Crown.

Fine, Gary Allen. 1993. "Ten Lies of Ethnography: Moral Dilemmas of Field Research." *Journal of Contemporary Ethnography* 22:267–94.

Fish, Stanley. 1980. *Is There a Text in This Class? The Authority of Interpretive Communities.* Cambridge, MA: Harvard University Press.

Fisher, Sue, and Kathy Davis, eds. 1993. *Negotiating at the Margins: The Gendered Discourses of Power and Resistance.* New Brunswick, NJ: Rutgers University Press.

Fiske, John. 1986. "Television: Polysemy and Popularity." *Critical Studies in Mass Communication* 3:391–408.

Frank, Arthur W. 1995. *The Wounded Storyteller: Body, Illness, and Ethics.* Chicago: University of Chicago Press.

Freud, Sigmund. 1959. "Inhibitions, Symptoms, and Anxiety." Pp. 87–156 in *The Standard Edition of the Complete Psychological Works of Sigmund Freud,* vol. 20, translated and edited by James Strachey. London: Hogarth Press.

Gagnon, John. 1984. "Success = Failure/Failure = Success." Pp. 97–108 in *Romanticism and Culture,* edited by H. W. Matalene. Columbia, SC: Camden House.

———. 1992. "The Self, Its Voices, and Their Discord." Pp. 221–43 in *Investigating Subjectivity,* edited by Carolyn Ellis and Michael Flaherty. Newbury Park, CA: Sage.

Gallup, George, Jr. 1988. *The Unchurched American—10 Years Later.* Princeton, NJ: Princeton Religion Research Center.

Gans, Herbert. 1982. *The Urban Villagers.* Updated and expanded edition. New York: Free Press.

Gergen, Kenneth. 1991. *The Saturated Self: Dilemmas of Identity in Contemporary Life.* New York: Basic Books.

Gergen, Kenneth, and Mary Gergen. 1988. "Narrative and Self as Relationship." *Advances in Experimental Social Psychology* 21:17–55.

Gerhards, Jürgen. 1989. "The Changing Culture of Emotions in Modern Society." *Social Science Information* 28:737–54.

Gerson, Judith M., and Kathy Peiss. 1985. "Boundaries, Negotiation, Consciousness: Reconceptualizing Gender Relations." *Social Problems* 32:317–31.

Gerstel, Naomi. 1987. "Divorce and Stigma." *Social Problems* 34:172–86.

Giddens, Anthony. 1991. *Modernity and Identity: Self and Society in the Late Modern Age.* Stanford, CA: Stanford University Press.

Glaser, Barney G. 1978. *Theoretical Sensitivity.* Mill Valley, CA: Sociology Press.

Glaser, Barney G., and Anselm L. Strauss. 1967. *The Discovery of Grounded Theory.* Chicago: Aldine.

Goffman, Erving. 1959. *The Presentation of Self in Everyday Life.* Garden City, NY: Anchor Books.

———. 1961. *Encounters.* Indianapolis: Bobbs-Merrill.

———. 1967. *Interaction Ritual.* Garden City, NY: Anchor Books.

Goldstein, Jonah, and Jeremy Rayner. 1994. "The Politics of Identity in Late Modern Society." *Theory and Society* 23:367–84.

Gray, Bradford. 1991. *The Profit Motive and Patient Care: The Changing Accountability of Doctors and Hospitals.* Cambridge, MA: Harvard University Press.

Greil, Arthur L., and David R. Rudy. 1984. "Social Cocoons: Encapsulation and Identity Transformation Organizations." *Sociological Inquiry* 54:260–78.

Gubrium, Jaber F., and James A. Hostein. 1998. "Narrative Practice and the Coherence of Personal Stories." *Sociological Quarterly* 39:163–87.

Haaken, Janice. 1993. "From Al-Anon to ACOA: Codependency and the Reconstruction of Caregiving." *Signs* 18:321-345.

———. 1995. "A Critical Analysis of the Codependency Construct." Pp. 53–69 in *Challenging Codependency: Feminist Critiques,* edited by Marguerite Babcock and Christine McKay. Toronto: University of Toronto Press. [Originally published in *Psychiatry* 53 (1990): 396–406.]

Hagan, Kay. 1995. "Codependency and the Myth of Recovery: A Feminist Scrutiny." Pp. 198–206 in *Challenging Codependency: Feminist Critiques,* edited by Marguerite Babcock and Christine McKay. Toronto: University of Toronto Press. [Originally published in Hagan's (1989) *Fugitive Information: Essays from a Feminist Hothead.* New York: HarperCollins.]

Hannerz, Ulf. 1969. *Soulside: Inquiries into Ghetto Culture and Community.* New York: Columbia University Press.

Harré, Rom. 1989. "Language Games and the Texts of Identity." Pp. 20–35 in *Texts of Identity,* edited by John Shotter and Kenneth Gergen. London: Sage.

Harper, Douglas. 1987. *Working Knowledge: Skill and Community in a Small Shop.* Chicago: University of Chicago Press.

Hewitt, John P. 1989. *Dilemmas of the American Self.* Philadelphia: Temple University Press.

―――. 1994. *Self and Society: A Symbolic Interactionist Perspective.* Sixth edition. Needham Heights, MA: Allyn and Bacon.

Hewitt, John P., and Randall Stokes. 1975. "Disclaimers." *American Sociological Review* 40:1–11.

Hochschild, Arlie Russell. 1975. "The Sociology of Feeling and Emotion: Selected Possibilities." Pp. 280–307 in *Another Voice: Feminist Perspectives on Social Life and Social Science,* edited by Marcia Millman and Rosabeth Moss Kanter. Garden City, NY: Anchor Books.

―――. 1983. *The Managed Heart: Commercialization of Human Feeling.* Berkeley: University of California Press.

―――. 1989. *The Second Shift.* New York: Avon Books.

Hoffman, Saul, and Greg Duncan. 1988. "What Are the Economic Consequences of Divorce?" *Demography* 25:641–45.

Humphreys, Laud. 1970. *Tearoom Trade.* Chicago: Aldine.

Irvine, Leslie. 1992. *The Pathologizing of Love: A Sociological Analysis of Codependency.* Unpublished master's thesis. Boca Raton, FL: Florida Atlantic University.

James, William. 1910. *Psychology: The Briefer Course.* New York: Henry Holt and Co.

Jimenez, Mary Ann, and Susan Rice. 1990. "Popular Advice to Women: A Feminist Perspective." *Affilia* 5:8–26.

Josselson, Ruthellen. 1996. *Ethics and Process.* Vol. 4, *The Narrative Study of Lives.* Thousand Oaks, CA: Sage.

Josselson, Ruthellen, and Amia Lieblich. 1993. *The Narrative Study of Lives.* Vol. 1, *The Narrative Study of Lives.* Thousand Oaks, CA: Sage.

―――. 1995. *Interpreting Experience.* Vol. 3, *The Narrative Study of Lives.* Thousand Oaks, CA: Sage.

Kaminer, Wendy. 1990. "Chances Are You're Codependent Too." *New York Times Book Review,* 11 February, pp. 1, 26–27.

―――. 1991. *I'm Dysfunctional, You're Dysfunctional: The Recovery Movement and Other Self-Help Fashions.* Reading, MA: Addison-Wesley.

Kanter, Rosabeth Moss. 1972. *Commitment and Community: Communes and Utopias in Sociological Perspective.* Cambridge, MA: Harvard University Press.

―――. 1977. *Men and Women of the Corporation.* New York: Basic Books.

Kaplan, Janice. 1990. "The Trouble with Codependency." *Self* (July): 112–13, 148.

Karp, David A. 1996. *Speaking of Sadness: Depression, Disconnection, and the Meaning of Illness.* New York: Oxford University Press.

Katz, Stan J., and Aimee E. Liu. 1991. *The Codependency Conspiracy.* New York: Warner Books.

Kaufman, Debra Renee. 1991. *Rachel's Daughters: Newly Orthodox Women.* New Brunswick, NJ: Rutgers University Press.

Kemper, Theodore D. 1978. *A Social Interactional Theory of Emotions.* New York: John Wiley and Sons.

Kimball, Gayle. 1983. *The 50/50 Marriage.* Boston: Beacon Press.

Kimmel, Michael. 1996. *Manhood in America: A Cultural History.* New York: Free Press.

Klapp, Orrin. 1969. *Collective Search for Identity.* New York: Holt, Rinehart, and Winston.

Kleinman, Arthur. 1988. *The Illness Narratives.* New York: Basic Books.

Krestan, Jo-Ann, and Claudia Bepko. 1990. "Codependency: The Social Reconstruction of Female Experience." *Smith College Studies in Social Work* 60: 216–32. [Also reprinted in Babcock and McKay 1995.]

Kristol, Elizabeth. 1990. "Declarations of Codependence: People Who Need People Are the Sickliest People in the World—And That's Just for Starters." *American Spectator* (June): 21–23.

Kurtz, Ernest. 1979. *Not-God: A History of Alcoholics Anonymous.* Center City, MN: Hazelden.

La Gaipa, John J. 1982. "Rules and Rituals in Disengaging from Relationships." Pp. 189–210 in *Personal Relationships,* vol. 4, *Dissolving Personal Relationships,* edited by Steve Duck. London: Academic Press.

Larsen, Earnie. 1983. *Basics of Co-Dependency.* Brooklyn Park, MN: Earnie Larsen Enterprises.

Lasch, Christopher. 1979. *The Culture of Narcissism: American Life in an Age of Diminishing Expectations.* New York: W. W. Norton.

———. 1984. *The Minimal Self: Psychic Survival in Troubled Times.* Princeton, NJ: Princeton University Press.

Latané, Bibb, and John M. Darley. 1970. *The Unresponsive Bystander: Why Doesn't He Help?* New York: Appleton-Century-Crofts.

Leo, Richard A. 1995. "Trial and Tribulations: Courts, Ethnography, and the Need for an Evidentiary Privilege for Academic Researchers." *American Sociologist* 26:113–34.

———. 1996. "The Ethics of Deceptive Research Roles Reconsidered: A Response to Kai Erikson." *American Sociologist* 27:122–28.

Lewis, Lisa. 1990. *Gender Politics and MTV: Voicing the Difference.* Philadelphia: Temple University Press.

Lidz, Charles W., and Alan Meisel, with Janice L. Holden, John H. Marx, and Mark Munetz. 1982. "Informed Consent and the Structure of Medical Care," in President's Commission for the Study of Ethical Problems in Medicine and Biomedical and Behavioral Research, *Making Health Care Decisions.* Vol. 2, *Appendices, Empirical Studies of Informed Consent.* Washington, DC: Government Printing Office.

Lidz, Charles W., Alan Meisel, Eviatar Zerubavel, Mary Carter, Regina Sestak, and Loren Roth. 1984. *Informed Consent.* New York: Guilford Press.

Lieblich, Amia, and Ruthellen Josselson. 1994. *Exploring Identity and Gender.* Vol. 2, *The Narrative Study of Lives.* Thousand Oaks, CA: Sage.

Lifton, Robert Jay. 1968. "Protean Man." *Partisan Review* 35, no. 1, pp. 13–27.

Lodl, Karen. 1995. "A Feminist Critique of Codependency." Pp. 207–18 in *Challenging Codependency: Feminist Critiques,* edited by Marguerite Babcock and Christine McKay. Toronto: University of Toronto Press.

MacIntyre, Alasdair. 1984. *After Virtue: A Study in Moral Theory.* Second edition. Notre Dame, IN: University of Notre Dame Press.

Maines, David R. 1993. "Narrative's Moment and Sociology's Phenomena: Toward a Narrative Sociology." *Sociological Quarterly* 34:17–38.

Marris, Peter. 1974. *Loss and Change.* New York: Pantheon.

Martin, Denise. 1988. "A Review of the Popular Literature on Co-Dependency." *Contemporary Drug Problems* (Fall): 383–98.

McAdams, Dan P. 1993. *The Stories We Live By: Personal Myths and the Making of the Self.* New York: Guilford Press.

McCall, George J. 1982. "Becoming Unrelated: The Management of Bond Dissolution." Pp. 211–32 in *Personal Relationships,* vol. 4, *Dissolving Personal Relationships,* edited by Steve Duck. London: Academic Press.

McCall, George J., and J. L. Simmons. 1978. *Identities and Interactions: An Examination of Human Associations in Everyday Life.* New York: Free Press.

McKay, Christine. 1995. "Codependency: The Pathologizing of Female Oppression." Pp. 219–40 in *Challenging Codependency: Feminist Critiques,* edited by Marguerite Babcock and Christine McKay. Toronto: University of Toronto Press.

Mills, C. Wright. 1940. "Situated Actions and Vocabularies of Motive." *American Sociological Review* 5:904–13.

Mitchell, W. J. T., ed. 1981. *On Narrative.* Chicago: University of Chicago Press.

Mitchell-Norberg, Jean, Carol A. B. Warren, and Stephanne L. Zale. 1995. "Gender and Codependents Anonymous." Pp. 121–47 in *Social Perspectives on Emotion,* edited by Michael Flaherty and Carolyn Ellis. Greenwich, CT: JAI.

National Association of Alcoholism and Drug Abuse Counselors (NAADAC). 1986. *Development of Model Professional Standards for Counselor Credentialing.* Dubuque, IA: Kendall-Hunt.

National Institute on Drug Abuse and National Institute on Alcohol Abuse and Alcoholism (NIDA and NIAAA). 1990. "Highlights from the 1989 National Drug and Alcoholism Treatment Unit Survey." *National Drug and Alcoholism Treatment Unit Survey.* Washington, DC: Government Printing Office.

Neisser, Ulric, and Robyn Fivush, eds. 1994. *The Remembering Self: Construction and Accuracy in the Self-Narrative.* Cambridge, UK: Cambridge University Press.

Norris, John L. 1976. "Alcoholics Anonymous and Other Self-Help Groups." In

Alcoholism, edited by Ralph Tarter and Arthur Sugerman. Reading, MA: Addison-Wesley.

Norwood, Robin. 1986. *Women Who Love Too Much*. New York: Simon and Schuster.

Obst, Lynda Rosen, ed. 1977. *The Sixties: The Decade Remembered Now, by the People Who Lived It Then*. New York: Random House/Rolling Stone.

Parsons, Talcott. 1951. *The Social System*. New York: Free Press.

———. 1978. *Action Theory and the Human Condition*. New York: Free Press.

Paules, Greta Foff. 1991. *Dishing It Out: Power and Resistance among Waitresses in a New Jersey Restaurant*. Philadelphia: Temple University Press.

Peterson, Richard C. 1996. "A Re-evaluation of the Economic Consequences of Divorce." *American Sociological Review* 61:528–36.

Philipson, Ilene J. 1993. *On the Shoulders of Women: The Feminization of Psychotherapy*. New York: Guilford.

Plummer, Ken. 1983. *Documents of Life: An Introduction to the Problems and Literature of a Humanistic Method*. London, UK: George Allen and Unwin.

———. 1990. "Herbert Blumer and the Life History Tradition." *Symbolic Interaction* 13:125–44.

———. 1995. *Telling Sexual Stories: Power, Change, and Social Worlds*. London and New York: Routledge.

Polkinghorne, Donald. E. 1988. *Narrative Knowing and the Human Sciences*. Albany: State University of New York Press.

———. 1991. "Narrative and the Self-Concept." *Journal of Narrative and Life History* 1:135–53.

Punch, Maurice. 1983. *The Politics and Ethics of Fieldwork*. Sage University Paper Series on Qualitative Research Methods (vol. 3). Beverly Hills, CA: Sage.

Putnam, Robert D. 1995. "Bowling Alone: America's Declining Social Capital." *Journal of Democracy* 6:65–78.

Radway, Janice. 1984. *Reading the Romance: Women, Patriarchy, and Popular Literature*. Chapel Hill: University of North Carolina Press.

Rapping, Elayne. 1996. *The Culture of Recovery: Making Sense of the Self-Help Movement in Women's Lives*. Boston: Beacon Press.

Rice, John Steadman. 1992. "Discursive Formation, Life Stories, and the Emergence of Co-Dependency: 'Power/Knowledge' and the Search for Identity." *Sociological Quarterly* 33:337–64.

———. 1996. *A Disease of One's Own: Psychotherapy, Addiction, and the Emergence of Co-Dependency*. New Brunswick: Transaction.

Rieff, David. 1991. "Victims All?" *Harper's Magazine* (October): 49–56.

Rieff, Philip. 1966. *The Triumph of the Therapeutic: Uses of Faith after Freud*. Second edition. New York: Harper and Row.

Riesman, David. 1981. "Egocentrism: Is the American Character Changing?" *Encounter* 55:19–28.

Riesman, David, with Nathan Glazer and Reuel Denney. 1950. *The Lonely Crowd: A Study of the Changing American Character.* New Haven: Yale University Press.

Riessman, Catherine Kohler. 1990. *Divorce Talk: Men and Women Make Sense of Personal Relationships.* New Brunswick, NJ: Rutgers University Press.

Rosenwald, George C. 1992. "Conclusion: Reflections on Narrative Self-Understanding." Pp. 265–89 in *Storied Lives: The Cultural Politics of Self-Understanding,* edited by George C. Rosenwald and Richard L. Ochberg. New Haven: Yale University Press.

Rosenwald, George C., and Richard L. Ochberg. 1992. "Introduction: Life Stories, Cultural Politics, and Self-Understanding." Pp. 1–18 in *Storied Lives: The Cultural Politics of Self-Understanding,* edited by George C. Rosenwald and Richard L. Ochberg. New Haven: Yale University Press.

Roth, Julius. 1962. "Comments on 'Secret Observation.'" *Social Problems* 9:283–84.

Rubin, Herbert J., and Irene S. Rubin. 1995. *Qualitative Interviewing: The Art of Hearing Data.* Thousand Oaks, CA: Sage.

Rudy, David R., and Arthur L. Greil. 1989. "Is Alcoholics Anonymous a Religious Organization? Meditations on Marginality." *Sociological Analysis* 50:41–51.

Russell, Cheryl. 1993. *The Master Trend: How the Baby Boom Generation is Remaking America.* New York: Plenum.

Ryan, Mary. 1979. *Womanhood in America.* Second edition. New York: New Viewpoints.

———. 1981. *The Cradle of the Middle Class: The Family in Oneida County, New York.* New York: Cambridge University Press.

Sarbin, Theodore R. 1986. *Narrative Psychology: The Storied Nature of Human Conduct.* New York: Praeger.

Sartre, Jean Paul. 1948. *The Emotions: Outline of a Theory.* Translated by Bernard Frechman. New York: Philosophical Library.

Schaef, Ann Wilson. 1986. *Co-Dependence: Misunderstood-Mistreated.* New York: Harper and Row.

Schafer, Roy. 1981. "Narration in the Psychoanalytic Dialogue." Pp. 25–49 in *On Narrative,* edited by W. J. T. Mitchell. Chicago: University of Chicago Press.

———. 1992. *Retelling a Life: Narration and Dialogue in Psychoanalysis.* New York: Basic Books.

Schur, Edwin. 1976. *The Awareness Trap: Self-Absorption Instead of Social Change.* New York: Quadrangle.

Scott, Anne Farrer. 1991. "The Codependency Cop-Out." *Family Circle,* 23 July, 140.

Scott, James. 1990. *Domination and the Arts of Resistance: Hidden Transcripts.* New Haven: Yale University Press.

Scott, Marvin B., and Stanford M. Lyman. 1968. "Accounts." *American Sociological Review* 33:46–62.

Secunda, Victoria. 1990. "The 12-Stepping of America." *New Woman* (June): 49–54.

Seidman, Steven. 1990. *Romantic Longings: Love in America 1883–1980.* New York: Routledge.

Sennett, Richard. 1977. *The Fall of Public Man.* New York: Knopf.

Shaw, C. R. 1930. *The Jack Roller: A Delinquent Boy's Own Story.* Chicago: University of Chicago Press.

———. 1931. *The Natural History of a Delinquent Career.* Chicago: University of Chicago Press.

———. 1936. *Brothers in Crime.* Chicago: University of Chicago Press.

Simonds, Wendy. 1992. *Women and Self-Help Culture: Reading between the Lines.* New Brunswick, NJ: Rutgers University Press.

Slavney, Phillip R., and Paul R. McHugh. 1984. "Life Stories and Meaningful Connections: Reflections on a Clinical Method in Psychiatry and Medicine." *Perspectives in Biology and Medicine* 27:279–88.

Slater, Phillip. 1970. *The Pursuit of Loneliness.* Boston: Beacon Press.

Somers, Margaret R. 1994. "The Narrative Constitution of Identity: A Relational and Network Approach." *Theory and Society* 23:605–49.

Sommers, Shula. 1984. "Adults Evaluating Their Emotions: A Cross-Cultural Perspective." Pp. 319–38 in *Emotion and Adult Development,* edited by Carol Zander Malatesta and Carroll E. Izard. Beverly Hills, CA: Sage.

Spanier, Graham, and Linda Thompson. 1983. "Relief and Distress after Marital Separation." *Journal of Divorce* 7:31–49.

Starr, Paul. 1982. *The Social Transformation of Medicine.* New York: Basic Books.

Stearns, Carol Zisowitz, and Peter N. Stearns. 1986. *Anger: The Struggle for Emotional Control in America's History.* Chicago: University of Chicago Press.

Stearns, Peter N. 1989a. "Suppressing Unpleasant Emotions: The Development of a Twentieth-Century American Style." Pp. 230–61 in *Social History and Issues in Human Consciousness: Some Interdisciplinary Connections,* edited by Andrew E. Burns and Peter N. Stearns. New York: New York University Press.

———. 1989b. *Jealousy: The Evolution of an Emotion in American History.* New York: New York University Press.

———. 1994. *American Cool: Constructing a Twentieth-Century Emotional Style.* New York: New York University Press.

Stokes, Randall, and John P. Hewitt. 1976. "Aligning Actions." *American Sociological Review* 41:838–49.

Strauss, Anselm, and Juliet Corbin, eds. 1997. *Grounded Theory in Practice.* Thousand Oaks, CA: Sage.

Stryker, Sheldon. 1980. *Symbolic Interactionism: A Social Structural Version.* Reading, MA: Benjamin-Cummings.

Swidler, Ann. 1980. "Love and Adulthood in American Culture." Pp. 120–47 in *Themes of Love and Adulthood in American Culture,* edited by Neil J. Smelser and Erik H. Erikson. Cambridge, MA: Harvard University Press.

———. 1986. "Culture in Action: Symbols and Strategies." *American Sociological Review* 51:273–86.

Sykes, Charles J. 1992. *A Nation of Victims: The Decay of the American Character.* New York: St. Martin's.

Tallen, Bette. 1990. "Co-Dependency: A Feminist Critique." *Sojourner* (January): 20–21. [Reprinted in Babcock and McKay 1995.]

Tavris, Carol. 1989. "The Politics of Codependency." *Family Therapy Networker* 14:43.

———. 1990. "Do Codependency Theories Explain Women's Unhappiness—or Exploit Their Insecurities?" *Vogue* (December): 220, 224–26. [Reprinted in Babcock and McKay 1995.]

Taylor, Charles. 1989. *Sources of the Self: The Making of the Modern Identity.* Cambridge, MA: Harvard University Press.

Teodori, Massimo, ed. 1969. *The New Left: A Documentary History.* Indianapolis and New York: Bobbs-Merrill.

Thomas, W. I., and Znaniecki, Florian. [1918–1920] 1958. *The Polish Peasant in Europe and America.* New York: Dover.

Thorne, Barrie. 1980. "'You Still Takin' Notes?' Fieldwork and Problems of Informed Consent." *Social Problems* 27:284–97.

Tocqueville, Alexis de. [1832] 1969. *Democracy in America.* New York: Anchor.

Trilling, Lionel. 1972. *Sincerity and Authenticity.* Cambridge, MA: Harvard University Press.

Turner, Ralph H. 1976. "The Real Self: From Institution to Impulse." *American Journal of Sociology* 81:989–1016.

Van Wormer, Katherine. 1989. "Codependency: Implications for Women and Therapy." Pp. 117–28 in *Challenging Codependency: Feminist Critiques,* edited by Marguerite Babcock and Christine McKay. Toronto: University of Toronto Press. [Previously published in *Women and Therapy* 8 (1989): 51–63.]

Vaughan, Diane. 1986. *Uncoupling: Turning Points in Intimate Relationships.* New York and Oxford: Oxford University Press.

Veroff, Joseph, Elizabeth Douvan, and Richard A. Kulka. 1981a. *The Inner American: A Self-Portrait from 1957–1976.* New York: Basic Books.

———. 1981b. *Mental Health in America: Patterns of Help-Seeking from 1957–1976.* New York: Basic Books.

Vidich, Arthur J., and Joseph Bensman. [1958] 1968. *Small Town in Mass Society:*

Class, Power, and Religion in a Rural Community. Princeton: Princeton University Press.

Vinitzky-Seroussi, Vered, and Robert Zussman. 1996. "High School Reunions and the Management of Identity." *Symbolic Interaction* 19:225–39.

Walters, Marianne. 1995. "The Codependent Cinderella Who Loves Too Much . . . Fights Back." Pp. 181–91 in *Challenging Codependency: Feminist Critiques,* edited by Marguerite Babcock and Christine McKay. Toronto: University of Toronto Press. [Previously published in *Family Networker* (July/August 1990): 53–57.]

Wax, Murray L. 1980. "Paradoxes of 'Consent' to the Practices of Fieldwork." *Social Problems* 27:272–83.

———.1983. "On Fieldworkers and Those Exposed to Fieldwork." Pp. 288–99 in *Contemporary Field Research: A Collection of Readings,* edited by Robert Emerson. Boston: Little, Brown and Co.

Weber, Max. [1922–23] 1946. "The Social Psychology of the World Religions." Pp. 267–301 in *From Max Weber,* edited by Hans Gerth and C. Wright Mills. New York: Oxford University Press.

Wegscheider-Cruse, Sharon. 1985. *Choicemaking: For Co-Dependents, Adult Children, and Spirituality Seekers.* Deerfield Beach, FL: Health Communications.

Wegscheider-Cruse, Sharon, and Joseph Cruse. 1990. *Understanding Co-Dependency.* Deerfield Beach, FL: Health Communications.

Weiss, Robert S. 1975. *Marital Separation.* New York: Basic Books.

Weitzman, Lenore. 1985. *The Divorce Revolution.* New York: Free Press.

Whitfield, Charles. 1991. *Co-Dependence: Healing the Human Condition.* Deerfield Beach, FL: Health Communications.

Whyte, William H., Jr. 1956. *The Organization Man.* New York: Simon and Schuster.

Wilkinson, Rupert. 1988. *The Pursuit of American Character.* New York: Harper and Row.

———. 1992. *American Social Character: Modern Interpretations from the 40s to the Present.* New York: HarperCollins.

Woititz, Janet. [1983] 1990. *Adult Children of Alcoholics.* Deerfield Beach, FL: Health Communications.

Wouters, Cas. 1991. "On Status Competition and Emotion Management." *Journal of Social History* 24:699–717.

Wrong, Dennis. 1961. "The Oversocialized Conception of Man in Modern Sociology." *American Sociological Review* 26:183–93.

Wuthnow, Robert. 1994. *Sharing the Journey: Support Groups and America's New Quest for Community.* New York: Free Press.

Yankelovich, Daniel. 1981. *New Rules: Searching for Self-Fulfillment in a World Turned Upside Down.* New York: Random House.

Zaretsky, Eli. 1976. *Capitalism, the Family, and Personal Life.* New York: Harper and Row.

Zimet, Carl N. 1989. "The Mental Health Care Revolution: Will Psychology Survive?" *American Psychologist* 44:703–8.

Zilbergeld, Bernie. 1983. *The Shrinking of America: Myths of Psychological Change.* Boston: Little, Brown and Co.

Zimmerman, Don H., and Melvin Pollner. 1970. "The Everyday World as a Phenomenon." Pp. 80–104 in *Understanding Everyday Life: Toward the Reconstruction of Sociological Knowledge,* edited by J. D. Douglas. Chicago: Aldine.

Zurcher, Louis A. 1977. *The Mutable Self: A Self-Concept for Social Change.* Beverly Hills, CA: Sage.

Zussman, Robert. 1992. *Intensive Care: Medical Ethics and the Medical Profession.* Chicago: University of Chicago Press.

———. 1996. "Autobiographical Occasions." *Contemporary Sociology* 25:143–48.